EYEWITNESS TO THE CIVIL WAR
Volume I

The Opening Guns

Fort Sumter to Bull Run, 1861

Edited by
Albert A. Nofi

GALLERY BOOKS
An imprint of W.H. Smith Publishers Inc.
112 Madison Avenue
New York, New York 10016

For my father,
who taught me to love books.

ACKNOWLEDGMENTS

Several people were of considerable help in the preparation of this volume and their mention here is my small way of expressing my thanks.

Helena Rubenstein, Daniel Scott Palter, and the staff of West End Games generously allowed me access to the company library, with its extensive Civil War collection. The fine people at the New York Public Library and the Brooklyn College Library were of enormous assistance in helping me track down a number of works which were rather rare.

As always, special thanks are due to my wife, Mary S. Nofi, who once more endured the mounds of books and the many hours spent in the preparation of yet a new volume, and to my daughter, Marilyn J. Spencer, who escaped most of it, this time around.

Prepared by Combined Books
26 Summit Grove, Suite 207
Bryn Mawr, PA 19010

Project Director: Robert L. Pigeon
Project Coordinator: Antoinette Bauer
Editor of the Series: Albert A. Nofi
Photographic Research: John Cannan
Photographs: Tim Scott
Layout: Lizbeth Nauta

Produced by Wieser and Wieser, Inc.
118 East 25th Street, New York, NY 10010

Library of Congress Cataloging-in-Publication Data

The Opening guns.

(Eyewitness history of the Civil War; v. 1)
Bibliography: p. 176
1. United States—History—Civil War, 1861-1865—Campaigns.   2. Fort Sumter (Charleston, S.C.)—Siege, 1861—Personal narratives.   3. Bull Run, 1st Battle, 1861—Personal narratives.   4. United States—History—Civil War, 1861-1865—Personal narratives.   I. Nofi, Albert A.   II. Series.
E471.056   1988   973.7'31   88-5056
ISBN 0-8317-3081-1

South Carolinians build floating battery, designed to capture Fort Sumter.

CONTENTS

PREFACE TO THE SERIES

Well over a century after its conclusion, the Civil War still remains the gravest crisis in the history of the Republic since the attainment of independence. It was a vast complex struggle which touched the lives of far more Americans than any other war in which the nation has fought. A conflict of momentous import, it still retains an immediate and continuing impact on the life of the nation. The story of the Civil War has been told on numerous occasions and in numerous ways. The literature is enormous, ranging from erudite scholarly tomes to dry official reports, from informative popular histories to vicious partisan tracts. All these have their value. Yet none can ever be entirely satisfactory. After all these years there exists no better way of looking at the Civil War than to see it through the eyes of those who lived through it, the thousands upon thousands for whom the war was a daily reality.

The Civil War was probably the first war in history in which most of the troops could read and write. As a result, there exists an enormous number of firsthand accounts. The range of materials is equally large, from private letters to multi-volume memoirs. These cover everything from the minutia of daily life to serious historical treatments, from amusing anecdotes to vituperative personal attacks. Nothing surpasses such original documents for developing an understanding of the events as they were perceived by the people who lived through them, for the flavor of the times, the emotions of the struggle, the force of the issues, the impact of the events. Such materials have been drawn upon several times already for the creation of a number of anthologies of firsthand accounts of the war, or of particular aspects of it. Yet the amount of material available is so vast, the stories to be told so numerous, that there still remains much material which has not received wide circulation. It was an awareness of this fact which led to the creation of the present series, *Eyewitness to the Civil War.*

Each volume in *Eyewitness to the Civil War* covers a distinct aspect of the war as seen by the people who lived through it, as expressed in their personal letters, private diaries, historical accounts, and even in their songs. The typical volume contains around two dozen items selected from among many thousands. These items deal with events ranging from small, otherwise forgotten, incidents to great historic battles. In almost every case, the events depicted were personally witnessed by the authors. In a few instances accounts by contemporary authors who did not personally witness the events have been included, especially when the writer was someone of particularly interesting identity or possessed an unusual perspective on the events.

In preparing *Eyewitness to the Civil War,* the editor has made no effort to attempt a "balanced" presentation. As a consequence, many events are treated from only a Northern point of view, while others have a Southern slant, and still others are seen from two or three different perspectives. The purpose of the work is neither to achieve historical accuracy nor political balance, but to see events as they were experienced and understood by some of the people who lived through them. There will thus be redundancies, contradictions, and errors, not to mention outright falsehoods.

All of the selections appear almost exactly as they did on their original publication, save for the occasional eliding of extraneous materials. Where necessary, the editor has created titles for selections which lacked such. For the most part, he has avoided the inclusion of explanatory notes, confining himself to the insertion of occasional comments in brackets. Where explanatory notes appear in the original, they have been included only when they seemed of particular importance. In addition, the editor has refrained from modernizing the many little differences in spelling, capitalization, grammar, usage and syntax, which have developed since the Civil War. Needless to say, there has been no attempt to impose a uniformity of style. Thus, in *Eyewitness to the Civil War* the participants speak for themselves in their own voices.

Introduction

THE IRREPRESSIBLE CONFLICT

Politically, the issue in dispute during the American Civil War was a simple one: secession. It was an issue on which the Constitution was silent. Historically, morally, and philosophically, the implied existence of such a right was undeniable. As recently as 1776 the British colonies in America had themselves seceded from the Crown. But the "Right to Rebellion" has historically been hedged with moral strictures. And in 1860 the matter was by no means as simple as a straight-forward issue of political preference.

Secession became a divisive issue in American politics because of significant social, cultural, and economic differences between the Southern states and the rest of the Union. The South, rural, agricultural, and aristocratic, saw its interests threatened as the rest of the nation became increasingly urban, industrial, and democratic. This divergence of interests between the South and the rest of the country began to appear almost as soon as the Revolution was won, and the differences increased during the early nineteenth century. There were disputes over tariffs, over government sponsored internal improvements, and over the distribution of public land, all of which the Northerners and Westerners favored, and the Southerners opposed. Complicating the issue was the fact that the population of the North and the West grew at a rate faster than did that of the South, a development itself largely a result of the divergent character of the regions. Even without further complications the differences between the sections would have been sufficient to raise tensions. But there was as yet another factor, one of overwhelming importance. There was slavery.

Slavery was at the root of the differences between the South and the rest of the Union. Slavery had created the planter aristocracy of the South. Slavery, which had made the South one the preeminent agricultural regions of the world, had hampered its industrialization. Slavery retarded the growth of the Southern population by discouraging the immigration which swelled the ranks of Northerners and Westerners.

Moved by practical and moral considerations, many perceptive Southerners had raised objections to slavery in the period after the Revolution, not least among them Thomas Jefferson and George Washington. And, indeed, the institution seemed in decline in the early years of the nineteenth century. But the character of the society created by slaveholding, the enormous profits, the gentility, the elegance, blinded most to the pernicious effects of the institution on the South. By the middle of the nineteenth century, though relatively few Southerners actually owned slaves—and those who did usually had but one or two—most of the white people of the South had come to view slavery as vital to the survival of Southern society. By mid-century there had developed in the South an almost spiritual belief in the righteousness of slavery. The slaveholders represented wealth and status, something to which the non-slaveholders could aspire. The fact that slavery had a racial dimension enhanced the status of the impoverished white: whatever else he was, he was "free, white, and twenty-one." During this same period, however, the notion that slavery was inherently wrong was spreading rapidly through Western Civilization.

By the mid-nineteenth century the United States was the only major Western country in which slavery was still legal. Nor was there an absence of opposition to slavery.

Active resistance to slavery was remarkably widespread, among both blacks and whites. The underground railroad operated everywhere, involving people from every level of society, both North and South. Through the early decades of the century the Abolitionist movement grew steadily. Slavery came under fire in books and plays and songs, in sermons and editorials and lectures. Southerners would continuously defend the institution, but slavery was indefensible, regardless of the arguments advanced. The impact of the debate over slavery was tremendous.

Slavery was the overriding issue of the age. Families were broken up, friendships dissolved. Every major Protestant church in the nation split in two, one branch opposing slavery and one favoring it. While Northerners snapped up 400,000 copies of Harriet Beecher Stowe's *Uncle Tom's Cabin* within a few years of its publication in 1851, Southerners avidly read detailed rebuttals composed by pro-slavery authors. While Abolitionists and former slaves like Frederick Douglass and Harriet Tubman stumped the North pointing out the evils of slavery, pro-slavery advocates toured the South, lecturing on its importance to "civilized living," sometimes even advocating the reopening of the trans-Atlantic slave trade. And violence became commonplace. It became impossible to publicly express anti-slavery views in the South, and an incipient Southern Abolitionist movement was destroyed in a series of lynchings and riots. Compromise was several times attempted, but each time came to nought. The fundamental issue was individual freedom, and the institution was inherently incompatible with the promise of America, despite constitutional sanction. In a sense the Supreme Court dealt the final blow to any possibility of compromise in 1857, when, in the infamous Dred Scott decision, it effectively ruled that no state could bar slavery from within its borders and went on to declare that even free blacks could not be citizens, both provisions alike being viewed as gross violations of states' rights throughout the North and West. By then the issue had become one without reasonable solution.

THE UNION COMES TO PIECES

BY THE LATE 1850S, THE LINES WERE DRAWN, THE TINDER WAS READY. NEVERTHELESS, few people really understood the danger. But events were beginning to move too fast. Emotions were becoming too strong. In a sense, the spark which ignited the whole was set by a tall, inelegant lawyer from Illinois.

In the 1850s, slave auctions were an institution in the South.

In 1858 Lincoln was certain that conflicting attitudes towards slavery would bring about a crisis in the country.

★★★

ABRAHAM LINCOLN
A House Divided

In 1858 Abraham Lincoln, a relatively un-known lawyer and unsuccessful politician from Illinois, attempted to unseat the redoubtable Stephen A. Douglas from his seat in the Senate. He had been led to this by Douglas' sponsorship of the Kansas-Nebraska Act in 1854, which undermined the Compromise of 1850, threaten-ing to throw open new territories to slavery on the basis of "popular sovereignty." In a speech, delivered before the state Republican convention on 16 June, Lincoln succinctly expressed his views on the issues dividing the nation. He went on to win the Republican nomination, and challenged Douglas to a series of debates. Though he lost the election, his campaign made him a national figure and helped to secure the Republican presidential nomination two years later. But in his words the pro-slavery faction was an inveterate foe of the South's "peculiar institution."

Mr. President and Gentlemen of the Convention.

If we could first know where we are, and whither we are tending, we could then better judge what to do, and how to do it.

We are now far into the fifth year, since a policy was initiated, with the avowed object, and confident promise, of putting an end to slavery agitation.

Under the operation of that policy, that agitation has not only not ceased, but has constantly aug-mented.

In my opinion, it will not cease, until a crisis shall have been reached, and passed.

"A house divided against itself cannot stand."

I believe this government cannot endure, perma-nently half slave and half free.

I do not expect the Union to be dissolved—I do not expect the house to fall—but I do expect it will cease to be divided.

It will become all one thing, or all the other.

Either the opponents of slavery, will arrest the further spread of it, and place it where the public mind shall rest in the belief that it is in the course of ultimate extinction; or its advocates will push it forward, till it shall become alike lawful in all the States, old as well as new—North as well as South.

Have we no tendency to the latter condition?

Let any one who doubts, carefully contemplate that now almost complete legal combination—piece of machinery so to speak—compounded of the Nebraska doctrine, and the Dred Scott decision. Let him consider not only what work the machinery is adapted to do, and how well adapted; but also, let him study the history of its construction, and trace, if he can, or rather fail, if he can, to trace the evidences of design, and concert of action, among its chief bosses, from the beginning.

But, so far, Congress only, had acted; and an indorsement by the people, real or apparent, was indispensable, to save the point already gained, and give chance for more.

The new year of 1854 found slavery excluded from more than half the States by State Constitutions, and from most of the national territory by Congressional prohibition.

Four days later, commenced the struggle, which ended in repealing that Congressional prohibition.

This opened all the national territory to slavery; and was the first point gained.

This necessity had not been overlooked; but had been provided for, as well as might be, in the notable argument of "squatter sovereignty," otherwise called "sacred right of self government," which latter phrase, though expressive of the only rightful basis of any government, was so perverted in this attempted use of it as to amount to just this: That if any one man, choose to enslave another, no third man shall be allowed to object.

That argument was incorporated into the Nebraska bill itself, in the language which follows: "It being the true intent and meaning of this act not to legislate slavery into any Territory or state, not exclude it therefrom; but to leave the people thereof perfectly free to form and regulate their domestic institutions in their own way, subject only to the Constitution of the United States."

Then opened the roar of loose declamation in favor of "Squatter Sovereignty," and "Sacred right of self government."

"But," said opposition members, "let us be more specific—let us amend the bill so as to expressly declare that the people of the territory may exclude slavery." "Not we," said the friends of the measure; and down they voted the amendment.

While the Nebraska bill was passing through congress, a law case, involving the question of a negroe's freedom, by reason of his owner having voluntarily taken him first into a free state and then a territory covered by the congressional prohibition, and held him as a slave, for a long time in each, was passing through the U.S. Circuit Court for the District of Missouri; and both Nebraska bill and law suit were brought to a decision in the same month of May, 1854. The negroe's name was "Dred Scott," which name now designates the decision made in the case.

Before the then next Presidential election, the law case came to, and was argued in the Supreme Court of the United States; but the decision of it was deferred until after the election. Still, before the election, Senator Trumbull, on the floor of the Senate, requests the leading advocate of the Nebraska bill to state his opinion whether the people of a territory can constitutionally exclude slavery from their limits; and the latter answers, "That is a question for the Supreme Court."

The election came. Mr. Buchanan was elected, and the indorsement, such as it was, secured. That was the second point gained. The indorsement, however, fell short of a clear popular majority by nearly four hundred thousand votes, and so, perhaps, was not overwhelmingly reliable and satisfactory.

The outgoing President, in his last annual message, as impressively as possible echoed back upon the people the weight and authority of the indorsement.

The Supreme Court met again; did not announce their decision, but ordered a re-argument.

The Presidential inauguration came, and still no decision of the court; but the incoming President, in his inaugural address, fervently exhorted the people to abide by the forthcoming decision, whatever it might be.

Then, in a few days, came the decision.

The reputed author of the Nebraska bill finds an early occasion to make a speech at this capitol indorsing the Dred Scott Decision, and vehemently denouncing all opposition to it.

The new President, too, seizes the early occasion of the Silliman letter to indorse and strongly construe that decision, and to express his astonishment that any different view had ever been entertained.

At length a squabble springs up between the President and the author of the Nebraska bill, on the mere question of fact, whether the Lecompton constitution was or was not, in any just sense, made by the people of Kansas; and in that squabble the latter declares that all he wants is a fair vote for the people, and that he cares not whether slavery be voted down or voted up. I do not understand his declaration that he cares not whether slavery be voted down or voted up, to be intended by him other than as an apt definition of the policy he would impress upon the public mind—the principle for which he declares he has suffered much, and is ready to suffer to the end.

And well may he cling to that principle. If he has any parental feeling, well may he cling to it. That principle, is the only shred left of his original Nebraska doctrine. Under the Dred Scott decision, "squatter sovereignty" squatted out of existence, tumbled down like temporary scaffolding—like the mould at the foundry served through one blast and fell back into loose sand—helped to carry an election, and then was kicked to the winds. His late joint struggle with the Republicans, against the Lecompton Constitution, involved nothing of the original Nebraska doctrine. That struggle was made on a point, the right of a people to make their own

Stephen A. Douglas held the Senate seat Lincoln sought in 1858.

constitution, upon which he and the Republicans have never differed.

The several points of the Dred Scott decision, in connection with Senator Douglas' "care not" policy, constitute the piece of machinery, in its present state of advancement. This was the third point gained.

The working points of that machinery are:

First, that no negro slave, imported as such from Africa, and no descendant of such slave can ever be a citizen of any State, in the sense of that term as used in the Constitution of the United States.

This point is made in order to deprive the negro, in every possible event, of the benefit of this provision of the United States Constitution, which declares that—

"The citizens of each State shall be entitled to all privileges and immunities of citizens in the several States."

Secondly, that "subject to the Constitution of the United States," neither Congress nor a Territorial Legislature can exclude slavery from any United States territory.

This point is made in order that individual men may fill up the territories with slaves, without danger of losing them as property, and thus to enhance the chances of permanency to the institution through all the future.

Thirdly, that whether the holding a negro in actual slavery in a free State, makes him free, as against the holder, the United States courts will not decide, but will leave to be decided by the courts of any slave State the negro may be forced into by the master.

This point is made, not to be pressed immediately; but, if acquiesced in for a while, and apparently indorsed by the people at an election, then to sustain the logical conclusion that what Dred Scott's master might lawfully do with Dred Scott, in the free State of Illinois, every other master may lawfully do with any other one, or one thousand slaves, in Illinois, or in any other free State.

Auxiliary to all this, and working hand in hand with it, the Nebraska doctrine, or what is left of it, is to educate and mould public opinion, at least Northern public opinion, to not care whether slavery is voted down or voted up.

This shows exactly where we now are; and partially also, whither we are tending.

It will throw additional light on the latter, to go back, and run the mind over the string of historical facts already stated. Several things will now appear less dark and mysterious than they did when they were transpiring. The people were to be left "perfectly free" "subject only to the Constitution." What the Constitution had to do with it, outsiders could not then see. Plainly enough now, it was an exactly fitted niche, for the Dred Scott decision to afterwards come in, and declare the perfect freedom of the people, to be just no freedom at all.

Why was the amendment, expressly declaring the right of the people to exclude slavery, voted down? Plainly enough now, the adoption of it, would have spoiled the niche for the Dred Scott decision.

Why was the court decision held up? Why, even a Senator's individual opinion withheld, till after the Presidential election? Plainly enough now, the speaking out then would have damaged the "perfectly free" argument upon which the election was to be carried.

Why the outgoing President's felicitation on the indorsement? Why the delay of a reargument? Why the incoming President's advance exhortation in favor of the decision?

These things look like the cautious patting and petting a spirited horse, preparatory to mounting him, when it is dreaded that he may give the rider a fall.

"And why the hasty after indorsements of the decision by the President and others?

We can not absolutely know that all these exact adaptations are the result of preconcert. But when we see a lot of framed timbers, different portions of what we know have been gotten out at different times and places and by different workmen—Stephen, Franklin, Roger and James, for instance—and when we see these timbers joined together, and see they exactly make the frame of a house or a mill, all the tenons and mortices exactly fitting, and all the lengths and proportions of the different pieces exactly adapted to their respective places, and not a piece too many or too few—not omitting even scaffolding—or, if a single piece be lacking, we can see the place in the frame exactly fitted and prepared to yet being such piece in—in such a case, we find it impossible to not believe that Stephen and Franklin and Roger and James all understood one another from the beginning, and all worked upon a common plan or draft drawn up before the first lick was struck.

Abraham Lincoln addresses the people from the Astor House balcony in February 1861.

It should not be overlooked that, by the Nebraska bill, the people of a State as well as Territory, were to be left "perfectly free" "subject only to the Constitution."

Why mention a State? They were legislating for territories, and not for or about States. Certainly the people of a State are and ought to be subject to the Constitution of the United States; but why is mention of this lugged into this merely territorial law? Why are the people of a territory and the people of a state therein lumped together, and their relation to the Constitution therein treated as being precisely the same?

While the opinion of the Court, by Chief Justice Taney, in the Dred Scot case, and the separate opinions of all the concurring Judges, expressly declare that the Constitution of the United States neither permits Congress nor a Territorial legislature to exclude slavery from any United States territory, they all omit to declare whether or not the same Constitution permits a state, or the people of a State, to exclude it.

Possibly, this was a mere omission; but who can be quite sure, if McLean or Curtis had sought to get into the opinion a declaration of unlimited power in the people of a state to exclude slavery from their limits, just as Chase and Macy sought to get such declaration, in behalf of the people of a territory, into the Nebraska bill—I ask, who can be quite sure that it would not have been voted down, on the one case, as it had been in the other.

The nearest approach to the point of declaring the power of a State over slavery, is made by Judge Nelson. He approaches it more than once, using the precise idea, and almost the language too, of the Nebraska act. On one occasion his exact language is, "except in cases where the power is restrained by the Constitution of the United States, the law of the State is supreme over the subject of slavery within its jurisdiction."

In what cases the power of the states is so restrained by the U.S. Constitution, is left an open question, precisely as the same question, as to the restraint on the power of the territories was left open in the Nebraska act. Put that and that together, and we have another nice little niche, which we may, ere long, see filled with another Supreme Court decision, declaring that the Constitution of the United States does not permit a state to exclude slavery from its limits.

And this may especially be expected if the doctrine of "care not whether slavery be voted down or voted up," shall gain upon the public mind sufficiently to give promise that such a decision can be maintained when made.

Such a decision is all that slavery now lacks of being alike lawful in all the States.

Welcome or unwelcome, such decision is probably coming, and will soon be upon us, unless the power of the present political dynasty shall be met and overthrown.

We shall lie down pleasantly dreaming that the people of Missouri are on the verge of making their State free; and we shall awake to the reality, instead, that the Supreme Court has made Illinois a slave State.

To meet and overthrow the power of that dynasty, is the work now before all those who would prevent that consummation.

This is what we have to do.

But how can we best do it?

There are those who denounce us openly to their own friends, and yet whisper us softly, that Senator Douglas is the aptest instrument there is, with which to effect that object. They do not tell us, nor has he told us, that he wishes any such object to be effected. They wish us to infer all, from the facts, that he now has a little quarrel with the present head of the dynasty; and that he has regularly voted with us, on a single point, upon which, he and we, have never differed.

They remind us that he is a very great man, and that the largest of us are very small ones. Let this be granted. But "a living dog is better than a dead lion." Judge Douglas, if not a dead lion for this work, is at least a caged and toothless one. How can he oppose the advances of slavery? He don't care anything about it. His avowed mission is impressing the "public heart" to care nothing about it.

A leading Douglas Democratic newspaper thinks Douglas' superior talent will be needed to resist the revival of the African slave trade.

Does Douglas believe an effort to revive that trade is approaching? He has not said so. Does he really think so? But if it is, how can he resist it? For years he has labored to prove it a sacred right of white men to take negro slaves into the new territories. Can he possibly show that it is less a sacred right to buy them where they can be bought the cheapest? And, unquestionably they can be bought cheaper in Africa than in Virginia.

He has done all in his power to reduce the whole question of slavery to one of a mere right of property; and as such, how can he oppose the foreign slave trade—how can he refuse that trade in that "property" shall be "perfectly free"—unless he does it as a protection to the home production? And as the home producers will probably not ask the protection, he will be wholly without a ground of opposition.

Senator Douglas holds, we know, that a man may rightfully be wiser to-day than he was yesterday—that he may rightfully change when he finds himself wrong.

But, can we for that reason, run ahead, and infer that he will make any particular change, of which he, himself, has given no intimation? Can we safely base our action upon any such vague inference?

Now, as ever, I wish to not misrepresent Judge Douglas' position, question his motives, or do ought that can be personally offensive to him.

Whenever, if ever, he and we can come together on principle so that our great cause may have assistance from his great ability, I hope to have interposed no

Lincoln is inaugurated under the incomplete Capitol dome on March 4, 1861.

adventitious obstacle.

But clearly, he is not now with us—he does not pretend to be—he does not promise to ever be.

Our cause, then, must be intrusted to, and conducted by its own undoubted friends—those whose hands are free, whose hearts are in the work—who do care for the result.

Two years ago the Republicans of the nation mustered over thirteen hundred thousand strong.

We did this under the single impulse of resistance to a common danger, with every external circumstance against us.

Of strange, discordant, and even, hostile elements, we gathered from the four winds, and formed and fought the battle through, under the constant hot fire of a disciplined, proud, and pampered enemy.

Did we brave all then, to falter now?—now—when that same enemy is wavering, dissevered, and belligerent?

The result is not doubtful. We shall not fail—if we stand firm, we shall not fail.

Wise counsels may accelerate or mistakes delay it, but, sooner or later the victory is sure to come.

John Brown seized the arsenal at Harpers Ferry in an attempt to spark a slave insurrection.

★★★

JAMES REDPATH

John Brown's Speech on Being Sentenced to Death

The Kansas-Nebraska Act led to outright civil war in the Kansas Territory over whether the new state should be slave or free. Pro-slavery groups throughout the South sent bands of thugs to overawe the largely anti-slavery settlers. Abolitionist extremists replied in kind. A great deal of blood was shed before the Army could restore order. Kansas became a free state, but in 1859 one of the revolutionary Abolitionist veterans of "Bleeding Kansas," John Brown, seized the United States arsenal at Harpers Ferry in Virginia in an attempt to spark a slave insurrection throughout the South.

Brown's bold gesture failed and he was taken prisoner by a detachment of Marines under Col. Robert E. Lee. On 2 November 1859 John Brown was sentenced to death. An eyewitness recounted the scene to James Redpath, a journalist, who incorporated it in his The Public Life of Capt. John Brown *(Boston, 1860). Brown's dignified and eloquent response to the sentence moved many, establishing him as a martyr to the Abolitionist cause. But his actions, and his words, convinced the pro-slavery elements that the people of the North were determined to end slavery by any means possible.*

John Brown was brought in from jail to be sentenced. He walked with considerable difficulty, and every movement appeared to be attended with pain, although his features gave no expression of it. It was late, and the gaslights gave an almost deathly pallor to his face. He seated himself near his counsel, and, after once resting his head upon his right hand, remained entirely motionless, and for a time appeared unconscious of the execrations audibly whis-

pered by spectators. . . . While the Judge read his decision . . . Brown sat very firm with lips tightly compressed but with no appearance of affectation of sternness. He was like a block of stone. When the clerk directed him to stand and say why sentence should not be passed upon him, he rose and leaned slightly forward, his hands resting on the table. He spoke timidly—hesitatingly, indeed—and in voice singularly gentle and mild. But his sentences came confused from his mouth, and he seemed to be wholly unprepared to speak. . . .

"I have, may it please the court, a few words to say.

"In the first place, I deny everything but what I have all along admitted—the design on my part to free the slaves. . . . That was all I intended. I never did intend murder, or treason, or the destruction of property, or to excite or incite slaves to rebellion, or to make insurrection.

"I have another objection: and that is, it is unjust that I should suffer such a penalty. Had I interfered in the manner which I admit, and which I admit has been fairly proved—(for I admire the truthfulness and candor of the greater portion of the witnesses, who have testified in this case)—had I so interfered in behalf of the rich, the powerful, the intelligent, the so-called great, or in behalf of any of their friends, either father, mother, brother, sister, wife, or children, or any of that class, and suffered and sacrificed what I have . . . it would have been all right, and every man in this court would have deemed it an act worthy of reward rather than punishment.

"This court acknowledges, as I suppose, the validity of the Law of God. I see a book kissed here which I suppose to be the Bible, or at least the New Testament. That teaches me that all things 'whatsoever I would that men should do unto me I should do even so to them.' It teaches me, further, to 'remember them that are in bonds as bound with them.' I endeavored to act up to that instruction. I say I am yet too young to understand that God is any respecter of persons. I believe that to have interfered as I have done, as I have always freely admitted I have done, in behalf of His despised poor, was not wrong, but right. Now, if it is deemed necessary that I should forfeit my life for the furtherance of the ends of justice and mingle my blood with the blood of my children and with the blood of millions in this slave country whose rights are disregarded by wicked, cruel, and unjust enactments—I say, so let it be done.

"Let me say one word further. I feel entirely satisfied with the treatment I have received on my trial. Considering all the circumstances, it has been more generous than I expected. But I feel no consciousness of guilt. I have stated from the first what was my intention and what was not. I never had any design against the life of any person, nor any disposition to commit treason, or excite slaves to rebel, or make any general insurrection. I never encouraged any man to do so but always discouraged any idea of that kind.

"Let me say, also, a word in regard to the statements made by some of those connected with me. I hear it has been stated by some of them that I have induced them to join me. But the contrary is true. I do not say this to injure them, but as regretting their weakness. . . . Not one of them but joined me of his own accord, and the greater part at their own expense. A number of them I never saw, and never had a word of conversation with till the day they came to me, and that was for the purpose I have stated.

"Now I have done."

Perfect quiet prevailed while this speech was delivered; and, when he finished, the Judge proceeded to pass sentence on him. After a few preliminary remarks, he stated that no doubt could exist of the guilt of the prisoner and sentenced him to be hanged by the neck till he was dead on Friday the 2d day of December.

"At the announcement," said a spectator, "that, for the sake of example, the execution would be more than usually public, one indecent fellow behind the Judge's chair shouted and clapped hands jubilantly; but he was indignantly checked and in a manner that induced him to believe that he would do best to retire. It is a question, nevertheless, if the general sentiment were not fairly expressed by this action. John Brown was soon after led away again to his place of confinement."

Harpers Ferry was located at the confluence of the Shenandoah and Potomac Rivers.

Francis W. Pickens was governor of South Carolina, the first state to secede.

★★★

Declaration of Causes which Induced the Secession of South Carolina

The election of 1860 found tensions over slavery at their highest. There were four major candidates, because the Democratic Party had split. Stephen A. Douglas might well have won had he been supported by the South. But he had alienated the slaveholders by some relatively innocuous remarks concerning the rights of individual states to abolish slavery. The outraged South backed John C. Breckenridge, a pro-slavery man and former Vice-President. A third candidate was put forward as a compromise, John Bell, of Tennessee. And then there was the Republican candidate, Abraham Lincoln. Lincoln was neither a pro-slavery man nor an Abolitionist. He believed slavery was wrong, but he also believed that precipitous action to abolish it would inevitably lead to disaster. Opposing the extension of slavery to new territories, he believed that it should be permitted to continue where it already existed. Although his thoughts on the subject are somewhat unclear, it appears that he believed slavery would eventually disappear. These were hardly rabid anti-slavery views. Unfortunately they were too radical for the more extreme pro-slavery elements which dominated the political life of the South. Lincoln's relatively mild opposition to the institution was enough to spark the secession of the principal slaveholding states.

The first state to secede was South Carolina, which adopted the Ordinance to Dissolve the Union between the State of South Carolina and other States at a special convention on 20 December 1860. On the 24th the convention explained the reasons for secession in the Declaration of the Causes which Induced the Secession of South Carolina. This presents the legal case for secession, while also giving a good insight into the moral bankruptcy of that case.

The people of the State of South Carolina in Convention assembled, on the 2d day of April, A.D. 1852, declared that the frequent violations of the Constitution of the United States by the Federal Government, and its encroachments upon the reserved rights of the States, fully justified this State in their withdrawal from the Federal Union; but in deference to the opinions and wishes of the other Slaveholding States, she forbore at that time to exercise this right. Since that time these encroachments have continued to increase, and further forbearance ceases to be a virtue.

And now the State of South Carolina, having resumed her separate and equal place among nations, deems it due to herself, to the remaining United States of America, and to the nations of the world, that she should declare the immediate causes which have led to this act.

Government thus established is subject to the two great principles asserted in the Declaration of Independence; and we hold further that the mode of its formation subjects it to a third fundamental principle, namely, the law of compact. We maintain that in every compact between two or more parties, the obligation is mutual; that the failure of one of the contracting parties to perform a material part of the agreement, entirely releases the obligation of the other; and that where no arbiter is provided, each party is remitted to his own judgment to determine the fact of failure, with all its consequences.

In the present case, that fact is established with certainty. We assert that fourteen of the States have deliberately refused for years past to fulfill their constitutional obligations, and we refer to their own statutes for the proof.

The Constitution of the United States, in its fourth Article, provides as follows:

> No person held to service or labor in one State under the laws thereof, escaping into another, shall, in consequence of any law or regulation therein, be discharged from such service or labor, but shall be delivered up, on claim of the party to whom such service or labor may be due.

This stipulation was so material to the compact that without it that compact would not have been made. The greater number of the contracting parties held slaves, and they had previously evinced their estimate of the value of such a stipulation by making it a condition in the Ordinance for the government of the territory ceded by Virginia, which obligations, and the laws of the General Government, have ceased to effect the objects of the Constitution. The States of Maine, New Hampshire, Vermont, Massachusetts, Connecticut, Rhode Island, New York, Pennsylvania, Illinois, Indiana, Michigan, Wisconsin, and Iowa, have enacted laws which either nullify the acts of Congress, or render useless any attempt to execute them. In many of these States the fugitive is discharged from the service of labor claimed, and in none of them has the State Government complied with the stipulation made in the Constitution. The State of New Jersey, at an early day, passed a law in conformity with her constitutional obligation; but the current of Anti-Slavery feeling has led her more recently to enact laws which render inoperative the remedies provided by her own laws and by the laws of Congress. In the State of New York even the right of transit for a slave has been denied by her tribunals; and the States of Ohio and Iowa have refused to surrender to justice fugitives charged with murder, and with inciting servile insurrection in the State of Virginia. Thus the constitutional compact has been deliberately broken and disregarded by the non-slaveholding States; and the consequence follows that South Carolina is released from her obligation.

The ends for which this Constitution was framed are declared by itself to be "to form a more perfect union, to establish justice, insure domestic tranquillity, provide for the common defense, promote the general welfare, and secure the blessings of liberty to ourselves and our posterity."

These ends it endeavored to accomplish by a Federal Government, in which each State was recognized as an equal, and had separate control over its own institutions. The right of property in slaves was recognized by giving to free persons distinct political rights, by giving them the right to represent, and burdening them with direct taxes for, three-fifths of their slaves; by authorizing the importation of slaves for twenty years; and by stipulating for the rendition of fugitives from labor.

We affirm that these ends for which this Government was instituted have been defeated, and the Government itself has been destructive of them by the action of the non-slaveholding States. Those States have assumed the right of deciding upon the propriety of our domestic institutions; and have denied the rights of property established in fifteen of the States and recognized by the Constitution; they have denounced as sinful the institution of Slavery; they have permitted the open establishment among them of societies, whose avowed object is to disturb the peace of and eloin the property of the citizens of other States. They have encouraged and assisted thousands of our slaves to leave their homes; and those who remain, have been incited by emissaries, books, and pictures, to servile insurrection.

For twenty-five years this agitation has been steadily increasing, until it has now secured to its aid the power of the common Government. Observing the forms of the Constitution, a sectional party has found within that article establishing the Executive Department, the means of subverting the Constitution itself. A geographical line has been drawn across the Union, and all the States north of that line have united in the election of a man to the high office of

The people of South Carolina receive news of the election of Lincoln.

President of the United States whose opinions and purposes are hostile to Slavery. He is to be intrusted with the administration of the common Government, because he has declared that that "Government cannot endure permanently half slave, half free," and that the public mind must rest in the belief that Slavery is in the course of ultimate extinction.

This sectional combination for the subversion of the Constitution has been aided, in some of the States, by elevating to citizenship persons who, by the supreme law of the land, are incapable of becoming citizens; and their votes have been used to inaugurate a new policy, hostile to the South, and destructive of its peace and safety.

On the 4th of March next this party will take possession of the Government. It has announced that the South shall be excluded from the common territory, that the Judicial tribunal shall be made sectional, and that a war must be waged against Slavery until it shall cease throughout the United States.

The guarantees of the Constitution will then no longer exist; the equal rights of the States will be lost. The Slaveholding States will no longer have the power of self-government, or self-protection, and the Federal Government will have become their enemy.

Sectional interest and animosity will deepen the irritation; and all hope of remedy is rendered vain, by the fact that the public opinion at the North has invested a great political error with the sanctions of a more erroneous religious belief.

We, therefore, the people of South Carolina, by our delegates in Convention assembled, appealing to the Supreme Judge of the world for the rectitude of our intentions, have solemnly declared that the Union heretofore existing between this State and the other States of North America is dissolved, and that the State of South Carolina has resumed her position among the nations of the world, as a separate and independent state, with full power to levy war, conclude peace, contract alliances, establish commerce, and to do all other acts and things which independent States may of right do.

★★★

GEORGE B. McCLELLAN
The Causes of the Civil War

George B. McClellan, a West Point graduate, left the army after distinguishing himself in Mexico and embarked upon a successful business career in railroading. Upon the outbreak of the Civil War he returned to active duty. Rising to create and command the famed Army of the Potomac, McClellan demonstrated considerable talents as an organizer, but was generally unsuccessful in the field. Relieved of duty in late 1862, he ran for President in 1864 and went down to resounding defeat at Lincoln's hands. *Thereafter he resumed his business career. For all his many virtues and faults, he has certainly never been considered a thoughtful political analyst. His views were so decidedly mild that he was charged with sympathizing with the South. Yet his memoirs,* McClellan's Own Story *(New York, 1887), contain one of the most perceptive summations of the causes of the Civil War.*

After all that has been said and written upon the subject, I suppose none now doubt that slavery was the real knot of the question and the underlying cause of the war. It is now easy to preceive how the war might have been avoided if for two or three generations back all the men of both sections had been eminently wise, calm, unselfish, and patriotic. But with men as they are, it would be difficult indeed to indicate how a permanent pacific solution could have been reached. It is no doubt true that events were precipitated, perhaps rendered inevitable, by the violent course of a comparatively small number of men, on both sides of the line, during the thirty years preceding the war.

But it is the distinct lesson of history that this is always so; that the great crises in the world's history are induced by the words and actions of a few earnest or violent men, who stir up the masses and induce them blindly to follow their lead, whether for good or evil. As a rule the masses of civilized men, if left to themselves, are not prone to disturb the existing order of things or to resort to violent measures, unless suffering under intense evils which come home to each man individually and affect either his personal safety or personal possessions and prosperity; and even in such cases spontaneous uprisings of the masses are rare.

In our own case the people of the two sections did not understand each other before the war, and probably neither section regarded the other as seriously in earnest. The wide difference existing in social organization and habits had much to do with this.

In the South the habit of carrying, and using on slight provocation, deadly weapons, the sparse settlement of the country, the idle and reckless habits of the majority of the illiterate whites, the self-assertion natural to the dominant race in a slave-holding country, all conspired to impress them with an ill-founded assumption of superior worth and courage over the industrious, peaceful, law-abiding Northerners. On the other hand, the men of the North had become somewhat habituated to the boastful assertions too common among the Southerners, and had learned to believe that no real purpose of using force lay concealed beneath their violent language. Both were mistaken. The Southerner, with all his gasconading, was earnest in his intention to fight to the last for slavery and the right of secession. The peaceful Northerner, unaccustomed to personal warfare and prone to submit his disputes to the regular ordeal of law, was ready to lay down his life for the cause of the Union.

More gallant foes never met on the field of battle than these men of the same race, who had so long lived under the ample folds of the same flag; more desperate battles were never fought than those now about to occur. The military virtues of patriotism, patience, endurance, self-abnegation, and heroism were about to receive their most striking illlustrations. . . .

While giving due weight to all said or done by the ultra abolitionists of the North, I hold the South directly accountable for the war. If the election of Mr. Lincoln meant a more determined attack upon slavery, they of the South were responsible for the result, in consequence of their desertion of Mr. Douglas and the resulting rupture of the Democratic party. Even after that, if they had chosen to draw near the Northern Democrats again, seeking their remedy and protection within the Union, the Constitution, and the laws, they would have retained the right on their side. If left to their own cool judgment it is probable that slavery could not exist much longer, and that their wisest course was to recognize that fact, consent that it should not be extended beyond its existing limits, and provide for its gradual extinction. But, for various reasons, more reckless counsels prevailed. The Southern States rallied to the support of their peculiar institution, declared it to be a holy ordinance, demanded that it might be extended over the Territories, and bitterly opposed the idea that general manumission should be provided for in any form. Thus a state of feeling arose, more particularly in the South, which could only be quieted by the drastic methods of war.

Jefferson Davis was president of the Confederacy.

★★★

JEFFERSON DAVIS
There Would Be War

Jefferson Davis, a Mississippian, was one of the most prominent political leaders in the South in the years prior to the outbreak of the Civil War. A West Point graduate with an impressive record in the War with Mexico, he had served in the House of Representatives, as Secretary of War, and in the Senate, from which he resigned upon the secession of Mississippi in January of 1861. Returning to his home state he briefly served as head of the militia before being elected provisional president of the Confederate states. The account which follows, from his The Rise and Fall of the Confederate Government *(New York, 1881) expresses Davis' views on his receiving the call to serve and on the inevitability of war over secession, a view not shared by the majority of his fellow Southerners.*

The congress of delegates from the seceding States convened at Montgomery, Alabama, according to appointment, on the 4th of February, 1861. Their first work was to prepare a provisional Constitution for the new Confederacy, to be formed of the States which had withdrawn from the Union, for which the style "Confederate States of America" was adopted. The powers conferred upon them were adequate for the performance of this duty,, the immediate necessity for which was obvious and urgent. This Constitution was adopted on the 8th of February, to continue in force for one year, unless superseded at an earlier date by a permanent organization. . . .

On the next day (9th of February) an election was held for the chief executive offices, resulting, as I afterward learned, in my election to the Presidency, with the Hon. Alexander H. Stephens, of Georgia, as Vice-President. Mr. Stephens was a delegate from Georgia to the congress.

While these events were occurring, having completed the most urgent of my duties at the capital of Mississippi, I had gone to my home, Brierfield, in Warren County, and had begun, in the homely but expressive language of Mr. Clay, "to repair my fences." While thus engaged, notice was received of my election ot the Presidency of the Confederate

States, with an urgent request to proceed immediately to Montgomery for inauguration.

As this had been suggested as a probable event, and what appeared to me adequate precautions had been taken to prevent it, I was surprised, and, still more, disappointed. For reasons which it is not now necessary to state, I had not believed myself as well suited to the office as some others. I thought myself better adapted to command in the field; and Mississippi had given me the position which I preferred to any other—the highest rank in her army. It was, therefore, that I afterward said, in an address delivered in the Capitol, before the Legislature of the State, with reference to my election to the Presidency of the Confederacy, that the duty to which I was thus called was temporary, and that I expected soon to be with the Army of Mississippi again.

While on my way to Montgomery, and waiting in Jackson, Mississippi, for the railroad train, I met the Hon. William L. Sharkey, who had filled with great distinction the office of Chief-Justice of the State. He said he was looking for me to make an inquiry. He desired to know if it was true, as he had just learned, that I believed there would be war. My opinion was freely given, that there would be war, long and bloody, and that it behooved every one to put his house in order. He expressed much surprise, and said that he had not believed the report attributing this opinion to me. He asked how I supposed war could result from the peaceable withdrawal of a sovereign State. The answer was, that it was not my opinion that war should be occasioned by the exercise of that right, but that it would be.

Judge Sharkey and I had not belonged to the same political party, he being a Whig, but we fully agreed with regard to the question of the sovereignty of the States. He had been an advocate of nullification—a

doctrine to which I had never assented, and which had at one time been the main issue in Mississippi politics. He had presided over the well-remembered Nashville Convention in 1849, and had possessed much influence in the State, not only as an eminent jurist, but as a citizen who had grown up with it, and held many offices of honor and trust.

On my way to Montgomery, brief addresses were made at various places, at which there were temporary stoppages of the trains, in response to calls from the crowds assembled at such points. Some of these addresses were grossly misrepresented in sensational reports made by irresponsible persons, which were published in Northern newspapers, and were not considered worthy of correction under the pressure of the momentous duties then devolving upon me. These false reports, which represented me as invoking war and threatening devastation of the North, have since been adopted by partisan writers as authentic history. It is a sufficent answer to these accusations to refer to my farewell address to the Senate, as . . . reported for the press at the time, and, in connection therewith, to my inaugural address at Montgomery, on assuming the office of President of the Confederate States, on the 18th of February. These two addresses, delivered at an interval of a month, during which no material change of circumstances had occurred, being one before and the other after the date of the sensational reports referred to, are sufficient to stamp them as utterly untrue. The inaugural was deliberately prepared, and uttered as written, and, in connection with the farewell speech to the Senate, presents a clear and authentic statement of the principles and purposes which actuated me on assuming the duties of the high office to which I had been called.

The Confederate cabinet met in Montgomery, Alabama, in February 1861.

Jefferson Davis addresses citizens of the new Southern Confederacy prior to his inauguration.

FORT SUMTER

THROUGH THE WINTER OF 1860–1861 SECESSION FEVER SWEPT THROUGH THE LOWER tier of Southern states. By early February Mississippi, Florida, Alabama, Georgia, Louisiana, and Texas had joined South Carolina, forming the Confederate States of America. President Franklin Buchanan, well-meaning but untalented, proved incapable of acting with decision, seeking, on the one hand, to preserve the prerogatives of the Federal government, while not precipitating an open break with the secessionists in the hope that a peaceful solution might be found. Many others, both North and South, shared this hope. But it was a futile hope. Though several last-ditch compromises were proposed, none had any chance of success. Meanwhile, the seceded states occupied—had to occupy if they were to assert their sovereignty—Federal installations on their territory, so that by the time Lincoln was inaugurated, in early March, the Stars and Stripes could be found flying over only three places in the entire South, all alike isolated posts on islands: Fort Pickens off Pensacola Harbor, Fort Jefferson in the Dry Tortugas, and Fort Sumter in Charleston Harbor. And it was at Sumter that the issue boiled over into war.

Fort Sumter was a Federal fort in Charleston Harbor.

***

STEPHEN D. LEE

The First Step in the War

Stephen D. Lee, a native of South Carolina and a West Point graduate, resigned from the Old Army early in 1861 and entered Confederate service. He was shortly appointed an aide-de-camp to Pierre G. T. Beauregard, commanding Confederate forces in Charleston Harbor, whose mission it was to secure control of Fort Sumter. Here Lee—who saw much distinguished service during the war, rising to the rank of lieutenant general—recounts what happened in an article originally written for The Century Magazine *and subsequently published in the famed collection by Robert U. Johnson and Clarence C. Buel,* Battles and Leaders of the Civil War *(New York, 1887).*

In the month of December, 1860, the South itself had no more realizing sense than the North of the magnitude of events about to be entered into so lightly. Even the Southern leaders did not realize that there could be any obstacle to "peaceable secession." Many at the North were willing to "let the wayward sisters depart in peace." Only a few on either side expected that blood would be shed. When, in the first Confederate Congress at Montgomery, one prudent debater exclaimed, "What if we really have a war?" the general response was, "There will be no war." "But," he persisted, "if there is a war, what are our resources?" and when one man in reply expressed his conviction that if the worst came, the South could put fifty thousand men into the field, he was looked upon as an enthusiast. The expectation of "peaceable secession" was the delusion that precipitated matters in the South; and it was on this expectation, when the crisis came, that South Carolina seceded. Her first step was to organize troops and assert the sovereignty in which she believed, by the occupation of her territory.

After the evacuation of Fort Moultrie, although Major Anderson was not permitted by the South Carolina authorities to receive any large supply of provisions, yet he received a daily mail, and fresh beef and vegetables from the city of Charleston, and was unmolested at Fort Sumter. He continued industriously to strengthen the fort. The military authorities of South Carolina, and afterward of the Confederate States, took possession of Fort Moultrie, Castle Pinckney, the arsenal, and other United States property in the vicinity. They also remounted the guns at Fort Moultrie, and constructed batteries on Sullivan's, Morris, and James islands, and at other places, looking to the reduction of Fort Sumter if it should become necessary; meantime leaving no stone unturned to secure from the authorities at Washington a quiet evacuation of the fort. Several arrangements to accomplish this purpose were almost reached, but failed. Two attempts were made to reënforce and supply the garrison: one by the steamer *Star of the West*, which tried to reach the fort, January 9th, 1861, and was driven back by a battery on Morris Island, manned by South Carolina troops; the other just before the bombardment of Sumter, April 12th. The feeling of the Confederate authorities was that a peaceful issue would finally be arrived at; but they had a fixed determination to use force, if necessary, to occupy the fort. They did not desire to intend to take the initiative, if it could be avoided. So soon, however, as it was clearly understood that the authorities at Washington had abandoned peaceful views, and would assert the power of the United States to supply Fort Sumter, General Beauregard, the commander of the Confederate forces at Charleston, in obedience to the command of his Government at Montgomery, proceeded to reduce the fort. His arrangements were about complete, and on April 11th he demanded of Major Anderson the evacuation of Fort Sumter. He offered to transport Major Anderson and his command to any port in the United States; and to allow him to move out of the fort with company arms and property, and all private property, and to salute his flag in lowering it. This demand was delivered to Major Anderson at 3:45 P.M., by two aides of General Beauregard, James Chesnut, Jr., and myself. At 4:30 P.M. he handed us his reply, refusing to accede to the demand; but added, "Gentlemen, if you do not batter the fort to pieces about us, we shall be starved out in a few days."

> Do not desire needlessly to bombard Fort Sumter. If Major Anderson will state the time at which, as indicated by him, he will evacuate, and agree that in the meantime he will not use his guns against us, unless ours should be employed against Fort Sumter, you are authorized thus to avoid the effusion of blood. If this, or its equivalent, be refused, reduce the fort as your judgment decides to be most practicable.

The same aides bore a second communication to Major Anderson, based on the above instructions, which was placed in his hands at 12:45 A.M., April

Pierre G.T. Beauregard commanded Confederate forces in Charleston Harbor.

12th. His reply indicated that he would evacuate the fort on the 15th, provided he did not in the meantime receive contradictory instructions from his Government, or additional supplies, but he declined to agree not to open his guns upon the Confederate troops, in the event of any hostile demonstration on their part against his flag. Major Anderson made every possible effort to retain the aides till daylight, making one excuse and then another for not replying. Finally, at 3:15 A.M., he delivered his reply. In accordance with their instructions, the aides read it and, finding it unsatisfactory, gave Major Anderson this notification:

> Fort Sumter, S.C., April 12, 1861, 3:20 A.M.—SIR: By authority of Brigadier-General Beauregard, commanding the Provisional Forces of the Confederate States, we have the honor to notify you that we will open the fire of his batteries on Fort Sumter in one hour from this time. We have the honor to be very respectfully, Your obedient servants, James Chesnut, Jr., Aide-de-camp. Stephen D. Lee, Captain C.S. Army, Aide-de-camp.

The above note was written in one of the casemates of the fort, and in the presence of Major Anderson and several of his officers. On receiving it, he was much affected. He seemed to realize the full import of the consequences, and the great responsibility of his position. Escorting us to the boat at the wharf, he cordially pressed our hands in farewell, remarking, "If we never meet in this world again, God grant that we may meet in the next."

The boat containing the two aides and also Roger A. Pryor, of Virginia, and A. R. Chisolm, of South Carolina, who were also members of General Beauregard's staff, went immediately to Fort Johnson on James Island, and the order to fire the signal gun was given to Captain George S. James, commanding the battery at that point. It was then 4 A.M. Captain James at once aroused his command, and arranged to carry out the order. He was a great admirer of Roger A. Pryor, and said to him, "You are the only man to whom I would give up the honor of firing the first gun of the war"; and he offered to allow him to fire it. Pryor, on receiving the offer, was very much agitated. With a husky voice he said, "I could not fire the first gun of the war." His manner was almost similar to that of Major Anderson as we left him a few moments before on the wharf at Fort Sumter. Captain James would allow no one else but himself to fire the gun.

The boat with the aides of General Beauregard left Fort Johnson before arrangements were complete for the firing of the gun, and laid on its oars, about one-third the distance between the fort and Sumter, there to witness the firing of "the first gun of the war" between the States. It was fired from a ten-inch mortar at 4:30 A.M., April 12th, 1861. Captain James was a skillful officer, and the firing of the shell was a success. It burst immediately over the fort, apparently about one hundred feet above. The firing of the mortar woke the echoes from every nook and corner of the harbor, and in this dead hour of night, before dawn, that shot was a sound of alarm that brought every soldier in the harbor to his feet, and every man, woman, and child in the city of Charleston from their beds. A thrill went through the whole city. It was felt that the Rubicon was passed. No one thought of going home; unused as their ears were to the appalling sounds, or the vivid flashes from the batteries, they stood for hours fascinated with horror. After the second shell the different batteries opened their fire on Fort Sumter, and by 4:45 A.M. the firing was general and regular. It was a hazy, foggy morning. About daylight, the boat with the aides reached Charleston, and they reported to General Beauregard.

Fort Sumter did not respond with her guns till 7:30 A.M. The firing from this fort, during the entire bombardment, was slow and deliberate, and marked with little accuracy. The firing continued without intermission during the 12th, and more slowly during the night of the 12th and 13th. No material

change was noticed till 8 A.M. on the 13th, when the barracks in Fort Sumter were set on fire by hot shot from the guns of Fort Moultrie. As soon as this was discovered, the Confederate batteries redoubled their efforts, to prevent the fire being extinguished. Fort Sumter fired at little longer intervals, to enable the garrison to fight the flames. This brave action, under such a trying ordeal, aroused great sympathy and admiration on the part of the Confederates for Major Anderson and his gallant garrison; this feeling was shown by cheers whenever a gun was fired from Sumter. It was shown also by loud reflections on the "men-of-war" outside the harbor.

About 12:30 the flag-staff of Fort Sumter was shot down, but it was soon replaced. As soon as General Beauregard heard that the flag was no longer flying,

he sent three of his aides, William Porcher Miles, Roger A. Pryor, and myself, to offer, and also to see if Major Anderson would receive or needed, assistance, in subduing the flames inside the fort. Before we reached it, we saw the United States flag again floating over it, and began to return to the city. Before going far, however, we saw the Stars and Stripes replaced by a white flag. We turned about at once and rowed rapidly to the fort. We were directed, from an embrasure, not to go to the wharf, as it was mined, and the fire was near it. We were assisted through an embrasure and conducted to Major Anderson. Our mission being made known to him, he replied, "Present my compliments to General Beauregard, and say to him I thank him for his kindness, but need no assistance." He further remarked that

A floating battery fires on Fort Sumter.

he hoped the worst was over, that the fire had settled over the magazine, and, as it had not exploded, he thought the real danger was about over. Continuing, he said, "Gentlemen, do I understand you come direct from General Beauregard?" The reply was in the affirmative. He then said, "Why! Colonel Wigfall has just been here as an aide too, and by authority of General Beauregard, and proposed the same terms of evacuation offered on the 11th instant." We informed the major that we were not authorized to offer terms; that we were direct from General Beauregard, and that Colonel Wigfall, although an aide-de-camp to the general, had been detached, and had not seen the general for several days. Major Ander-

son at once stated, "There is a misunderstanding on my part, and I will at once run up my flag and open fire again." After consultation, we requested him not to do so, until the matter was explained to General Beauregard, and requested Major Anderson to reduce to writing his understanding with Colonel Wigfall, which he did. However, before we left the fort, a boat

arrived from Charleston, bearing Major D. R. Jones, assistant adjutant-general on General Beauregard's staff, who offered substantially the same terms to Major Anderson as those offered on the 11th, and also by Colonel Wigfall, and which were now accepted.

Thus fell Fort Sumter, April 13th, 1861. At this time fire was still raging in the barracks, and settling steadily over the magazine. All egress was cut off except through the lower embrasures. Many shells from the Confederate batteries, which had fallen in the fort and had not exploded, as well as the hand-grenades used for defense, were exploding as they were reached by the fire. The wind was driving the heat and smoke down into the fort and into the casemates, almost causing suffocation. Major Anderson, his officers, and men were blackened by smoke and cinders, and showed signs of fatigue and exhaustion, from the trying ordeal through which they had passed.

It was soon discovered, by conversation, that it was a bloodless battle; not a man had been killed or seriously wounded on either side during the entire bombardment of nearly forty hours. Congratulations were exchanged on so happy a result. Major Anderson stated that he had instructed his officers only to fire on the batteries and forts, and not to fire on private property.

The terms of evacuation offered by General Beauregard were generous, and were appreciated by Major Anderson. The garrison was to embark on the 14th, after running up and saluting the United States flag, and to be carried to the United States fleet. A soldier killed during the salute was buried inside the fort, the new Confederate garrison uncovering during the impressive ceremonies. Major Anderson and his command left the harbor, bearing with them the respect and admiration of the Confederate soldiers. It was conceded that he had done his duty as a soldier holding a most delicate trust.

This first bombardment of Sumter was but its "baptism of fire." During subsequent attacks by land and water, it was battered by the heaviest Union artillery. Its walls were completely crushed, but the tons of iron projectiles imbedded in its ruins added strength to the inaccessible mass that surrounded it and made it impregnable. It was never taken, but the operations of General Sherman, after his march to the sea, compelled its evacuation, and the Stars and Stripes were again raised over it, April 14th, 1865.[1]

The people of Charleston watch the bombardment of Sumter from the roof tops.

---

1. Under an order from Secretary Stanton, the same flag that was lowered, April 14th, 1861, was raised again over Sumter, by Major (then General) Anderson, on April 14, 1865, the day President Lincoln was shot. Of Major Anderson's former officers, Generals Abner Doubleday and Norman J. Hall and Chaplain Matthias Harris were present. The Rev. Henry Ward Beecher delivered an oration, and other prominent anti-slavery men attended the ceremony.

ABNER DOUBLEDAY
From Moultrie to Sumter

Abner Doubleday—who had a long and varied career during the war, rising to major general by brevet—was a native of New York widely credited for his reputed invention of baseball. The fortunes of the service found him, West *Point graduate and career soldier, attached to the defenses of Charleston Harbor in late 1860. His account of the events prior to the bombardment of Fort Sumter is drawn from* Battles and Leaders of the Civil War.

As senior captain of the 1st Regiment of United States Artillery, I had been stationed at Fort Moultrie, Charleston Harbor, two or three years previous to the outbreak of 1861. There were two other forts in the harbor. Of these, Fort Sumter was unoccupied, being in an unfinished state, while Castle Pinckney was in charge of a single ordnance sergeant. The garrision of Fort Moultrie consisted of 2 companies that had been reduced to 65 men, who with the band raised the number in the post to 73. Fort Moultrie had no strength; it was merely a sea battery. No one ever imagined it would be attacked by our own people; and if assailed by foreigners, it was supposed that an army of citizen-soldiery would be there to defend it. It was very low, the walls having about the height of an ordinary room. It was little more, in fact, than the old fort of Revolutionary time of which the father of Major Robert Anderson had been a defender. The sand had drifted from the sea against the wall, so that cows would actually scale the ramparts. In 1860 we applied to have the fort put in order, but the quartermaster-general, afterward the famous Joseph E. Johnston, said the matter did not pertain to his department. We were then apprehending trouble, for the signs of the times indicated that the South was drifting toward secession, though the Northern people could not be made to believe this, and regarded our representation to this effect as nonsense. I remember that at that time our engineer officer, Captain J. G. Foster, was alone, of the officers, in thinking there would be no trouble. We were commanded by a Northern man of advanced age, Colonel John L. Gardner, who had been wounded in the war of 1812 and had served with credit in Florida and Mexico. November 15th, 1860, Mr. Floyd, the Secretary of War, relieved him and put in command Major Robert Anderson of Kentucky, who was a regular officer. Floyd thought the new commander could be relied upon to carry out the Southern programme, but we never believed that Anderson took command with a knowledge of that programme or a desire that it should succeed. He simply obeyed orders; he had to obey or leave the army. Anderson was a Union man, and, in the incipiency, was perfectly willing to chastise South Carolina in case she should attempt any revolutionary measures. His feeling as to coercion changed when he found that all the Southern States had joined South Carolina, for he looked upon the conquest of the South as hopeless.

Soon after his arrival, which took place on the 21st of November, Anderson wanted the sand removed from the walls of Moultrie, and urged that it be done. Suddenly the Secretary of War seemed to adopt this view. He pretended there was danger of

Major Robert Anderson.

war with England, with reference to Mexico, which was absurd; and under this pretext was seized with a sudden zeal to put the harbor of Charleston in condition,—to be turned over to the Confederate forces. He appropriated $150,000 for Moultrie and $80,000 to finish Sumter. There was not much to be made out of Fort Moultrie, with all our efforts, because it was hardly defensible; but Major Anderson strove to strengthen it. He put up heavy gates to prevent Charleston secessionists from entering, and made a little man-hole through which visitors had to crawl in and out.

We could get no additional ammunition, but Colonel Gardner had managed to procure a six months' supply of food from the North before the trouble came. The Secretary of War would not let us have a man in the way of reënforcement, the plea being that reënforcements would irritate the people. The secessionists could hardly be restrained from attacking us, but the leaders kept them back, knowing that our workmen were laboring in their interests, at the expense of the United States. When Captain Truman Seymour was sent with a party to the United States arsenal in Charleston to get some friction primers and a little ammunition, a crowd interfered and drove his men back. It became evident, as I told Anderson, that we could not defend the fort, because the houses around us on Sullivan's Island looked down into Moultrie, and could be occupied by our enemies. At last it was rumored that two thousand riflemen had been detailed to shoot us down from the tops of those houses. I proposed to anticipate the enemy and burn the dwellings, but Anderson would not take so decided a step at a time when the North did not believe there was going to be war. It was plain that the only thing to be done was to slip over the water to Fort Sumter, but Anderson said he had been assigned to Fort Moultrie, and that he must stay there. We were then in a very peculiar position. It was commonly believed that we would not be supported even by the North, as the Democrats had been bitterly opposed to the election of Lincoln; that at the first sign of war twenty thousand men in sympathy with the South would rise in New York. Moreover, the one to whom we soldiers always looked up as to a father,—the Secretary of War, seemed to be devising arrangements to have us made away with. We believed that in the event of an outbreak from Charleston few of us would survive; but it did not greatly concern us, since that risk was merely a part of our business, and we intended to make the best fight we could. The officers, upon talking the matter over, thought they might control any demonstration at Charleston by throwing shells into the city from Castle Pinckney. But, with only sixty-four soldiers and a brass band, we could not detach any force in that direction.

Finally, Captain Foster, who had misapprehended the whole situation, and who had orders to put both Moultrie and Sumter in perfect order, brought several hundred workmen from Baltimore. Unfortunately, these were nearly all in sympathy with the Charlestonians, many even wearing badges.

The officers in Anderson's command were depicted on the cover of the March 23, 1861, issue of *Harpers Weekly*.

Bands of secessionists were now patrolling near us by day and night. We were so worn out with guard-duty—watching them—that on one occasion my wife and Captain Seymour's relieved us on guard, all that was needed being some one to give the alarm in case there was an attempt to break in. Foster thought that out of his several hundred workmen he could get a few Union men to drill at the guns as a garrison in Castle Pinckney, but they rebelled the moment they found they were expected to act as artillerists, and said that they were not there as warriors. It was said that when the enemy took possession of the castle, some of these workmen were hauled from under beds and from other hiding-places.

The day before Christmas I asked Major Anderson for wire to make an entanglement in front of my part of the fort, so that any one who should charge would tumble over the wires and could be shot at our leisure. I had already caused a sloping picket fence to be projected over the parapet on my side of the works so that scaling-ladders could not be raised against us. The discussion in Charleston over our proceedings was of an amusing character. This wooden *fraise* puzzled the Charleston militia and editors; one of the latter said, "Make ready your sharpened stakes, but you will not intimidate free-men."

When I asked Anderson for the wire, he said I should have a mile of it, with a peculiar smile that puzzled me for the moment. He then sent for Hall, the post quaratermaster, bound him to secrecy, and told him to take three schooners and some barges which had been chartered for the purpose of taking the women and children and six months' supply of provisions to Fort Johnson, opposite Charleston. He was instructed when the secession patrols should ask what this meant, to tell them we were sending off the families of the officers and men to the North because they were in the way. The excuse was plausible, and no one interfered. We were so closely watched that we could make no movement without demands being made as to the reason of it. On the day we left—the day after Christmas—Anderson gave up his own mess, and came to live with me as my guest. In the evening of that day I went to notify the major that tea was ready. Upon going to the parapet for that purpose, I found all the officers there, and noticed something strange in their manner. The problem was solved when Anderson walked up to me and said: "Captain, in twenty minutes you will leave this fort with your company for Fort Sumter." The order was startling and unexpected, and I thought of the immediate hostilities of which the movement would be the occasion. I rushed over to my company quarters and informed my men, so that they might put on their knapsacks and have everything in readiness. This took about ten minutes. Then I went to my house, told my wife that there might be fighting, and that she must get out of the fort as soon as she could and take refuge behind the sand-hills. I put her trunks out of the sally-port,

and she followed them. Then I started with my company to join Captain Seymour and his men. We had to go a quarter of a mile through the little town of Moultrieville to reach the point of embarkation. It was about sunset, the hour of the siesta, and fortunately the Charleston militia were taking their afternoon nap. We saw nobody, and soon reached a low line of sea-wall under which were hidden the boats in charge of the three engineers, for Lieutenants Snyder and Meade had been sent by Floyd to

help Captain Foster do the work on the forts. The boats had been used in going back and forward in the work of construction, manned by ordinary work-men, who now vacated them for our use. Lieutenant Snyder said to me in a low tone: "Captain, those boats are for your men." So saying, he started with his own party up the coast. When my thirty men were embarked I went straight for Fort Sumter. It was getting dusk. I made slow work in crossing over, for my men were not expert oarsmen. Soon I saw the lights of the secession guard-boat coming down on us. I told the men to take off their coats and cover up their muskets, and I threw my own coat open to conceal my buttons. I wished to give the impression that it was an officer in charge of laborers. The guard-ship stopped its paddles and inspected us in the gathering darkness, but concluded we were all right and passed on. My party was the first to reach Fort Sumter.

We went up the steps of the wharf in the face of an

Major Anderson's command enters Fort Sumter on Christmas Night 1860.

excited band of secession workmen, some of whom were armed with pistols. One or two Union men among them cheered, but some of the others said angrily: "What are these soldiers doing here? what is the meaning of this?" Ordering my men to charge bayonets, we drove the workmen into the center of the fort. I took possession of the guard-room commanding the main entrance and placed sentinels. Twenty minutes after, Seymour arrived with the rest of the men. Meantime Anderson had crossed in one of the engineer boats. As soon as the troops were all in we fired a cannon, to give notice of our arrival to the quartermaster, who had anchored at Fort Johnson with the schooners carrying the women and children. He immediately sailed up to the wharf and landed his passengers and stores. Then the workmen of secession sympathies were sent aboard the schooners to be taken ashore.

Lieutenant Jefferson C. Davis of my company had been left with a rear-guard at Moultrie. These, with Captain Foster and Assistant-Surgeon Crawford,

stood at loaded columbiads during our passage, with orders to fire upon the guard-boats and sink them if they tried to run us down. On withdrawing, the rear-guard spiked the guns of the fort, burned the gun-carriages on the front looking toward Sumter, and cut down the flag-staff. Mrs. Doubleday first took refuge at the house of the post sutler, and afterward with the family of Chaplain Harris, with whom she sought shelter behind the sand-hills. When all was quiet they paced the beach, anxiously watching Fort Sumter. Finding that the South Carolinians were ignorant of what had happened, we sent the boats back to procure additional supplies.

The next morning Charleston was furious. Messengers were sent out to ring every door-bell and convey the news to every family. The governor sent two or three of his aides to demand that we return to Moultrie. Anderson replied in my hearing that he was a Southern man, but that he had been assigned to the defense of Charleston Harbor, and intended to defend it.

★★★

JAMES CHESTER
Inside Sumter in '61

James Chester was one of the many millions of ordinary people caught up in the Civil War. A junior officer of artillery, Chester was one of the small band of officers and men who defended

Fort Sumter. His account, taken from Battles and Leaders of the Civil War, *is one of the most detailed available on the defense of the fort.*

The transfer of Major Anderson's command from Moultrie to Sumter was neatly executed early in the evening of December 26th, 1860. It was a few minutes after sunset when the troops left Moultrie; the short twilight was about over when they reached the boats; fifteen or twenty minutes more carried them to Sumter. The workmen had just settled down to an evening's enjoyment when armed men at the door startled them. There was no parleying, no explaining; nothing but stern commands, silent astonishment, and prompt obedience. The workmen were on the wharf, outside the fort, before they were certain whether their captors were secessionists or Yankees.

Meantime the newly arrived troops were busy enough. Guards were posted, embrasures secured, and, as far as practicable, the place was put in a defensible condition against any storming-party which chagrin might drive the guard-boat people to send against it. Such an attempt was perfectly feasi-

ble. The night was very dark; the soldiers were on unknown ground and could not find their way about readily; many of the embrasures could not be closed; and there were at least a hundred willing guides and helpers already on the wharf and in a fine frame of mind for such work. But nothing was attempted, and when the soldiers felt themselves in a position to repel any attempt against them that night, two guns were fired as a signal to friends that the occupation had been successfully accomplished, and that they might proceed with their part of the programme. This was the first intimation the guard-boat people had of the transfer; and, indeed, it told them nothing, except that some soldiers must have got into Sumter. But they blew their alarm-whistle all the same, and burned blue-lights; signal-rockets were sent up from various points, and there was great excitement everywhere in the harbor until morning.

Troops join in prayer at Fort Sumter on December 27, 1860.

When the signal-guns were fired, the officer in charge of the two schooners which had carried provisions and ammunition to Fort Johnson (under the pretense that they were subsistence for the women and children, whom he had also carried there as a cloak) cast loose his lines and made all speed for Sumter, and the old sergeant who had been left in Moultrie for the purpose set fire to the combustibles which had been heaped around the gun-carriages, while another man spiked the guns. The garrison from the ramparts of its new nest grimly approved of the destruction of the old one.

At dawn of December 27th the men were up and ready for any emergency; indeed, most of them had been up all night. Captain Foster had been specially busy with his former employees. Among them he found several loyal men, and also some doubtful ones who were willing to share the fortunes of the garrison. These constituted an acceptable addition to our working strength, although those classed as doubtful would have been an element of weakness in case of a fight. However, they did much good work

before hostilities began, and the worst ones were weeded out before we were closely invested. Those who remained to the end were excellent men. They endured the hardships of the siege and the dangers of the bombardment without a murmur, and left Sumter with the garrison—one of them, John Swearer, severely wounded—with little besides the clothes they stood in. They were the first volunteers for the Union, but were barred from the benefits secured by legislation for the national soldiers, having never been "mustered in."

Fort Sumter was unfinished, and the interior was filled with building materials, guns, carriages, shot, shell, derricks, timbers, blocks and tackle, and coils of rope in great confusion. Few guns were mounted, and these few were chiefly on the lowest tier. The work was intended for three tiers of guns, but the embrasures of the second tier were incomplete, and guns could be mounted on the first and third tiers only.

The complete armament of the work had not yet arrived, but there were more guns on hand than we

The main battery at Fort Sumter bore on Fort Moultrie and the channel.

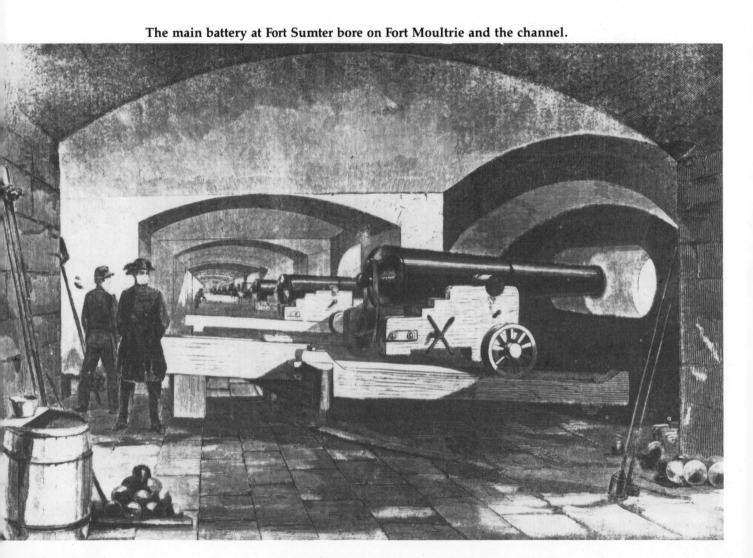

could mount or man. The first thing to be considered was immediate defense. The possibility of a sudden dash by the enemy, under cover of darkness and guided by the discharged workmen then in Charleston, demanded instant attention. It was impossible to spread 65 men over ground intended for 650, so some of the embrasures had to be bricked up. Selecting those, therefore, essential to artillery defense, and mounting guns in them, Anderson closed the rest. This was the work of many days; but we were in no immediate danger of an artillery attack. The armament of Moultrie was destroyed; its guns were spiked, and their carriages burned; and it would take a longer time to put them in condition than it would to mount the guns of Sumter.

On the parade were quantities of flag-stones standing on end in masses and columns everywhere. We dared not leave them where they were, even if they had not been in the way, because mortar shells bursting among them would have made the very bomb-proofs untenable. A happy idea occurred to some one in authority, and the flag-stones were arranged two tiers high in front of the casemates, and just under the arches, thus partly closing the casemates and making excellent splinter-proofs. This arrangement, no doubt, saved the garrison from many wounds similar to that inflicted on John Swearer, for it was in passing an opening unprotected by the screen that he was struck by a fragment of shell.

Moving such immense quantities of material, mounting guns, distributing shot, and bricking up embrasures kept us busy for many weeks. But order was coming out of chaos every day, and the soldiers began to feel that they were a match for their adversaries. Still, they could not shut their eyes to the fact that formidable works were growing up around them. The secessionists were busy too, and they had the advantage of unlimited labor and material. Fort Moultrie had its armament again in position, and was receiving the framework of logs which formed the foundation for its sandbag bomb-proofs. The Stevens's Point floating battery was being made impregnable by an overcoat of railroad iron; and batteries on Morris, James, and Sullivan's islands were approaching completion. But our preparations were more advanced than theirs; and if we had been permitted to open on them at this time, the bombardment of Sumter would have had very different termination. But our hands were tied by policy and instructions.

The heaviest guns in Sumter were three ten-inch columbiads—considered very big guns in those days. They weighed fifteen thousand pounds each, and were intended for the gorge and salient angles of the work. We found them skidded on the parade ground. Besides these there was a large number of eight-inch columbiads—more than we could mount or man—and a full supply of 42, 32, and 24-pounders, and some eight-inch sea-coast howitzers. There was an ample supply of shot and shell, and plenty of powder in the magazines, but friction primers were not

abundant and cartridge-bags were scarce. The scarcity of cartridge-bags drove us to some strange makeshifts. During the bombardment several tailors were kept busy making cartridge-bags out of soldiers' flannel shirts, and we fired away several dozen pairs of wollen socks belonging to Major Anderson. In the matter of friction primers strict economy had to be observed, as we had no means of improvising a substitute.

Our first efforts in preparation were directed toward mounting the necessary guns on the lowest tier. These consisted of 42 and 32-pounders, and as the necessary trucks, gins, and tackle were on hand, the work went on rapidly. The men were in fine condition and as yet well fed; besides, they had the assistance of the engineer workmen, who soon became experts at this kind of work. Meantime a party of mechanics were making the main gate secure. This was situated at the middle of the gorge or base of the pentagon (the trace of the work was pentagonal), which was also the south-west side. It was closed by two heavy iron-studded gates, the outer a folding pair, and the inner arranged on pulleys, so that it could be raised or lowered at will. It was clear that the enemy, if he meant to bombard us, would erect batteries on Morris Island, and thus would be able to deliver an oblique fire on the gate sufficient to demolish it in a very few minutes. The gate once demolished, a night assault would become practicable.

To meet this possible emergency the main entrance was closed by a substantial brick wall, with a man-hole in the middle two feet wide and opposite to the man-hole in the gate. This wall was about six feet high, and to increase the security and sweep the wharf, an eight-inch sea-coast howitzer was mounted on its upper carriage without any chassis, so as to fire through the man-hold. The howitzer was kept loaded with double canister. To induce the belief that the folding gates were our sole dependence at this point, their outer surface was covered with iron.

The lower tier of guns being mounted, the more difficult operation of sending guns up to the third tier began. The terre-plein of work was about fifty feet above parade level,—a considerable hoist,—but a pair of shears being already in position, and our tackle equal to the weight of eight-inch columbiads, the work went on amidst much good humor until all the guns of that caliber were in position.

We had now reached a problem more difficult to solve, namely, sending up our ten-inch columbiads. We were extremely desirous to have them—or at least two of them—on the upper tier. They were more powerful guns than any the enemy had at that time, and the only ones in our possession capable of smashing the iron-clad defenses which might be constructed against us. We had rumors that an iron-clad floating battery was being built in Charleston, which the enemy proposed to anchor in some convenient position so as to breach Sumter at his leisure. We had no faith in the penetrating power of the eight-inch guns, and if we wished to demolish this floating adversary, it was necessary that the ten-inch guns should be mounted. Besides, an iron-clad battery was well on the road to completion at Cumming's Point (twelve hundred yards from the weakest side of Sumter), which, from what we could see of it, would be impervious to any less powerful gun.

There was in the fort a large coil of very heavy rope, new, and strong enough to sustain fifteen thousand pounds, but some of the doubtful workmen had cut several strands of it at various points on the outside of the coil; at least we could account in no other way for the damage. Besides, we had no blocks large enough to receive the rope even if it had been uninjured. The rope was uncoiled and examined. The portion of the inner side of the coil was found uninjured, and a few splices gave rope enough for a triple tackle sixty feet long. The improvisation of blocks of sufficient size and strength now became the sole remaining difficulty, and it was overcome in this way: the gun-carriages of those days were made of well-seasoned oak, and one of them was cut up and the material used for the construction of blocks. When the blocks were finished the iron-clad battery was shorn of half its terrors.

The tackle thus improvised was rigged on the shears, the first gun was rolled into position for hoisting, the sling was attached, and the windlass was manned. After carefully inspecting every knot and lashing, the officer in charge gave the word, "Heave away," and the men bent to their work steadily and earnestly, feeling, no doubt, that the battle with the iron-clad had really begun. Every eye watched the ropes as they began to take the strain, and when the gun had fairly left the skids, and there was no accident, the song which anxiety had suspended was resumed, all hands joining in the chorus, "On the plains of Mexico," with a sonorous heartiness that might well have been heard at Fort Moultrie. The gun made the vertical passage of fifty feet successfully, and was safely landed on the terre-plein. The chassis and carriage were then sent up, transported to the proper emplacement, and put in position, and the gun was mounted.

The ten-inch columbiad threw a shot weighing one hundred and twenty-eight pounds, and it was now necessary that a supply of such should be raised. Of course, they could have been sent up at the derrick, but that would have been a slow process, and, moreover, it would have required the derrick and the men, when they were needed for other work. So after retreat roll-call, when the day's work was over, the men were bantered by some designing sergeant as to their ability to carry a ten-inch shot up the stairway. Some of the soldiers, full of confidence and energy, shouldered a shot each and started. They accomplished the feat, and the less confident, unwilling to be outdone by comrades no bigger than themselves, shouldered a shot each and made the passage. In a few minutes sixty shot were deposited near the gun; and it became the custom to carry up a ten-inch shot after retreat—just for fun—as long as there were any to carry.

These trivial incidents serve to show the spirit and humor of the men better than any description. There never was a happier or more contented set of men in any garrison than the Sumter soldiers. There was no sulkiness among them, and no grumbling until they had to try their teeth on spun yarn as a substitute for tobacco. This occurred long before the ration was reduced, and it produced some of the loudest grumbling ever listened to.

The second ten-inch columbiad was less fortunate than its fellow. It reached the level of the terre-plein without accident, but almost at the first haul on the watch tackle to swing it in, it broke away and fell with a dull thud. There was no mirth in the faces of the men at the watch tackle as they looked over the edge of the parade wall to see how many of the men at the windlass were left. The gun had descended, breech first, like a bolt from a catapult, and had buried itself in the sand up to the trunnions; but beyond breaking the transoms of the derrick, no damage was done. The cause of the accident was easily discovered. The amateur block-maker, unwilling to weaken the blocks by too much trimming, had left their upper edges too sharp, and the strap of the upper block had been cut in consequence. In four days the derrick was repaired, and the gun safely landed on the terre-plein.

The third ten-inch columbiad was not sent up. It was mounted as a mortar on the parade, for the purpose of shelling Charleston should that become advisable. A mortar platform already existed there. A ten-inch top carriage was placed on it and the gun mounted pointing toward the city.

A laughable incident occurred in connection with this gun soon after it was mounted. Some of the officers were anxious to try how it would work, and perhaps to see how true its alignment was, and to advertise to the enemy the fact that we had at least one formidable mortar in Fort Sumter. At any rate they obtained permission from Major Anderson to try the gun with a "very small charge." So, one afternoon the gun was loaded with a blind shell, and what was considered a "very small charge" of powder. The regulation charge for the gun, as a gun, was eighteen pounds. On this occasion two pounds only were used. It was not expected that the shell would be thrown over a thousand yards, and as the bay was clear no danger was anticipated. Everything being in readiness, the gun was fired, and the eyes of the garrison followed the shell as it described its graceful curve in the direction of the city. By the time it reached the summit of its trajectory, the fact that the charge used was not a "very small" one for the gun fired as a mortar became painfully apparent to every observer, and fears were entertained by some that the shell would reach the city, or at least the shipping near the wharves. But fortunately it fell short, and did no damage beyond scaring the secessionist guard-boat then leaving the wharf for her nightly post of observation. The guard-boat put back

A ten-inch columbiad was mounted as a mortar at Fort Sumter.

and Sumter was visited by a flag of truce, perhaps to find out the meaning of our performance. No doubt the explanations given were satisfactory. No more experiments for range were tried with that gun, but we knew that Charleston was within range.

Although the full armament of Sumter was not on hand, there were many more guns than places to put them. This resulted from the fact that no guns were mounted on the second tier, and because many embrasures on the first tier were bricked up. There were four unplaced eight-inch columbiads after the fort had been satisfactorily garnished with guns. But we were entirely without mortars. Perhaps this serious defect in our armament, and perhaps our success with the ten-inch gun mounted as a mortar, induced Major Anderson to mount his extra eight-inch guns in that way. Morris Island, twelve hundred yards away, was the nearest terra firma to Fort Sumter, and there the enemy would plant his most important batteries. The more searching and severe the fire that could be brought to bear upon that island, therefore, the better. So the four extra columbiads were mounted as mortars to fire in that direction. We had

no carriages for the guns and no platforms. So a trench was dug in the parade at right angles to the proposed line of fire. A heavy timber was then embedded in the sand at the bottom of the trench, and another on the Morris Island side of it, in such a way that a gun resting on the one and leaning on the other would be supported at an angle of forty-five degrees. The guns were then placed in notches at equal intervals along the trench. We had no opportunity to try this novel mortar battery, but everybody was satisfied that it could have done good service.

It was expected that the walls of Fort Sumter would be able to withstand the guns which we knew the enemy possessed, but we did not anticipate importations from abroad. During the bombardment a Whitworth gun of small caliber, just received from England, was mounted in one of the Morris Island batteries, and in a few rounds demonstrated its ability to breach the work. Fortunately its supply of ammunition was limited, and the fire stopped short of an actual breach. But a few hours more of that Whitworth 12-pounder would have knocked a hole in our defenses.

A breach was not dreaded by the garrison, for, weak as it was, it could have given a good account of itself defending a breach. The greatest danger was a simultaneous attack on all sides. Sixty-four men could not be made very effective at a dozen different points. The possibility of the enemy, under cover of darkness, getting a foothold in force on the narrow bit of riprapping between tide-water and the foundation of the scarp was ever present in our minds.

The most likely place to land was the wharf, a stone structure in front of the main entrance. There an assaulting column might be formed and the main gate stormed, while the bulk of the garrison was defending the embrasures. To checkmate any such attempt, means of blowing the wharf out of existence were devised. Two five-gallon demijohns filled with powder were planted as mines, well under the wharf pavement, in such a way as to insure the total demolition of the structure by their explosion. Those mines were arranged so that both should explode at the same instant. The means of firing were twofold: first, a powder-hose leading from the mines through a wooden trough buried under the pavement, and terminating in a dry well just inside the gate; second, a long lanyard connected with friction primers inserted in the corks of the powder demijohns, and extending through the trough into the well, whence it branched like a bell wire to convenient points inside the fort.

Another place offering special advantages to a storming party was the esplanade. This was a broad promenade extending the whole length of the gorge wall on the outside, and paved with immense blocks of dressed granite. As Fort Sumter was not designed to resist attack by storm, the esplanade was unswept by any fire. To remedy this defect the stone fougasse was resorted to. To the uninitiated the "fougasse" looked like a harmless pile of stones resting against the scarp wall. The only thing that would be likely to attract his attention was the bin-like inclosure of solid mansonry open at the outer side, which looked like an immense dust-pan, and which he might think was a rather elaborate arrangement to hold merely a pile of stones together. There was nothing to indicate that beneath the stones, in the angle close to the scarp wall, a magazine of gunpowder lay concealed, and that behind were arrangements for firing it from the inside of the works. These harmless-looking piles of stones were mines of the deadliest kind. In addition, two eight-inch sea-coast howitzers were mounted on their upper carriages only, and placed in front of the main entrance, pointing to the right and left so as to sweep the esplanade.

The possibility of a hostile landing on the narrow strip of riprapping between the scarp wall and tide-water still remained to be provided for. Before secondary defenses were constructed, this was a continuous dead space on which a thousand men could have found a safe lodgment perfectly screened from fire and observation. The danger from such a lodgment was, that from it all our embrasures could have been assulted at the same time. It was all-important, therefore, that the entrance by an embrasure should be made as difficult as possible. The ledge of riprapping was little more than four feet below the sills of the embrasures, and there would have been no difficulty in stepping in, if the two or three guards inside were disposed of. This fact was well known to the enemy, and we felt certain that, if he decided to attempt an assault in this way, he would consider scaling-ladders unnecessary. In order to disappoint him, therefore, we removed the riprapping in front of each embrasure to the depth of four or five feet, rolling the large stones into the water. This gave a height of eight or nine feet to the embrasure sills.

Machicoulis galleries were also erected on all the flanks and faces of the work. The machicoulis when completed looked like an immense dry-goods box, set upon the parapet so as to project over the wall some three or four feet. The beams upon which it rested extended inward to the terre-plein and were securely anchored down. But the dry-goods box was deceptive. Inside it was lined with heavy iron plates to make it bullet-proof. That portion of the bottom which projected beyond the wall was loop-holed for musketry, and a marksman in the machicoulis could shoot a man, however close he might be to the scarp wall. But musketry from the machicoulis could hardly be expected to beat off a determined assault upon the flanks and faces of the work. To meet this difficulty, hand-grenades were improvised. Shells of all sizes, from 12-pounders to 10-inch, were loaded, and the fuse-holes stopped with wooden plugs. The plugs were then bored through with a gimlet, and friction primers inserted. Behind the parapet at short intervals, and wherever it was thought they might be useful, numbers of these shell-grenades were stored under safe cover in readiness for any emergency. The method of throwing them was simple. Lanyards of sufficient length to reach to within about four feet of the riprapping were prepared, and fastened securely at the handle end near the piles of shell-grenades. To throw a grenade, the soldier lifted it on the parapet, hooked the lanyard into the eye of the friction primer, and threw the shell over the parapet. When the lanyard reached its length, the shell exploded. Thus a very few men would be more than a match for all that could assemble on the riprapping.

Another contrivance, the "flying fougasse," or bursting barrel, a device of Captain Truman Seymour, consisted of an ordinary cask or barrel filled with broken stones, and having in its center a canister of powder, sufficient to burst the barrel and scatter its contents with considerable force. A fuse connected the powder in the canister with a friction primer in the bung, and the barrel was exploded by attaching a lanyard to the eye of the primer, and letting the barrel roll over the parapet, as in the case of the shell-grenade. If one experiment can justify an opinion, the flying fougasse would have been a success. When it became known in the fort that one of the barrels was about to be fired as an experiment, the novelty of the thing attracted most of the men to the place, and the little crowd attracted the attention of the enemy. No doubt glasses were focused on the party from every battery within sight. When everything was ready the barrel was allowed to roll over the parapet, and an instant afterward a terrific explosion took place. The stones were thrown in every direction, and the surface of the water was lashed into foam for a considerable distance. The effect as seen by the secessionists must have appeared greater than it did to us, although we thought it quite satisfactory. The Charleston newspapers described the effect of the "infernal machine" as simply terrific. Only three of them were constructed, yet for moral effect an empty barrel set upon the parapet would have been just as good.

In war, plan as we may, much depends upon accident, and the moral effect of very insignificant incidents is often considerable. For this reason "Wittyman's Masterpiece" deserves to be mentioned. Wittyman was a German carpenter, not very familiar with English, and wholly ignorant of military engineering. His captain had conceived the idea that a *cheval-de-frise* across the riprapping at the salient angles of the fort would confine the enemy on whatever face he landed until he had been treated liberally with shell-grenades. So Wittyman was ordered to build a *cheval-de-frise* at the angle of the gorge nearest Morris Island. It was easy to see that Wittyman was not familiar with *chevaux-de-frise*, so the captain explained and roughly illustrated the construction. At last Wittyman seemed to grasp the idea and went to work upon it forthwith. Perhaps the work was not examined during construction, nor seen by any one but Wittyman until it was placed.

But from that day forward it was the fountain of amusement for the men. No matter how sick or sad a man might be, let him look at the masterpiece and his ailments were forgotten. Not a steamer passed,— and they were passing almost every hour,—but every glass on board was leveled at the masterpiece. But it baffled every one of them. Not one could guess what it was, or what it was intended to be; and after the bombardment was over we learned, quite accidentally, that it had been set down by the enemy as a means of exploding the mines.

Any description of the siege of Sumter would be incomplete without some sort of reference to the *Star of the West* fiasco. At reveille on the 9th of January, it became generally known among the men that a large steamer flying the United States flag was off the bar, seemingly at anchor. There had been some talk among the men, based upon rumors from Charleston, that the garrison would either be withdrawn from the harbor or returned to Fort Moultrie; and there were some who believed the rumors. These believers were now confident that withdrawal had been determined on, and that the steamer off the bar was the transport come to take them away. There was no denying that appearances favored the theory, yet there was no enthusiasm. The men were beginning to feel that they were a match for their adversaries, and they were loath to leave without proving it. And, indeed, at that time Sumter was master of the situation. Moultrie had very few guns mounted,—only one, according to report,—and that fact ought to have been known to the people on the

The *Star of the West* carried men and supplies to reinforce Sumter.

Star of the West. It was known officially in Washington that fourteen days previously Major Anderson had spiked the guns and burned the carriages at Moultrie, and gun-carriages cannot be replaced in two weeks when they have to be fabricated. Hence Moultrie could not have been formidable, and as soon as it should have passed the battery on Morris Island, it would have been comparatively safe.

When the *Star of the West* was seen standing in, the novelty of a steamer carrying the national flag had more attractions for the men than the breakfast table. They soon made her out to be a merchant steamer, as the walking-beam, plainly visible as she rounded into the channel, was unknown on a man-of-war. She had taken the Morris Island channel, and was approaching at a fair rate of speed. Perhaps every man in Sumter was on the ramparts, but there was no excitement. But when the blue puff of smoke from a hidden battery on Morris Island advertised the fact that she was being fired on, there was great scurrying and scampering among the men. The long roll was beaten, and the batteries were manned almost before the guns of the hidden battery had fired their second shot. As she approached, a single gun at Fort Moultrie opened at extreme long range, its shot falling over half a mile short. There seemed to be much perplexity among our officers, and Major Anderson had a conference with some of them in a room used as a laundry which opened on the terreplein of the sea-flank. The conference was an impromptu one, as Captain Doubleday and Lieutenant Davis were not of it. But Captain Foster was there, and by his actions demonstrated his disappointment at the result. He left the laundry, bounding up the two or three steps that led to the terre-plein, smashing his hat, and muttering something about the flag, of which the words "trample on it" reached the ears of the men at the guns, and let them know that there was to be no fighting, on their part at least. Meantime the steamer had worn ship, and was standing out again, receiving the fire of the hidden battery in passing. This is about all the men saw or knew about the strange vessel at the time, although she came near enough for them to look down upon her decks and see that there were no troops visible on her.

With the exception of the mounting of the guns, the preparations described were chiefly intended to ward off assault. The actions of the enemy now indicated that he proposed to bombard the work at an early day. If we would meet Moultrie, and the numerous batteries which were being constructed against us, on anything like even terms, we must be prepared to shoot accurately.

Few artillerymen, without actual experience, have any idea of the difficulty of aiming a gun during a bombardment. They may be able to hit a target in ordinary practice with absolute certainty, and yet be unable to deliver a single satisfactory shot in a bombardment. The error from smoke is difficult to deal with, because it is a variable, depending upon the density of the smoke clouds which envelop your own and your adversary's batteries. (Within the writer's experience, a thin veil of fog protected a mass of army wagons—900, it was said—from the fire of some 8 or 10 guns, during a whole forenoon, although the guns were within easy range, and the wagons could be distinctly seen. Refraction saved them, every shot going over.) Then danger and its consequent excitement are also disturbing elements, especially where delicate instruments have to be used. It is easier to lead a forlorn hope than to set a vernier under a heavy artillery fire. Fortunately, we had officers of experience in Sumter, and fortunately, too, we had very few instruments; one gunner's level and two old quadrants being the extent of the outfit, with perhaps some breech-sights and tangent-scales. The paucity of aiming-instruments, and perhaps the experience of some of the officers, led to the devising of instruments and methods which neither smoke nor excitement could disturb; and as some of them, in a much more perfect form, have since been adopted, the rude originals may as well be described here. Aiming cannon consists of two distinct operations: namely, alignment and elevation. In the former, according to instructions and practice, the gunner depends upon his eye and the cannon-sights. But for night firing or when the enemy is enveloped in smoke,—as he is sure to be in any artillery duel,—the eye cannot be depended on. Visual aiming in a bombardment is a delusion and a snare. To overcome this difficulty, on clear days, when all the conditions were favorable to accuracy, and we could work at our leisure, every gun in the armament was carefully aimed at all the prominent objects within its field of fire, and its position marked on the traverse circle, the index being a pointer securely fastened to the traverse fork. After this had been done, alignment became as easy as setting a watch, and could be done by night or day, by the least intelligent soldier in the garrison.

The elevation was more difficult to deal with. The ordinary method by the use of a breech-sight could not be depended on, even if there had been a sufficient supply of such instruments, because darkness or smoke would render it inapplicable or inaccurate; and the two quadrants in the outfit could not be distributed all over the fort.

Before the correct elevation to carry a shot to a given object can be determined, it is necessary to know the exact distance of the object. This was obtained from the coast-survey chart of the harbor. The necessary elevation was then calculated, or taken from the tables, and the gun elevated accordingly by means of the quadrant. The question then became, How can the gunner bring the gun to this elevation in the heat of action, and without the use of a quadrant? There was an abundance of brass rods, perhaps a quarter-inch in diameter, in the fort. Pieces of such rods, eighteen inches long, were prepared by shaping one end to fit into a socket on the cheek of the carriage, and the other into a chisel edge. They were called by the men pointing rods. A vertical line was then drawn on the right breech of the gun, and painted white. The non-commissioned officer who attended to this preparation, having carefully elevated the gun with the quadrant for a particular object, set the pointing rod in the socket, and brought its chisel end down on the vertical. The point thus cut was marked and the initials of the object to be struck with that elevation written opposite. These arrangements, which originated with Captain Doubleday, were of great value during the bombardment.

The preparation of Sumter for defense afforded a fine field for ingenuity, because nothing connected with its equipment was complete. As another illustration of this ingenuity, the following is in point. It might become desirable to continue a bombardment into the night, and the casemates, owing to the partial closing up of the arches with flagstones, were as dark as dungeons, even on very clear nights. Lights of some kind were absolutely necessary, but there were no candles and no lamps. There was a light-house on the fort, however, and the light-keeper had several barrels of oil on hand. Small tubes of tin, to receive wicks, were made, and fitted into disks of cork sufficiently large to float them on the surface of the oil. Coffee-cups were then filled with oil and the floats laid on the surface.

Among the many incidents of the siege may be mentioned the mishap of an ice-laden Yankee schooner that strayed within range of the secession batteries; the accidental solid shot fired at Fort Sumter by an impatient secessionist in the Cumming's Point battery, and the daring generosity of McInerny, a warm-hearted and loyal Irishman, who did not "cross the broad Atlantic to become the citizen of only one State," and who cheerfully risked his life and ruined his Sunday shirt by tearing a white flag from it, that he might be able to deliver in person his donation of tobacco to the besieged soldiers. There is one other incident which should find a place in these reminiscences.

Major Anderson was fully impressed with the solemn responsibilities which rested upon him when he transferred his command to Sumter. When he reached Sumter there were no halliards to the flagstaff, and as there was more pressing work on hand for several days, some time elapsed before it became possible to display the national flag. At length, however, halliards were rigged, and everything was ready for the flag. The usual method of proceeding in such a case would have been to order the sergeant of the guard to send up the flag, but it was otherwise arranged on this occasion. A dress-parade was ordered, and the little garrison formed around the flag-staff, the officers in the center. Presently Major Anderson, with Chaplain Harris of Fort Moultrie, who perhaps had been summoned for the purpose, approached the flag-staff, and the command was brought to "Attention." The flag, already bent to the halliards, was held by one officer, and another held the hoisting end of the halliards. The chaplain then, in a few words, invited those present to join with him in prayer, and Major Anderson, receiving the halliards from the officer who till that time had held them,

knelt beside the chaplain, most of the officers and some of the men in the ranks following his example. Prayers being ended, all rose, and the flag of Fort Sumter was raised by Major Anderson, and the halliards secured. He then turned toward the officers and directed that the companies be dismissed. If any of those who doubted the loyalty to the Union of Major Anderson could have had but one glimpse of that impressive scene, they would have doubted no longer.

The weary waiting for war or deliverance which filled up the few weeks that intervened between the preparations and the actual bombardment developed no discontent among the men, although food and fuel were getting scarce. The latter was replenished from time to time by tearing down sheds and temporary workshops, but the former was a constantly diminishing quantity, and the men could count on their fingers the number of days between them and starvation. It was a favorite belief among the secessionists that the pinchings of hunger would arouse a spirit of mutiny among the soldiers, and compel Major Anderson to propose terms of evacuation. But no such spirit manifested itself. On the contrary, the men exhibited a devotion to their Government and the officers appointed over them which surprised their enemies, but attracted little attention from their friends.

The opening of the bombardment was a somewhat dramatic event. A relieving fleet was approaching, all unknown to the Sumter garrison, and General Beauregard, perhaps with the hope of tying Major Anderson's hands in the expected fight with that fleet, had opened negotiations with him on the 11th of April looking toward the evacuation of the fort. But Major Anderson declined to evacuate his post till compelled by hunger. The last ounce of breadstuffs had been consumed, and matters were manifestly approaching a crisis. It was evident from the activity of the enemy that something important was in the wind. That night we retired as usual. Toward half-past three on the morning of the 12th we were startled by a gun fired in the immediate vicinity of the fort, and many rose to see what was the matter. It was soon learned that a steamer from the enemy desired to communicate with Major Anderson, and a small boat under a flag of truce was received and delivered the message. Although no formal announcement of the fact was made, it became generally known among the men that in one hour General Beauregard would open his batteries on Sumter.

The men waited about for some time in expectation of orders, but received none, except an informal order to go to bed, and the information that reveille would be sounded at the usual hour. This was daylight, fully two hours off, so some of the men did retire. The majority perhaps remained up, anxious to see the opening, for which purpose they had all gone on the ramparts. Except that the flag was hoisted, and a glimmer of light was visible at the guard-house, the fort looked so dark and silent as to seem deserted. The morning was dark and raw. Some of the watchers surmised that Beauregard was "bluffing," and that there would be no bombardment. But promptly at 4:30 A.M. a flash as of distant lightning in the direction of Mount Pleasant, followed by the dull roar of a mortar, told us that the bombardment had begun. The eyes of the watchers easily detected and followed the burning fuse which marked the course of the shell as it mounted among the stars, and then descended with ever-increasing velocity, until it landed inside the fort and burst. It was a capital shot. Then the batteries opened on all sides, and shot and shell went screaming over Sumter as if an army of devils were swooping around it. As a rule the guns were aimed too high, but all the mortar practice was good. In a few minutes the novelty disappeared in a realizing sense of danger, and the watchers retired to the bomb-proofs, where they discussed probabilities until reveille.

Habits of discipline are strong among old soldiers.

The bombardment of Sumter began at 4:30 in the morning.

If it had not been for orders to the contrary, the men would have formed for roll-call on the open parade, as it was their custom to do, although mortar-shells were bursting there at the lively rate of about one a minute. But they were formed under the bomb-proofs, and the roll was called as if nothing unusual was going on. They were then directed to get breakfast, and be ready to fall in when "assembly" was beaten. The breakfast part of the order was considered a grim joke, as the fare was reduced to the solitary item of fat pork, very rusty indeed. But most of the men worried down a little of it, and were "ready" when the drum called them to their work.

By this time it was daylight, and the effects of the bombardment became visible. No serious damage was being done to the fort. The enemy had concentrated their fire on the barbette batteries, but, like most inexperienced gunners, they were firing too high. After daylight their shooting improved, until at 7:30 A.M., when "assembly" was beaten in Sumter, it had become fairly good. At "assembly" the men were again paraded, and the orders of the day announced. The garrison was divided into two reliefs, and the tour of duty at the guns was to be four hours. Captain Doubleday being the senior captain, his battery took the first tour.

There were three points to be fired upon,—the Morris Island batteries, the James Island batteries, and the Sullivan's Island batteries. With these last was included the famous iron-clad floating battery, which had taken up a position off the western end of Sullivan's Island to command the left flank of Sumter. Captain Doubleday divided his men into three parties: the first, under his own immediate command, was marched to the casemate guns bearing on Morris Island; the second, under Lieutenant Jefferson C. Davis, manned the casemate guns bearing on the James Island batteries; and the third—without a commissioned officer until Dr. Crawford joined it—was marched by a sergeant to the guns bearing on Sullivan's Island. The guns in the lower tier, which were the only ones used during the bombardment,—except surreptitiously without orders,—were 32 and 42-pounders, and some curiosity was felt as to the effect of such shot on the iron-clad battery. The gunners made excellent practice, but the shot were seen to bounce off its sides like peas. After battering it for about an hour and a half, no visible effect had been produced, although it had perceptibly slackened its fire, perhaps to save ammunition. But it was evident that throwing 32-pounder shot at it, at a mile range, was a waste of iron, and the attention of the gunners was transferred to Fort Moultrie.

Moultrie was, perhaps, a less satisfactory target than the iron-clad. It was literally buried under sand-bags, the very throats of the embrasures being closed with cotton-bales. The use of cotton-bales was very effective as against shot, but would have been less so against shell. The fact that the embrasures were thus closed was not known in Sumter til after the bombardment. It explained what was otherwise inexplicabale. Shot would be seen to strike an embrasure, and the gunner would feel that he had settled one gun for certain, but even while he was receiving the congratulations of his comrades the supposed disabled gun would reply. That the cotton-bales could not be seen from Sumter is not surprising. The sand-bag casemates which covered the guns were at least eighteen feet thick, and the cotton-bale shutter was no doubt arranged to slide up and down like a portcullis inside the pile of sand-bags. The gunners of Sumter, not knowing of the existence of these shutters, directed their shot either on the embrasures for the purpose of disabling the enemy's guns, or so as to graze the sand-bag parapet for the purpose of reaching the interior of the work. The practice was very good, but the effect, for reasons already stated, was inconsiderable.

At the end of the first four hours, Doubleday's men were relieved from the guns and had an opportunity to look about them. Not a man was visible near any of the batteries, but a large party, apparently of non-combatants, had collected on the beach of Sullivan's Island, well out of the line of fire, to witness the duel between Sumter and Moultrie. Doubleday's men were not in the best of temper. They were irritated at the thought that they had been unable to inflict any serious damage on their adversary, and although they had suffered no damage in return they were dissatisfied. The crowd of unsympathetic spectators was more than they could bear, and two veteran sergeants determined to stir them up a little. For this purpose they directed two 42-pounders on the crowd, and, when no officer was near, fired. The first shot struck about fifty yards short, and, bounding over the heads of the astonished spectators, went crashing through the Moultrie House. The second followed an almost identical course, doing no damage except to the Moultrie House, and the spectators scampered off in a rather undignified manner. The Moultrie House was flying a yellow flag at the time, and the Charleston newspapers discoursed upon the barbarity of firing upon a hospital flag, forgetting, perhaps, that we also had a hospital in Sumter, which they treated to red-hot shot during the bombardment. Of course, none of the officers of Sumter knew anything about the two 42-pounder shot.

The smoke which enveloped the Confederate batteries during the first day, while not so thick as entirely to obscure them, was sufficiently so to make visual aiming extremely unreliable; and during the second day, when Sumter was on fire, nothing could be seen beyond the muzzles of our own guns. But the aiming arrangements, due to the foresight and ingenuity of Captain Doubleday, enabled us to fire with as much accuracy when we could not see the object as when we could.

Early on the first day several vessels of the fleet were observed off the bar, and orders were given to dip the flag to them. This was done, and the salute was returned, but while our flag was being hoisted after the third dip, a shell burst near the flag-staff and cut the halliards. This accident put the flag beyond our control. It ran down until the kinky halliards jammed in the pulley at the mast-head, and the flag remained at about half-staff. This has been interpreted as a signal of distress, but it was only an accident. There was no special distress in Sumter, and no signal to that effect was intended.

Major Anderson had given orders that only the casemate batteries should be manned. While this was undoubtedly prompted by a desire to save his men, it operated also, in some degree, to save the Confederates. Our most powerful batteries and all our shell guns were on the barbette tier, and, being forbidden their use, we were compelled to oppose a destructive shell fire with solid shot alone. This, especially as we had no mortars, was a great disadvantage. Had we been permitted to use our shell guns we could have set fire to the barracks and quarters in Moultrie; for, as it was, we wrecked them badly with solid shot, although we could not see them. Then the cotton-bale shutters would have been destroyed, and we could have made it much livelier generally for our adversaries. This was so apparent to the men, that one of them—a man named Carmody—stole up on the ramparts and deliberately fired every barbette gun in position on the Moultrie side of the work. The guns were already loaded and roughly aimed, and Carmody simply discharged them in succession; hence, the effect was less than it would have been if the aim had been carefully rectified. But Carmody's effort aroused the enemy to a sense of his danger. He supposed, no doubt, that Major Anderson had determined to open his barbette batteries, so he directed every gun to bear on the barbette tier of Fort Sumter, and probably believed that the vigor of his fire induced Major Anderson to change his mind. But the contest was merely Carmody against the Confederate States; and Carmody had to back down, not because he was beaten, but because he was unable, single-handed, to reload his guns.

Another amusing incident in this line occurred on the Morris Island side of the fort. There, in the gorge angle, a ten-inch columbiad was mounted, *en barbette*, and as the 42-pounders of the casemate battery were making no impression on the Cumming's Point iron battery, the two veteran sergeants who had surreptitiously fired upon the spectators, as already related, determined to try a shot at the iron battery from the big gun. As this was a direct violation of orders, caution was necessary. Making sure that the major was out of the way, and that no officers were near, the two sergeants stole upstairs to the ten-inch gun. It was loaded and aimed already, they very well knew, so all they would have to do was to fire it. This was the work of a few seconds only. The gun was fired, and those in the secret down below watched the flight of the shot in great expectations of decided results. Unfortunately the shot missed; not a bad shot—almost grazing the crest of the battery—but a miss. A little less elevation, a very little, and the battery would have been

smashed: so thought the sergeants, for they had great faith in the power of their gun; and they determined to try a second shot. The gun was reloaded, a feat of some difficulty for two men, but to run it "in battery" was beyond their powers. It required the united efforts of six men to throw the carriage "in gear," and the two sergeants could not budge it. Things were getting desperate around them. The secessionists had noticed the first shot, and had now turned every gun that would bear on that ten-inch gun. They were just getting the range, and it was beginning to be uncomfortable for the sergeants, who in a fit of desperation determined to fire the gun "as she was." The elevating screw was given half a turn less elevation, and the primer was inserted in the vent. Then one of the sergeants ran down the spiral stairs to see if the coast were clear, leaving his comrade in a very uncomfortable position at the end of the lanyard, and lying flat on the floor. It was getting hotter up there every second, and a perfect hurricane of shot was sweeping over the prostrate soldier. Human nature could stand it no longer. The lanyard was pulled and the gun was fired. The other sergeant was hastening up the stairway, and he almost reached the top, when he met the gun coming down, or at least trying to. Having been fired "from battery," it had recoiled over the counter-hurters, and, turning a back somersault, had landed across the head of the stairway. Realizing in a moment what had happened, and what would be to pay if they were found out, the second sergeant crept to the head of the stairway and called his comrade, who, scared almost to death,—not at the danger he was in, but at the accident,—was still hugging the floor with the lanyard in his hand. Both got safely down, swearing eternal secrecy to each other; and it is doubtful if Major Anderson ever knew how that ten-inch gun came to be dismounted. It is proper to add that the shot was a capital one, striking just under the middle embrasure of the iron battery and half covering it with sand. If it had been a trifle higher it would have entered the embrasure.

The first night of the bombardment was one of great anxiety. The fleet might send reënforcements; the enemy might attempt an assault. Both would come in boats; both would answer in English. It would be horrible to fire upon friends; it would be fatal not to fire upon enemies. The night was dark and chilly. Shells were dropping into the fort at regular intervals, and the men were tired, hungry, and out of temper. Any party that approached that night would have been rated as enemies upon general principles. Fortunately nobody appeared; reveille sounded, and the men oiled their appetites with the fat pork at the usual hour by way of breakfast.

The second day's bombardment began at the same hour as did the first; that is, on the Sumter side. The enemy's mortars had kept up a very slow fire all night, which gradually warmed up after daylight as their batteries seemed to awaken, until its vigor was about equal to their fire of the day before. The fleet was still off the bar—perhaps waiting to see the end.

Fire broke out once or twice in the officers' quarters, and was extinguished. It broke out again in several places at once, and we realized the truth and let the quarters burn. They were firing red-hot shot. This was about 9 o'clock. As soon as Sumter was noticed to be on fire the secessionists increased the fire of their batteries to a maximum. In the perfect storm of shot and shell that beat upon us from all sides, the flag-staff was shot down, but the old flag was rescued and nailed to a new staff. This, with much difficulty, was carried to the ramparts and lashed to some chassis piled up there for a traverse.

We were not sorry to see the quarters burn. They were a nuisance. Built for fire-proof buildings, they were not fire-proof. Neither would they burn up in a cheerful way. The principal cisterns were large iron tanks immediately under the roof. These had been riddled, and the quarters below had been deluged with water. Everything was wet and burned badly, yielding an amount of pungent piney smoke which almost suffocated the garrison.

The scene inside the fort as the fire gained headway and threatened the magazine was an exciting one. It had already reached some of our stores of loaded shells and shell-grenades. These must be saved at all hazard. Soldiers brought their blankets and covered the precious projectiles, and thus the most of them were saved. But the magazine itself was in danger. Already it was full of smoke, and the flames were rapidly closing in upon it. It was evident that it must be closed, and it would be many hours before it could be opened again. During these hours the fire must be maintained with such powder as we could secure outside the magazine. A number of barrels were rolled out for this purpose, and the magazine door—already almost too hot to handle—was closed.

It was the intention to store the powder taken from the magazine in several safe corners, covering it with damp soldiers' blankets. But safe corners were hard to find, and most of the blankets were already in use covering loaded shells. The fire was raging more fiercely than ever, and safety demanded that the uncovered powder be thrown overboard. This was instantly done, and if the tide had been high we should have been well rid of it. But the tide was low, and the pile of powder-barrels rested on the riprapping in front of the embrasure. This was observed by the enemy, and some shell guns were turned upon the pile, producing an explosion which blew the gun at that embrasure clear out of battery, but did no further damage.

The fire had now enveloped the magazine, and the danger of an explosion was imminent. Powder had been carried out all the previous day, and it was more than likely that enough had sifted through the cartridge-bags to carry the fire into the powder-chamber. Major Anderson, his head erect as if on parade, called the men around him; directed that a shot be fired every five minutes; and mentioned that there was some danger of the magazine exploding. Some of the men, as soon as they learned what the

real danger was, rushed to the door of the magazine and hurriedly dug a trench in front of it, which they kept filled with water until the danger was considered over.

It was during this excitement that ex-Senator Wigfall of Texas visited the fort. It came the turn of one of the guns on the left face of the work to fire,—we were now firing once in five minutes,—and as the cannoneer approached for the purpose of loading, he discovered a man looking in at the embrasure. The man must have raised himself to the level of the embrasure by grasping the sill with his hands. A short but lively altercation ensued between the man and the cannoneer, the man pleading to be taken in lest he should be killed with his own shot and shell. He was hauled in, Thompson, the cannoneer, first receiving his sword, to the point of which a white handkerchief was attached, not by way of surrender, but for convenience. Once inside, the bearer asked to see Major Anderson. The major was soon on the spot and opened the conversation by asking, "To what am I indebted for this visit?" The visitor replied, "I am Colonel Wigfall, of General Beauregard's staff. For God's sake, Major, let this thing stop. There has been enough bloodshed already." To which the major replied, "There has been none on my side, and besides, your batteries are still firing on me." At which Wigfall exclaimed, "I'll soon stop that," and turning to Thompson, who still held the sword under his arm, he said, pointing to the handkerchief, "Wave that out there." Thompson then handed the sword to Wigfall, saying, in substance, "Wave it yourself." Wigfall received back his sword and took a few steps toward the embrasure, when the major called him back, saying, "If you desire that to be seen you had better send it to the parapet." There was a good deal more said on the subject of the white flag both by Wigfall and the major which the writer cannot recall, but the end of it all was that a white flag was ordered to be displayed from the parapet at the request of Colonel Wigfall, and pending negotiations with him, which was instantly done, a hospital sheet being used for the purpose. Then the firing gradually ceased, and the major and his officers and Colonel Wigfall retired into the hospital bomb-proof, the only habitable room left. This was about 3 o'clock in the afternoon.

Wigfall's conference was not of long duration. He left the fort in the small boat which brought him from Morris Island, and which was manned by negroes. Shortly after his departure another small boat from Sullivan's Island, containing officers in full uniform (Wigfall wore citizen's dress with the sword), approached the fort. The officers in this boat were very much astonished and annoyed at being warned off by the sentinel, and compelled to show a white flag before they were permitted to approach. They were received by the officer of the day, who apologized for not meeting them afloat, saying that all our boats had been destroyed by shot or burned up. They were indignant at their reception, and demanded to know whether or not the fort had surrendered. What was said in reply was not distinctly heard by the writer, but it was believed to be a negative. The officer then asked what the white flag meant, and Wigfall's name was mentioned in reply. About this time Major Anderson made his appearance, and the visitors, still talking in an indignant tone, addressed themselves to him. What was said seemed to be a repetition of what had just been said to the officer of the day. The major's replies were inaudible where the writer of this stood, except when he raised his hand in a sweeping sort of gesture in the direction of Fort Moultrie, and said, "Very well, gentlemen, you can return to your batteries."

They did not return, however, immediately, but were conducted into the hospital where Wigfall had been, and remained there some time. When they left we learned that there would be no more firing until General Beauregard had time to hear from his Government at Montgomery.

About 7 o'clock in the evening another white flag brought the announcement that the terms agreed upon between General Beauregard and Major Anderson had been confirmed, and that we would leave Fort Sumter the following day; which we did, after saluting our flag with fifty guns.

★★★

JOHN GIBBON

The Rumblings of Civil War Reach a Frontier Garrison

The secession winter found John Gibbon—a talented young officer whose Artillerist's Manual *(Washington, 1860) would be used by gunners on both sides—at an isolated frontier post. Gibbon, a Pennsylvania-born North Carolinian who had three brothers in Confederate service, cast his lot with the Union. He eventually rose to brigadier general in the Regular Army and had a distinguished career during the Civil War—it*

was his corps which received Pickett's Charge at Gettysburg—and afterwards, spending some 20 years of his 44 years in the service on the frontier. Here, in an excerpt from his Personal Recollections of the Civil War *(New York, 1928) Gibbon recounts how news of the momentous events in the East was received in Utah.*

Camp Floyd, Utah Territory, established in 1858 by Gen. Albert Sidney Johnston, was my station when, in the early spring of 1861, the rumblings of civil war first began to be heard in our country. In those days the stage coach and the pony express were the only means of communication across the continent; but a telegraph line had already been projected and a portion, as far as old Fort Kearney, on the Platte, was completed. To Fort Kearney the news of the country was "wired," and from there copies on manifold paper were sent by pony express to California and intermediate points. . . .

The road leading to Camp Floyd, located on a broad level sage-brush plain, was a wide and dusty one. On a clear, bright day anything moving along this road could be seen for miles, for the pony would leave behind him a streamer of dust almost as marked as the smoke of a moving engine. Arrangement had been made at the post to receive one copy of the news, sent from Fort Kearney; and every "pony day" at the specified hour the officers would assemble at the Post Trader's store and as soon as the

bag was opened an eager crowd gathered round to listen as one of the number read the latest news from "the States." Were the pony ever late the crowd was there all the same, some of them on the roof of the store, straining their eyes eastward anxious to be the first to cry: "Here he comes." As the spring advanced and the approaching storm in the east became more threatening, all wore an anxious, earnest look on "pony day" and the few absent ones hurried quickly to the Trader's store when the cry went through the camp "The pony is coming." Well do I remember the day the news was received of the firing on Fort Sumter. Looking back now and reading in the official records the correspondence between Beauregard and Anderson the whole scene comes up before me like a long forgotten dream. There were the silent anxious faces as the reader told of Beauregard's summons and Anderson's reply, the threat to open fire and the announcement that at the end of the specified time the guns did open, and that the harbor of Charleston reverberated with the sound of cannon, manned on both sides by brothers and life-long friends firing at each other! All were quiet, serious and thoughtful, as we wended our way back to our quarters to tell our wives and children that all our hopes of peace were blasted, and that our once happy and prosperous country was plunged into the horrors of civil war, the end of which no man could foretell.

Days and weeks now dragged their slow length along and all eyes were turned eagerly eastward for more news, while orders for our recall to the States were anxiously awaited. The attendance at the Trader's store on "pony days" was now more prompt than ever and the eager faces became more anxious as the dispatches described in succession the attempt and failure to relieve Fort Sumter, the final surrender of the Fort, the excitement throughout the country, the peril of Washington, the marshalling of forces, and the general preparations everywhere for the great struggle which all now saw was coming. Every succeeding dispatch added to the excitement at the post. There were a number of southern officers in the garrison, some of whom resigned and went home, and all of them, probably with one exception, were looked upon with a certain amount of suspicion and distrust not calculated to add to the social feeling among us.

The basic design of Washington as the Civil War broke out.

THE LEAP TO ARMS

FORT SUMTER WAS THE SIGNAL FOR WAR. THE TINY REGULAR ARMY NUMBERED LITTLE more than 16,000 and could scarcely muster 5,000 men in one place, at a time when the Confederacy had already some 35,000 under arms. On 15 April, the day after the fall of Sumter, Lincoln issued a call for 75,000 volunteers to put down "combinations too powerful to be supressed by the ordinary course of judicial proceedings." Shocked at the threat of force against the secessionists, the remaining slaveholding states, hitherto tentatively loyal to the Union, wavered. Most soon threw their lot in with the Confederacy: Virginia on 17 April, followed within weeks by Arkansas, North Carolina, and Tennessee, while Maryland, Kentucky, and Missouri were held to their loyalty only by desperate measures. In the North and South men sprang to arms by the thousands, all anxious to take part in the glorious adventure to come.

JOHN G. NICOLAY
Lincoln Calls for Volunteers

John G. Nicolay immigrated from Bavaria as a child, and settled with his family in Illinois. A journalist, ardent Republican, and early supporter of Lincoln, he became the latter's private secretary in 1860 and served in that capacity throughout the war. After the war Nicolay held a variety of diplomatic and civil service posts, and, in collaboration with John Hay, wrote a multi-volume biography of Lincoln and edited his complete works. Nicolay's account of Lincoln's call for volunteers is taken from his The Outbreak of the Rebellion *(New York, 1882).*

The news of the assault on Sumter reached Washington on Saturday, April 13th; on Sunday morning, the 14th, the President and Cabinet were met to discuss the surrender and evacuation. Sunday, though it was, Lincoln with his own hand immediately drafted the following proclamation, which was dated, issued, telegraphed, and published to the whole country on Monday morning, April 15th.

The possible contingency foreshadowed by Lincoln in his Trenton address had come; and he not only redeemed his promise to "put the foot down firmly," but he took care to place it on a solid foundation. Nominally the call of the militia was based on the act of 1795. But the broad language of the proclamation was an "appeal to all loyal citizens to favor, facilitate, and aid this effort to maintain the

PROCLAMATION

BY THE PRESIDENT OF THE UNITED STATES

Whereas, the laws of the United States have been for some time past and now are opposed, and the execution thereof obstructed in the States of South Carolina, Georgia, Alabama, Florida, Mississippi, Louisiana, and Texas, by combinations too powerful to be suppressed by the ordinary course of judicial proceedings, or by the powers vested in the marshals by law: now therefore, I ABRAHAM LINCOLN, President of the United States, in virtue of the power in me vested by the Constitution and the laws, have thought fit to call forth, and hereby do call forth the militia of the several States of the Union, to the aggregate number of seventy-five thousand, in order to suppress said combinations and to cause the laws to be duly executed.

The details for this object will be immediately communicated to the State authorities through the War Department. I appeal to all loyal citizens to favor, facilitate, and aid this effort to maintain the honor, the integrity, and existence of our National Union, and the perpetuity of popular government, and to redress wrongs already long enough endured. I deem it proper to say that the first service assigned to the forces hereby called forth will probably be to repossess the forts, places, and property which have been seized from the Union; and in every event the utmost care

will be observed, consistently with the objects aforesaid, to avoid any devastation, any destruction of, or interference with property, or any disturbance of peaceful citizens in any part of the country; and I hereby command the persons composing the combinations aforesaid to disperse and retire peaceably to their respective abodes within twenty days from this date.

Deeming that the present condition of public affairs presents an extraordinary occasion, I do hereby, in virtue of the power in me vested by the Constitution, convene both Houses of Congress. Senators and Representatives are therefore summoned to assemble at their respective chambers at twelve o'clock, noon, on Thursday, the fourth day of July next, then and there to consider and determine such measures as, in their wisdom, the public safety and interest may seem to demand.

In witness whereof, I have hereunto set my hand and caused the seal of the United States to be affixed.

Done at the City of Washington, this fifteenth day of April, in the year of our Lord one thousand eight hundred and sixty-one, and of the independence of the United States the eighty-fifth.

ABRAHAM LINCOLN

By the President.
William H. Seward, *Secretary of State*

honor, the integrity, and existence of our National Union, and the perpetuity of popular government." The President had taken care to so shape the issue— so to strip it of all provocation or ingenious excuse, as to show the reckless malignity of the rebellion in showering red-hot shot on a starving garrison; he now asked the people to maintain their assaulted dignity and outraged authority; touching not merely the machinery of forms and statutes, but invoking directly that spirit of free government to preserve itself, against which in his opinion "the gates of hell" could not prevail.

The correctness of his faith was equal to the wisdom of his policy; for now there was seen one of those mighty manifestations of national will and national strength that mark the grand epochs of civilized history. The whole country seemed to awaken as from the trouble of a feverish dream, and once again men entered upon a conscious recognition of their proper relations to the Government. Cross-purpose and perplexed counsel faded from the public mind. Parties vanished from politics. Universal opinion recognized but two rallying-points—the camps of the South which gathered to assail the Union, and the armies of the North that rose to defend it.

A parade recruits New York Zouaves.

EDWARD DICEY
The Union Creates an Army

Edward Dicey was a British journalist of liberal persuasions who spent six months in the United States during the war. Upon his return to England he wrote Six Months in the Federal States *(London, 1863). In the selection here, he addresses the capacity of the unmilitary North to create an army in a passage which might as readily serve to describe the exertions of the South.*

Surely no nation in the world has gone through such a baptism of war as the people of the United States underwent in one short year's time. With the men of the Revolution the memories of the revolutionary wars had died out. Two generations had passed away to whom war was little more than a name. The Mexican campaign was rather a military demonstration than an actual war, and the sixteen years which had elapsed since its termination form a long period in the life of a nation whose whole existence has not completed its first century. Twenty months ago there were not more than 12,000 soldiers in a country of 31,000,000. A soldier was as rare an object throughout America as in one of our country hamlets. I recollect a Northern lady telling me that, till within a year before, she could not recall the name of a single person whom she had ever known in the army, and that now she had sixty friends and relatives who were serving in the war; and her case was by no means an uncommon one.

Once in four years, on the fourth of March, two or three thousand troops were collected in Washington to add to the pomp of the Presidential inauguration; and this was the one military pageant the country had to boast of. Almost in a day this state of things passed away. Our English critics were so fond of repeating what the North could not do—how it could not fight, nor raise money, nor conquer the South—that they omitted to mention what the North had done. There was no need to go farther than my windows at Washington to see the immensity of the war. It was curious to me to watch the troops as they came marching past. Whether they were regulars or volunteers, it was hard for the unprofessional critic to discern; for all were clad alike, in the same dull, grey-blue overcoats, and most of the few regular regiments were filled with such raw recruits that the difference between volunteer and regular was not a marked one.

Of course it was easy enough to pick faults in the aspect of such troops. As each regiment marched, or rather waded through the dense slush and mud which covered the roads, you could observe many inaccuracies of military attire. One man would have his trousers rolled up almost to his knees; another would wear them tucked inside his boots; and a third would appear with one leg of his trousers hang-ing down, and the other gathered tightly up. It was not unfrequent, too, to see an officer with his epaulettes sewed on to a common plain frock-coat. Then there was a slouching gait about the men, not soldierlike to English eyes. They used to turn heads round when on parade, with an indifference to rule which would drive an old drill-sergeant out of his senses. There was an absence, also, of precision in the march. The men kept in step; but I always was at a loss to discover how they ever managed to do so. The system of march, it is true, was copied rather from the French than the English or Austrian fashion; but still it was something very different from the orderly disorder of a Zouave march. That all these, and a score of similar irregularities, are faults, no one—an American least of all—would deny. But there are two sides to the picture.

One thing is certain, that there is no physical degeneracy about a race which could produce such regiments as those which formed the Army of the Potomac. Men of high stature and burly frames were rare, except in the Kentucky troops; but, on the other hand, small, stunted men were almost unknown. I have seen the armies of most European countries; and I have no hesitation in saying that, as far as the average raw material of the rank and file is concerned, the American army is the finest.

The officers are, undoubtedly, the weak point of the system. They have not the military air, the self-possession which long habit of command alone can give; while the footing of equality on which they inevitably stand with the volunteer privates, deprives them of the esprit de corps belonging to a ruling class. Still they are active, energetic, and constantly with their troops.

Wonderfully well equipped too, at this period of the war, were both officers and men. Their clothing was substantial and fitted easily, their arms were good, and the military arrangements were as perfect as money alone could make them.

It was remarkable to me how rapidly the new recruits fell into the habits of military service. I have seen a Pennsylvanian regiment, raised chiefly from the mechanics of Philadelphia, which, six weeks after its formation, was, in my eyes, equal to the average of our best-trained volunteer corps, as far as marching and drill-exercise went. Indeed, I often asked myself what it was that made the Northern volunteer troops look, as a rule, so much more soldier-like than our own. I suppose the reason is, that across the Atlantic there was actual war, and that at home there was at most only a parade. I have no doubt that, in the event of civil war or invasion, England would raise a million volunteers as rapidly as America has done—more rapidly she could not; and that, when fighting had once begun, there would only be too much of grim earnestness about our soldiering; but it is not want of patriotism to say that the American volunteers looked to me more businesslike than our own. At the scene of war itself there was no playing at soldiering. No gaudy uniforms or crack companies, no distinction of classes. From every part of the North; from the ports of New York and Boston; from the homesteads of New England; from the mines of Pennsylvania and the factories of Pittsburgh; from the shores of the great lakes; from the Mississippi valley; and from the far-away Texas prairies, these men had come to fight for the Union.

The bulk of the native volunteers consisted of men who had given up good situations in order to enlist, and who had families to support at home; and for such men the additional pay was not an adequate inducement to incur the dangers and hardships of war. Of course, wherever there is an army, the scum of the population will always be gathered together; but the average morale and character of the couple of hundred thousand troops collected round Washington was extremely good. There was very little outward drunkenness, and less brawling about the streets than if half a dozen English militia regiments had been quartered there. The number of papers purchased daily by the common soldiers, and the amount of letters which they sent through the military post, was astonishing to a foreigner, though less strange when you considered that every man in that army, with the exception of a few recent immigrants, could both read and write. The ministers, also, of the different sects, who went out on the Sundays to preach to the troops, found no difficulty in obtaining large and attentive audiences.

The Seventh Regiment, N.Y.S.M., gets a heart-warming send-off on its way to Washington, D.C.

JACOB D. COX
Ohio Goes to War

Jacob D. Cox was a young Republican member of the Ohio State Senate when the Civil War broke out. Totally without military experience, he nevertheless held the rank of brigadier general in the state militia. Cox proved to be one of the better amateur soldiers of the war, serving in a variety of posts including corps commander, and rising to the rank of major general of volunteers. After the war he had a distinguished political and business career, serving as Gover-nor of Ohio, Secretary of the Interior, and member of Congress, while becoming a railroad president and author of several books on the Civil War. The following selection, from Battles and Leaders of the Civil War, *gives a good picture of the spirit of the times and the con-fusion which prevailed as Ohio answered the call. It is a picture which was duplicated in various ways in every state, both North and South.*

When Mr. Lincoln issued his first call for troops, the existing laws made it necessary that these should be fully organized and officered by the several States. Then, the treasury was in no condition to bear the burden of war expenditures, and, till Congress could assemble, the president was forced to rely on the States for means to equip and transport their own men. This threw upon the governors and legislatures of the loyal States responsibilities of a kind wholly unprecedented. A long period of pro-found peace had made every military organization seem almost farcical. A few independent companies formed the merest shadow of an army, and the State militia proper was only a nominal thing. It hap-pened, however, that I held a commission as brig-adier in this State militia, and my intimacy with Governor Dennison led him to call upon me for such assistance as I could render in the first enroll-ment and organization of the Ohio quota. Arranging to be called to the Senate chamber when my vote might be needed, I gave my time chiefly to such military matters as the governor appointed. Al-though, as I have said, my military commission had been a nominal thing, and in fact I had never worn a uniform, I had not wholly neglected theoretic prepa-ration for such work. For some years, the possibility of a war of secession had been one of the things which were forced upon the thoughts of reflecting people, and I had given some careful study to such books of tactics and of strategy as were within easy reach. I had especially been led to read military history with critical care, and had carried away many valuable ideas from that most useful means of military education. I had, therefore, some notion of the work before us, and could approach its problems with less loss of time, at least, than if I had been wholly ignorant.

My commission as brigadier-general in the Ohio quota in national service was dated the 23d of April. Just about the same time Captain George B. Mc-Clellan was requested by Governor Dennison to come to Columbus for consultation, and, by the governor's request, I met him at the railway station and took him to the State House. I think Mr. Lars Anderson (brother of Major Robert Anderson) and Mr. L'Hommedieu of Cincinnati were with him. The intimation had been given me that he would probably be made major-general of the Ohio con-tingent, and this, naturally, made me scan him closely. He was rather under the medium height, but muscularly formed, with broad shoulders and a well-poised head, active and graceful in motion. His whole appearance was quiet and modest, but when drawn out he showed no lack of confidence in him-self. He was dressed in a plain traveling dress and wore a narrow-rimmed soft felt hat. In short, he seemed what he was, a railway superintendent in his business clothes. At the time, his name was a good deal associated with Beauregard's, and they were spoken of as young men of similar standing in the engineer corps of the army, and great things were expected of them both because of their scientific knowledge of their profession, though McClellan had been in civil life for some years. McClellan's report on the Crimean war was one of the few impor-tant memoirs our old army had produced, and was valuable enough to give a just reputation for com-prehensive understanding of military organization, and the promise of ability to conduct the operations of an army.

I was present at the interview which the governor had with him. The destitution of the State of every-thing like military material and equipment was very plainly put, and the magnitude of the task of build-ing up a small army out of nothing was not blinked. The governor spoke of the embarrassment he felt at every step from the lack of practical military experi-ence in his staff, and of his desire to have some one on whom he could properly throw the details of military work. McClellan showed that he fully un-derstood the difficulties there would be before him, and said no man could wholly master them at once, although he had confidence that if a few weeks' time for preparation were given, he would be able to put the Ohio division into reasonable form for taking the field. The command was then formally tendered and accepted. All of us who were present felt that the selection was one full of promise and hope, and that the governor had done the wisest thing practicable at the time.

The next morning McClellan requested me to accompany him to the State arsenal, to see what arms and material might be there. We found a few boxes of smooth-bore muskets which had once been issued to militia companies and had been returned rusted and damaged. No belts, cartridge-boxes, or other accounterments were with them. There were two or three smooth-bore brass field-pieces, 6-pounders, which had been honey-combed by firing salutes, and of which the vents had been worn out, bushed, and worn out again. In a heap in one corner lay a confused pile of mildewed harness which had been once used for artillery horses, but was now not worth carrying away. There had for many years been no money appropriated to buy military material or even to protect the little the State had. The Federal Government had occasionally distributed some arms which were in the hands of the independent uniformed militia, and the arsenal was simply an empty store-house. It did not take long to complete our inspection. At the door, as we were leaving the building, McClellan turned, and, looking back into its emptiness, remarked, half humorously and half sadly, "A fine stock of munitions on which to begin a great war!"

We went back to the State House where a room was assigned us, and we sat down to work. The first task was to make out detailed schedules and estimates of what would be needed to equip ten thousand men for the field. This was a unit which could be used by the governor and Legislature in estimating the appropriations needed then or subsequently. Intervals in this labor were used in discussing the general situation and plans of campaign. Before the close of the week McClellan drew up a paper embodying his own views, and forwarded it to Lieutenant-General Scott. He read it to me, and my recollection of it is that he suggested two principal lines of movement in the West: one to move eastward by the Kanawha Valley with a heavy column to coöperate with an army in front of Washington; the other to march directly southward and to open the Valley of the Mississippi. Scott's answer was appreciative and flattering, without distinctly approving his plan, and I have never doubted that the paper prepared the way for his appointment in the regular army, which followed at an early day.

But in trying to give a connected idea of the first military organization of the State, I have outrun some incidents of those days which are worth recollection. From the hour the call for troops was published, enlistments began, and recruits were parading the streets continually. At the capitol the restless impulse to be doing something military seized even upon the members of the Legislature, and a good many of them assembled every evening upon the east terrace of the State House to be drilled in marching and facing by one or two of their own number who had some knowledge of company tactics. Most of the uniformed independent companies in the cities of the State immediately tendered their services and began to recruit their numbers to the

Raw recruits submit to drill.

hundred men required for acceptance. There was no time to procure uniforms, nor was it desirable; for these companies had chosen their own, and would have to change it for that of the United States as soon as this could be furnished. For some days companies could be seen marching and drilling, of which part would be uniformed in some gaudy style such as is apt to prevail in holiday parades in time of peace, while another part would be dressed in the ordinary working garb of citizens of all degrees. The uniformed files would also be armed and accoutered, the others would be without arms or equipments, and as awkward a squad as could well be imagined. The material, however, was magnificent and soon began to take shape. The fancy uniforms were left at home, and some approximation to a simple and useful costume was made. The recent popular outburst in Italy furnished a useful idea, and the "Garibaldi uniform" of a red flannel shirt with broad falling collar, with blue trousers held by a leathern waist-belt, and a soft felt hat for the head, was extensively copied and served an excellent purpose. It could be made by the wives and sisters at home, and was all the more acceptable for that. The spring was opening and a heavy coat would not be much needed, so that with some sort of overcoat and a good blanket in an improvised knapsack, the new company was not badly provided. The warm scarlet color reflected from their enthusiastic faces as they stood in line made a picture that never failed to impress the mustering officers with the splendid character of the men.

The officering of these new troops was a difficult and delicate task, and, so far as company officers were concerned, there seemed no better way at the beginning than to let the enlisted men elect their own, as was in fact done. In most cases where entirely new companies were raised, it had been by the enthusiastic efforts of some energetic volunteers who were naturally made the commissioned officers. But not always. There were numerous examples of self-denial by men who remained in the ranks after expending much labor and money in recruiting, modestly refusing the honors, and giving way to some one supposed to have military knowledge or experience. The war in Mexico in 1846–7 had been our latest conflict with a civilized people, and to have served in it was a sure passport to confidence. It had often been a service more in name than in fact; but the young volunteers felt so deeply their own ignorance that they were ready to yield to any pretense of superior knowledge, and generously to trust themselves to any one who would offer to lead them. Hosts of charlatans and incompetents were thus put into responsible places at the beginning, but the sifting work went on fast after the troops were once in the field. The election of field-officers, however, ought not to have been allowed. Companies were necessarily regimented together of which each could have little personal knowledge of the officers of the others; intrigue and demagogy soon came into play, and almost fatal mistakes were made in selection. The evil worked its cure, but the ill effects of it were long visible.

The immediate need of troops to protect Washington caused most of the uniformed companies to be united into the first two regiments, which were quickly dispatched to the East. These off, companies began to stream in from all parts of the State. On their first arrival they were quartered wherever shelter could be had, as there were no tents or sheds to make a camp for them. Going to my evening work at the State House, as I crossed the rotunda I saw a company marching in by the south door, and another disposing itself for the night upon the marble pavement near the east entrance; as I passed on to the north hall, I saw another that had come a little earlier holding a prayer-meeting, the stone arches echoing with the excited supplications of some one who was borne out of himself by the terrible pressure of events around him, while, mingling with his pathetic, beseeching tones as he prayed for his country, came the shrill notes of the fife and the thundering din of the ubiquitous bass-drum from the company marching in on the other side. In the Senate chamber a company was quartered, and the senators were supplying them with paper and pens with which "the boys" were writing their farewells to mothers and sweethearts, whom they hardly dared hope they should see again. A similar scene was going on in the Representatives' hall, another in the Supreme Court-room. In the executive office sat the governor, the unwonted noises, when the door was opened, breaking in on the quiet, businesslike air of the room,—he meanwhile dictating dispatches, indicating answers to others, receiving committees of citizens, giving directions to officers of companies and regiments, accommodating himself to the willful democracy of our institutions which insists upon seeing the man in chief command, and will not take its answer from a subordinate, until in the small hours of the night the noises were hushed, and after a brief hour of effective, undisturbed work upon the matters of chief importance, he could leave the glare of his gas-lighted office and seek a few hours' rest, only to renew his wearing labors on the morrow.

On the streets the excitement was of a rougher if not more intense character. A minority of unthinking partisans could not understand the strength and sweep of the great popular movement, and would sometimes venture to speak out their sympathy with the rebellion, or their sneers at some party friend who had enlisted. In the boiling temper of the time the quick answer was a blow; and it was one of the common incidents of the day for those who came into the State House to tell of a knock-down that had occurred here or there, when this popular punishment had been administered to some indiscreet "rebel-sympathizer."

Various duties brought young army officers of the regular service to the State capital, and others sought a brief leave of absence to come and offer their services to the governor of their native State.

General Scott had planted himself firmly on the theory that the regular army must be the principal reliance for severe work, and that the volunteers could only be auxiliaries around this solid nucleus which would show them the way to perform their duty, and take the brunt of every encounter. The young regulars who asked leave to accept commissions in State regiments were therefore refused, and were ordered to their own subaltern positions and posts. There can be no doubt that the true policy would have been to encourage the whole of this younger class to enter at once the volunteer service. They would have been field-officers in the new regiments, and would have impressed discipline and system upon the organization from the beginning. The Confederates really profited by having no regular army. They gave to the officers who left our service, it is true, commissions in their so-called "provisional" army, to encourage them to expect permanent military positions if the war should end in the independence of the South; but this was only a nominal organization, and their real army was made up (as ours turned out practically to be) from the regiments of State volunteers. Less than a year afterward we changed our policy, but it was then too late to induce many of the regular officers to take regimental positions in the volunteer troops. I hesitate to declare that this was not, after all, for the best; for, although the organization of our army would have been more rapidly perfected, there are other considerations which have much weight. The army would not have been the popular thing it was, its close identification with the people's movement would have been weakened, and it, perhaps, would not so readily have melted again into the mass of the nation at the close of the war.

On the 29th of April I was ordered by McClellan to proceed next morning to Camp Dennison, near Cincinnati, where he had fixed the site for a permanent camp of instruction. I took with me one full regiment and half of another. The day was a fair one, and when about noon our railway train reached the camping ground, it seemed an excellent place for our work. The drawback was that the land was planted in wheat and corn, instead of being meadow or pasture land. Captain Rosecrans (later the well-known general) met us as McClellan's engineer officer, coming from Cincinnati with a trainload of lumber. With his compass and chain, and by the help of a small detail of men, he soon laid off the two regimental camps, and the general lines of the whole encampment for a dozen regiments. The men of the regiments shouldered the pine boards, and carried them up to the lines of the company streets which were close to the hills skirting the valley, and which opened into the parade and drill ground along the railway. Vigorous work housed all the men before night, and it was well that it did so, for the weather changed in the evening, a cold rain came on, and the next morning was a chill and dreary one. My own headquarters were in a little brick school-house of one story, and with a single aide (my only staff-officer) we bestowed ourselves for the night in the little spaces between the pupils' desks and the teacher's pulpit. The windy, cheerless night was a long one, but gave place at last to a fickle, changeable day of drifting showers and occasional sunshine, and we were roused by our first reveille in camp. A breakfast was made from some cooked provisions brought with us, and we resumed the duty of organizing and instructing the camp. With the vigorous outdoor life and the full physical and mental employment, the depression which had weighed upon me since the news of the guns at Sumter passed away, never to return.

General Winfield Scott.

Women make havelocks (capes with flap at back to protect neck) for volunteers.

New battalions arrived from day to day, the cantonments were built by themselves, like the first, and the business of instruction and drill was systematized. The men were not yet armed, so there was no temptation to begin too soon with the manual of the musket, and they were kept industriously employed in marching in single line, by file, in changing direction, in forming column of fours from double line, etc., before their guns were put into their hands. Each regiment was treated as a separate camp with its own chain of sentinels, and the officers of the guard were constantly busy inspecting the sentinels on post and teaching guard and picket duty theoretically to the reliefs off duty. Schools were established in each regiment for field and staff as well as for company officers, and Hardee's "Tactics" was in the hands of everybody who could procure a copy. One of the proofs of the unprecedented scale of our war preparation is found in the fact that the supply of the authorized "Tactics" was soon exhausted, making it difficult to get the means of instruction in the company schools. The arriving regiments sometimes had their first taste of camp life under circumstances well calculated to dampen their ardor. The 4th Ohio, under Colonel Lorin Andrews, president of Kenyon College, came just before a thunderstorm one evening, and the bivouac that night was as rough a one as his men were likely to experience for many a day. They made shelter by placing boards from the fence-tops to the ground, but the fields were level and soon became a mire under the pouring rain, so that they were a queer-looking lot when they crawled out in the morning. The sun was then shining bright, however, and they had better cover for their heads by the next night. The 7th Ohio, which was recruited in Cleveland and on the "Western Reserve," sent a party in advance to build some of their huts, and though they too came in a rain-storm, they were less uncomfortable than some of the others. In the course of a fortnight all the regiments of the Ohio contingent were in the camp, except the two that had been hurried to Washington. They were organized into three brigades. The brigadiers, besides myself, were Generals J. H. Bates and Newton Schleich. General Bates, who was the senior, and as such assumed command of the camp in McClellan's absence, was a graduate of West Point who had served some years in the regular army, but had resigned and adopted the profession of law. General Schleich was a Democratic senator, who had been in the State militia, and had been one of the drill-masters of the Legislative Squad, which had drilled upon the Capitol terrace. McClellan had intended to make his own headquarters in the camp; but the convenience of attending to official business in Cincinnati kept him in the city. His purpose was to make the brigade organizations permanent, and to take them as a division to the field when they were a little prepared for the work. Like many other good plans, it failed to be carried out. I was the only one of the brigadiers who remained in the service after the first enlistment for ninety days, and it was my fate

to take the field with new regiments, only one of which had been in my brigade in camp. After General Bates's arrival my own hut was built on the slope of the hillside behind my brigade, close under the wooded ridge, and here for the next six weeks was my home. The morning brought its hour of business correspondence relating to the command; then came the drill, when the parade ground was full of marching companies and squads. Officers' drill followed, with sword exercise and pistol practice, and the evening was allotted to schools of theoretic tactics, outpost duty, and the like.

The first fortnight in camp was the hardest for the troops. The plowed fields became deep with mud which nothing could remove till steady good weather should allow them to be packed hard under the continued tramp of thousands of men. The organization of camp-kitchens had to be learned by the hardest experience also, and the men who had some aptitude for cooking had to be found by a slow process of natural selection, during which many an unpalatable meal had to be eaten. A disagreeable bit of information soon came to us in the proof that more than half the men had never had the contagious diseases of infancy. The measles broke out, and we had to organize a camp-hospital at once. A large barn near by was taken for this purpose, and the surgeons had their hands full of cases, which, however trivial they might seem at home, were here aggravated into dangerous illness by the unwonted surroundings, and the impossibility of securing the needed protection from exposure. The good women of Cincinnati took promptly in hand the task of providing nurses for the sick and proper diet and delicacies for hospital use. The Sisters of Charity, under the lead of Sister Anthony, a noble woman, came out in force, and their black and white robes harmonized picturesquely with the military surroundings, as they flitted about under the rough timber framing of the old barn, carrying comfort and hope from one rude couch to another.

As to supplies, hardly a man in a regiment knew how to make out a requisition for rations or for clothing, and, easy as it is to rail at "red-tape," the necessity of keeping a check upon embezzlement and wastefulness justified the staff-bureaus at Washington in insisting upon regular vouchers to support the quartermasters' and commissaries' accounts. But here, too, men were gradually found who had special talent for the work. Where everybody had to learn a new business, it would have been miraculous if grave errors had not frequently occurred. Looking back at it, the wonder is that the blunders and mishaps had not been tenfold more numerous than they were.

By the middle of May the confusion had given way to reasonable system, but we now were obliged to meet the embarrassments of reorganization for three years, under the president's second call for troops (May 3d). In every company some discontented spirits wanted to go home, and, to avoid the odium of going alone, they became mischief-makers, seeking to prevent the whole company from reënlisting. The growing discipline was relaxed or lost in the solicitations, the electioneering, the speech-making, and the other common arts of persuasion. In spite of all these discouragements, however, the daily drills and instruction went on with some approach to regularity, and our raw volunteers began to look more like soldiers. Captain Gordon Granger, of the regular army, came to muster the reënlisted regiments into the three-years service, and as he stood at the right of the 4th Ohio, looking down the line of a thousand stalwart men, all in their Garibaldi shirts (for we had not yet got our uniforms), he turned to me and exclaimed, "My God! that such men should be food for powder!" It certainly was a display of manliness and intelligence such as had hardly ever been seen in the ranks of an army. There were in camp at that time, three if not four companies in different regiments that were wholly made up of under-graduates of colleges, who had enlisted together, their officers being their tutors and professors. And where there was not so striking evidence as this of the enlistment of the best of our youth, every company could still show that it was largely recruited from the best nurtured and most promising young men of the community.

Granger had been in the South-west when the secession movement began, and had seen the formation of military companies everywhere, and the incessant drilling which had been going on all winter; while we, in a strange condition of political paralysis, had been doing nothing. His information was eagerly sought by us all, and he lost no opportunity of impressing upon us the fact that the South was nearly six months ahead of us in organization and preparation. He did not conceal his belief that we were likely to find the war a much longer and more serious piece of business than was commonly expected, and that, unless we pushed hard our drilling and instruction, we should find ourselves at a disadvantage in our earlier encounters. What he said had a good effect in making officers and men take more willingly to the laborious routine of the parade ground and the regimental school; for such opinions as his soon ran through a camp, and they were commented upon by the enlisted men quite as earnestly as among the officers. Still, hope kept the upper hand, and I believe that three-fourths of us still cherished the belief that a single campaign would end the war.

Though most of our men were native Ohioans, we had in camp two regiments made up of other material. The 9th Ohio was recruited from the Germans of Cincinnati, and was commanded by Colonel Robert McCook. In camp, the drilling of the regiment fell almost completely into the hands of the adjutant, Lieutenant August Willich (afterward a general of division), and McCook, who humorously exaggerated his own lack of military knowledge, used to say that he was only "clerk for a thousand Dutchmen," so completely did the care of equipping and providing for his regiment engross his time and labor. The 10th Ohio was an Irish regiment, also from Cincinnati, and its men were proud to call themselves the "Bloody Tinth." The brilliant Lytle was its commander, and his control over them, even in the beginning of their service and near the city of their home, showed that they had fallen into competent hands. It happened, of course, that the guard-house pretty frequently contained representatives of the 10th, who, on the short furloughs that were allowed them, took a parting glass too many with their friends in the city, and came to camp boisterously drunk. But the men of the regiment got it into their heads that the 13th, which lay just opposite them across the railroad, took a malicious pleasure in filling the guard-house with the Irishmen. Some threats had been made that they would go over and "clean out" the 13th, and one fine evening these came to a head. I suddenly got orders from General Bates to form my brigade and march them at once between the 10th and 13th to prevent a collision that seemed imminent. The long-roll was beaten as if the drummers realized the full importance of the first opportunity to sound that warlike signal. We marched by the moonlight into the space between the belligerent regiments; but Lytle already had got his own men under control, and the less mercurial 13th were not disposed to be aggressive, so that we were soon dismissed, with a compliment for our promptness.

The six weeks of our stay in Camp Dennison seem like months in the retrospect, so full were they crowded with new experiences. The change came in an unexpected way. The initiative taken by the Confederates in West Virginia had to be met by prompt action, and McClellan was forced to drop his own plans and meet the exigency. The organization and equipment of the regiments for the three-years service was still incomplete, and the brigades were broken up, to take across the Ohio the regiments best prepared to go. This was discouraging to a brigade commander, for, even with veteran troops, acquaintanceship between the officer and his command is a necessary condition of confidence and a most important element of strength. My own assignment to the Great Kanawha district was one I had every reason to be content with, except that for several months I felt the disadvantage I suffered from having command of troops which I had never seen till we met in the field.

Rebels parade in camp.

JOHN H. LEWIS
Virginia Goes to War

John H. Lewis was a young carpenter who went to war early, as a private, when his militia regiment was mustered into service within days of the secession of his native Virginia. Lewis marched and fought in virtually all of the great battles of the Army of Northern Virginia until mid-1863. As a second lieutenant he took part in Pickett's Charge on the third day at Gettysburg, where he was captured, with the result that he spent the rest of the war as a prisoner. After the war he resumed his trade, leading, like millions of other veterans of the conflict from both sides, a quiet, undistinguished life, save that he wrote a slender but remarkably valuable little memoir, Recollections from 1860 to 1865 (Washington, 1895), from which the following selection is taken.

I well remember the receipt of the news [of the Virginia Ordinance of Secession] and its effect in my town, Portsmouth. Up to that time there had been differences of opinion; but immediately on the seceding of the State the whole population became united, as they had been taught from childhood that while it was a duty to love their country, it was obligatory to love their State and obey her decrees "first, last, and all the time." Believing thus, it is no wonder that when on April 20 the Government called out the Third Virginia Regiment of Volunteers seven hundred men promptly answered the call, and were ready to do battle for the State and the South.

This regiment was assembled at one o'clock on April 20, 1861, and on that night the war commenced in earnest; it is true that Sumter had been fired on and evacuated; but that night, at the Gosport navyyard, was seen the terrors of what war would be; the yard with all its shipping and buildings, and vast stores of ammunition, went up in flames; and amid the red glare of fire, with the boom of artillery from loaded guns left on the old battle ship Pennsylvania, and as the fire reached them were discharged; amid this glare and the passing of the Federal fleet down the river, with shotted guns and ports open for action, bearing on the two cities, that section of Virginia, and the whole State was firmly cemented to the cause of the South; and men who had been opposed to war, and were lukewarm, became hot advocates and rushed to do battle for their State and the cause of the South.

All of the border States soon followed Virginia, and the South became united "for weal or woe," and so remained until the final climax at Appomattox. There might have been, and probably was, mismanagement on the part of the civil Government of the Confederate States, but there was no weakness, no shrinking, in her soldiers. From each and every part of the South her sons came forward to the support of her cause, and from Manassas to Appomattox in the East, and from Shiloh to the surrender of Johnson in North Carolina, and beyond the mighty Mississippi, all stood shoulder to shoulder as they had bound themselves in the beginning, and they fell together in the mighty crash, everything gone save honor and the memory of the graves of their comrades. These were left them as a heritage, as a reminder of the heroic struggle, and it becomes the duty of the living to see that the memory of our dead does not suffer, and to teach our children and the youth of our southland their duty to the memories of their ancestors.

In a few days after Virginia joined hands with the Southern States troops began to arrive within her borders from the South, this being tidewater one of the important points they naturally were sent here. . . .

Naturally, all was bustle and hurry; war was new to us. With soldiers arriving and to be provided for, new officers to appoint, such as quartermasters and commissaries, the vast amount of camp equipage and rations, kept everybody on the move, but soon things began to assume shape, and quiet and order were restored. The Virginia troops and all of the material of war captured in the Gosport navyyard remained under the Virginia authorities for a time, about two months; the heavy guns were being shipped to various points south, and distributed to the different batteries in the harbor. Soon we were in condition in and around Norfolk and Portsmouth to resist any fleet that might attempt to enter. The troops as they arrived were placed in camp, and began the routine life of the soldier, drilling, doing guard duty, eating and sleeping; in fact, in a month or so a great many of the soldiers began to look on the matter as a holiday, and few thought they would ever be called on to fight. It seemed to [be] the great fear at this time with many of the soldiers that the war would close before they would have the pleasure of killing some one; many of us had in after years worried for fear somebody might kill us.

Thus the days went by, and with the pranks of the boys who were learning all kinds of deviltry, as soldiers in camp generally learn; even then camp hung heavy on all heads; but this was only the beginning. New things and new duties were to come, of which we little dreamed. Great numbers of soldiers had assembled in that vicinity, and were placed first under the command of General Gwynn, but at the time of which I write were under the command of General Huger, of South Carolina. There was possibly 10,000 men in that vicinity, and all seemed to be trying to do as little as they could, and get as much pleasure out of the situation, and all were always ready to draw their rations and pay. I recollect the first pay was paid Virginia troops by the State, and the next pay was by the Confederate States, in new Confederate notes, and the people were paying 20 per cent premium for it as souvenirs. Some of the people who bought at that time had boxes of it at the close of the war. One gentleman, a dealer in wood, at that time told me at the close of the war he had about $200,000 of it, and as Congress made no provision for its redemption I suppose he has it yet. But at the time of which I write there were few people who did not believe the war would be over in less than a year, with the independence of the South.

★★★

WARREN LEE GOSS
Going to the Front

Warren Lee Goss, a young man from Massachusetts, volunteered in the anger and enthusiasm of the first weeks of the war. He fought in most of the campaigns in the East, serving in the 2nd Massachusetts Artillery. Twice captured, he was both times exchanged. In later life he wrote several books and a number of articles about the war. The selection given here, *which first appeared in* Battles and Leaders of the Civil War, *and was subsequently incorporated in somewhat different form in his memoirs,* Recollections of a Private: A Story of the Army of the Potomac *(New York, 1890), tells the universal story of a young man getting his first taste of army life.*

Before I reached the point of enlisting, I had read and been "enthused" by General Dix's famous "shoot him on the spot" dispatch;[1] I had attended flag-raisings, and had heard orators declaim of "undying devotion to the Union." One speaker to whom I listened declared that "human life must be cheapened"; but I never learned that he helped on the work experimentally. When men by the hundred walked soberly to the front and signed the enlistment papers, he was not one of them. As I came out of the hall, with conflicting emotions, feeling as though I should have to go finally or forfeit my birthright as an American citizen, one of the orators who stood at the door, glowing with enthusiasm and patriotism, and shaking hands effusively with those who enlisted, said to me:

"Did you enlist?" "No," I said. "Did you?"

"No; they won't take me. I have got a lame leg and a widowed mother to take care of."

I remember another enthusiast who was eager to enlist others. He declared that the family of no man who went to the front should suffer. After the war he was prominent among those who at town-meeting voted to refund the money to such as had expended it to procure substitutes. He has, moreover, been fierce and uncompromising toward the ex-Confederates since the war.

From the first I did not believe the trouble would blow over in "sixty days"; nor did I consider eleven dollars a month, and the promised glory, large pay for the services of an able-bodied young man.

It was the news that the 6th Massachusetts regiment had been mobbed by roughs on their passage through Baltimore which gave me the war fever.[2] And yet when I read Governor John A. Andrew's instructions to have the hero martyrs "preserved in ice and tenderly sent forward," somehow, though I felt the pathos of it, I could not reconcil myself to the ice. Ice in connection with patriotism did not give me agreeable impressions of war, and when I came to think of it, the stoning of the heroic "Sixth" didn't suit me; it detracted from my desire to die a soldier's death.

---

1. January 18th, 1861, three days after he had entered on his duties as Secretary of the Treasury to President Buchanan, John A. Dix sent W. Hemphill Jones, chief clerk of one of the Treasury bureaus to the South, for the purpose of saving the revenue-cutters at New Orleans, Mobile, and Galveston. January 29th, Mr. Jones telegraphed from New Orleans that the captain of the revenue-cutter *McClelland* refused to obey the Secretary's orders. It was seven in the evening when the dispatch was received. Immediately, Secretary Dix wrote the following reply: "Treasury Department, January 29, 1861. Tell Lieutenant Caldwell to arrest Captain Breshwood, assume command of the cutter, and obey the order I gave through you. If Captain Breshwood, after arrest, undertakes to interfere with the command of the cutter, tell Lieutenant Caldwell to consider him a mutineer, and treat him accordingly. If any one attempts to haul down the American flag, shoot him on the spot. JOHN A. DIX, Secretary of the Treasury.

2. Concerning this encounter Colonel Edward F. Jones, of the 6th Massachusetts, says in his report:

"After leaving Philadelphia I received intimation that our passage through the city of Baltimore would be resisted. I caused ammunition to be distributed and arms loaded, and went personally through the cars, and issued the following order, viz., 'The regiment will march through Baltimore in column of sections, arms at will. You will undoubtedly be insulted, abused, and perhaps assaulted, to which you must pay no attention whatever, but march with your faces square to the front and pay no attention to the mob, even if they throw stones, bricks, or other missiles; but if you are fired upon and any one of you is hit, your officers will order you to fire. Do not fire into any promiscuous crowds, but select any man whom you may see aiming at you, and be sure you drop him.' Reaching Baltimore, horses were attached the instant that the locomotive was detached, and the cars were driven at a rapid pace across the city. After the cars containing seven companies had reached the Washington depot the track behind them was barricaded, and the cars containing . . . the following companies, viz., Company C, of Lowell, Captain Follansbee; Company D. of Lowell, Captain Hart; Company I, of Lawrence, Captain Pickering, and Company L, of Stoneham, Captain Dike, were vacated, and they proceeded but a short distance before they were furiously attacked by a shower of missiles, which came faster as they advanced. They increased their steps to double-quick, which seemed to infuriate the mob, as it evidently impressed the mob with the idea that the soldiers dared not fire or had no ammunition, and pistol-shots were numerously fired into the ranks, and one soldier fell dead. The order 'Fire' was given, and it was executed. In consequence, several of the mob fell, and the soldiers again advanced hastily. The mayor of Baltimore placed himself at the head of the column beside Captain Follansbee and proceeded with them a short distance."

This regiment, the 6th Massachusetts, were the first armed troops to reach Washington in response to the call of the President.

The 27th Pennsylvania Regiment (unarmed) arrived at Baltimore by the same train as the Massachusetts troops. It was attacked by a mob and obliged to remain at the President street station, from which point it was sent back the same day in the direction of Philadelphia. The same night, by order of the Board of Police Commissioners, with the concurrence of Governor Hicks and Mayor Brown, the railways from the north were obstructed, so that the 8th Massachusetts, with General B. F. Butler, and the 7th New York were compelled to go to Annapolis by water and march thence to Washington.

I lay awake all night thinking the matter over, with the "ice" and "brick-bats" before my mind. However, the fever culminated that night, and I resolved to enlist.

"Cold chills" ran up and down my back as I got out of bed after the sleepless night, and shaved, preparatory to other desperate deeds of valor. I was twenty years of age, and when anything unusual was to be done, like fighting or courting, I shaved.

With a nervous tremor convulsing my system, and my heart thumping like muffled drum-beats, I stood before the door of the recruiting-office, and, before turning the knob to enter, read and re-read the advertisement for recruits posted thereon, until I knew all its peculiarities. The promised chances for "travel and promotion" seemed good, and I thought I might have made a mistake in considering war so serious after all. "Chances for travel!" I must confess now, after four years of soldiering, that the "chances for travel" were no myth; but "promotion" was a little uncertain and slow.

I was in no hurry to open the door. Though determined to enlist, I was half inclined to put it off awhile; I had a fluctuation of desires; I was faint-hearted and brave; I wanted to enlist, and yet— Here I turned the knob, and was relieved. I had been more prompt, with all my hesitation, than the officer in his duty; he wasn't in. Finally he came, and said: "What do you want, my boy?" "I want to enlist," I responded, blushing deeply with upwelling patriotism and bashfulness. Then the surgeon came to strip and examine me. In justice to myself; it must be stated that I signed the rolls without a tremor. It is common to the most of humanity, I believe, that, when confronted with actual danger, men have less fear than in its contemplation. I will, however, make one exception in favor of the first shell I heard uttering its blood-curdling hisses, as though a steam locomotive were traveling the air. With this exception I have found the actual dangers of war always less terrible face to face than on the night before the battle.

My first uniform was a bad fit: my trousers were too long by three or four inches; the flannel shirt was coarse and unpleasant, too large at the neck and too short elsewhere. The forage cap was an ungainly bag with pasteboard top and leather visor; the blouse was the only part which seemed decent; while the overcoat made me feel like a little nubbin of corn in a large preponderance of husk. Nothing except "Virginia mud" ever took down my ideas of military pomp quite so low.

After enlisting I did not seem of so much consequence as I had expected. There was not so much excitement on account of my military appearance as I deemed justly my due. I was taught my facings, and at the time I thought the drill-master needlessly fussy about shouldering, ordering, and presenting arms. At this time men were often drilled in company and regimental evolutions long before they learned the manual of arms, because of the difficulty of obtaining muskets. These we obtained at an early

Volunteers pass Faneuil Hall.

day, but we would willingly have resigned them after carrying them for a few hours. The musket, after an hour's drill, seemed heavier and less ornamental than it had looked to be. The first day I went out to drill, getting tired of doing the same things over and over, I said to the drill-sergeant: "Let's stop this fooling and go over to the grocery." His only reply was addressed to a corporal: "Corporal, take this man out and drill him like h—l"; and the corporal did! I found that suggestions were not so well appreciated in the army as in private life, and that no wisdom was equal to a drill-master's "Right face," "Left wheel," and "Right, oblique, march." It takes a raw recruit some time to learn that he is not to think or suggest, but obey. Some never do learn. I acquired it at last, in humility and mud, but it was tough. Yet I doubt if my patriotism, during my first three weeks' drill, was quite knee-high. Drilling looks easy to a spectator, but it isn't. Old soldiers who read this will remember their green recruithood and smile assent. After a time I had cut down my

eat,—pies, cakes, doughnuts, and jellies. It was one way in which a mother's heart found utterance. The young ladies (sisters, of course) brought an invention, usually made of leather or cloth, containing needles, pins, thread, buttons, and scissors, so that nearly every recruit had an embryo tailor's shop, with the goose outside. One old lady, in the innocence of her heart, brought her son an umbrella. We did not see anything particularly laughable about it at the time, but our old drill-sergeant did. Finally we were ready to move; our tears were wiped away, our buttons were polished, and our muskets were as bright as emery paper could make them.

"Wad" Rider, a member of our company, had come from a neighboring State to enlist with us. He was about eighteen years of age, red-headed, freckled-faced, good-natured and rough, with a wonderful aptitude for crying or laughing from sympathy. Another comrade, whom I will call Jack, was honored with a call from his mother, a little woman, hardly reaching up to his shoulder, with a sweet, motherly, care-worn face. At the last moment, though she had tried hard to preserve her composure, as is the habit of New England people, she threw her arms around her boy's neck, and with an outburst of sobbing and crying, said: "My dear boy, my dear boy, what will your poor old mother do without you? You are going to fight for your country. Don't forget your mother, Jack; God bless you, God bless you!" We felt as if the mother's tears and blessing were a benediction over us all. There was a touch of nature in her homely sorrow and solicitude over her big boy, which drew tears of sympathy from my eyes as I thought of my own sorrowing mother at home. The sympathetic Wad Rider burst into tears and sobs. His eyes refused, as he expressed it, to "dry up," until, as we were moving off, Jack's mother, rushing toward him with a bundle tied like a wheat-sheaf, called out in a most pathetic voice, "Jack! Jack! you've forgotten to take your pennyroyal." We all laughed, and so did Jack, and I think the laugh helped him more than the cry did. Everybody had said his last word, and the cars were off. Handkerchiefs were waved at us from all the houses we passed; we cheered till we were hoarse, and then settled back and swung our handkerchiefs.

Just here let me name over the contents of my knapsack, as a fair sample of what all the volunteers started with. There were in it a pair of trousers, two pairs of drawers, a pair of thick boots, four pairs of stockings, four flannel shirts, a blouse, a looking-glass, a can of peaches, a bottle of cough-mixture, a button-stick, chalk, razor and strop, the "tailor's shop" spoken of above, a Bible, a small volume of Shakspere, and writing utensils. To its top was strapped a double woolen blanket and a rubber one. Many other things were left behind because of lack of room in or about the knapsack.

On our arrival in Boston we were marched through the streets—the first march of any consequence we had taken with our knapsacks and equipments. Our dress consisted of a belt about the

uniform so that I could see out of it, and had conquered the drill sufficiently to see through it. Then the word came: On to Washington!

Our company was quartered at a large hotel near the railway station in the town in which it had been recruited. Bunks had been fitted up within a part of the hotel but little used. We took our meals at the public table, and found fault with the style. Six months later we would have considered ourselves aristocratic to have slept in the hotel stables with the meal-bin for a dining-table. One morning there was great excitement at the report that we were going to be sent to the front. Most of us obtained a limited pass and went to see our friends for the last time, returning the same night. Many of our schoolmates came in tears to say good-bye. We took leave of them all with heavy hearts, for, lightly as I may here seem to treat the subject, it was no light thing for a boy of twenty to start out for three years into the unknown dangers of a civil war. Our mothers—God bless them!—had brought us something good to body, which held a cartridge-box and bayonet, a cross-belt, also a haversack and tin drinking-cup, a canteen, and, last but not least, the knapsack strapped to the back. The straps ran over, around, and about one, in confusion most perplexing to our unsophisticated shoulders, the knapsack constantly giving the wearer the feeling that he was being pulled over backward. My canteen banged against my bayonet, both tin cup and bayonet badly interfered with the butt of my musket, while my cartridge-box and haversack were constantly flopping up and down—the whole jangling like loose harness and chains on a runaway horse. As we marched into Boston Common, I involuntarily cast my eye about for a bench. But for a former experience in offering advice, I should have proposed to the captain to "chip in" and hire a team to carry our equipments. Such was my first experience in war harness. Afterward, with hardened muscles, rendered athletic by long marches and invigorated by hardships, I could look back upon those days and smile, while carrying a knapsack as lightly as my heart. That morning my heart was as heavy as my knapsack. At last the welcome orders came: "Prepare to open ranks! Rear, open order, march! Right dress! Front! Order arms! Fix bayonets! Stack arms! Unsling knapsacks! In place, rest!"

The tendency of raw soldiers at first is to overload themselves. On the first long march the reaction sets in, and the recruit goes to the opposite extreme, not carrying enough, and thereby becoming dependent upon his comrades. Old soldiers preserve a happy medium. I have seen a new regiment start out with a lot of indescribable material, including sheet-iron stoves, and come back after a long march covered with more mud than baggage, stripped of everything except blankets, haversacks, canteens, muskets, and cartridge-boxes.

During that afternoon in Boston, after marching and countermarching, or, as one of our farmer-boy recruits expressed it, after "hawing and geeing" about the streets, we were sent to Fort Independence for the night for safekeeping. A company of regulars held the fort, and the guards walked their post with an uprightness that was astonishing. Our first impression of them was that there was a needless amount of "wheel about and turn about, and walk just so," and of saluting, and presenting arms. We were all marched to our quarters within the fort, where we unslung our knapsacks. After the first day's struggle with a knapsack, the general verdict was, "got too much of it." At supper-time we were marched to the dining-barracks, where our bill of

The 8th Massachusetts is quartered in the unfinished rotunda of the Capitol.

fare was beefsteak, coffee, wheat bread, and potatoes, but not a sign of milk or butter. It struck me as queer when I heard that the army was never provided with butter and milk.

The next day we started for Washington, by rail. We marched through New York's crowded streets without awakening the enthusiasm we thought our due; for we had read of the exciting scenes attending the departure of the New York 7th for Washington, on the day the 6th Massachusetts was mobbed in Baltimore, and also of the march of the 12th Massachusetts down Broadway on the 24th of July, when the regiment sang the then new and always thrilling lyric, "John Brown's Body." The following morning we took breakfast in Philadelphia, where we were attended by matrons and maidens, who waited upon us with thoughtful tenderness, as if they had been our own mothers and sweethearts instead of strangers. They feasted us and then filled our haversacks. God bless them! If we did not quite appreciate them then, we did afterward. After embarking on the cars at Philadelphia, the waving of handkerchiefs was less and less noticeable along the route. We arrived in Baltimore late at night; Union troops now controlled the city, and we marched through its deserted streets unmolested. On our arrival at Washington

the next morning, we were marched to barracks, dignified by the name of "Soldiers' Retreat," where each man received a half loaf of "softtack," as we had already begun to call wheat bread, with a piece of "salt junk," about as big and tough as the heel of my government shoe, and a quart of coffee,—which constituted our breakfast. Our first day in Washington was spent in shaving, washing, polishing our brasses and buttons, and cleaning-up for inspection. A day or two later we moved to quarters not far from the armory, looking out on the broad Potomac, within sight of Long Bridge and the city of Alexandria.

Here and there the sound of a gun broke the serenity, but otherwise the quiet seemed inconsistent with the war preparations going on around us. In the distance, across the wide river, we could see the steeples and towers of the city of Alexandria, while up stream, on the right, was the Long Bridge. Here and there was to be seen the moving panorama of armed men, as a regiment crossed the bridge; a flash of sunlight on the polished muskets revealed them to the eye; while the white-topped army baggage-wagons filed over in constant procession, looking like sections of whitewashed fence in motion. The overgrown country village of that period, called Washington, can be described in a few words. There

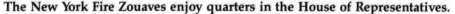

The New York Fire Zouaves enjoy quarters in the House of Representatives.

Recruits parade before the White House.

were wide streets stretching out from a common center like a spider's web. The Capitol, with its unfinished dome; the Patent Office, the Treasury, and the other public buildings, were in marked and classic contrast with the dilapidated, tumble-down, shabby look of the average homes, stores, groceries, and groggeries, which increased in shabbiness and dirty dilapidation as they approached the suburbs. The climate of Washington was genial, but in the winter months the mud was fearful. I have drilled in it, marched in it, and run from the provost-guard in it, and I think I appreciate it from actual and familiar knowledge. In the lower quarter of the city there was not a piece of sidewalk. Even Pennsylvania Avenue, with its sidewalks, was extremely dirty; and the cavalcade of teams, artillery caissons, and baggage-wagons, with their heavy wheels, stirred the mud into a stiff batter for the pedestrian.

Officers in tinsel and gold lace were so thick on Pennsylvania Avenue that it was a severe trial for a private to walk there. The salute exacted by officers, of bringing the hand to the visor of the cap, extending the arm to its full length, and then letting it drop by the side, was tiresome when followed up with the industry required by this horde. Perhaps I exaggerate, but in a half-hour's walk on the avenue I think I have saluted two hundred officers. Brigadier-generals were more numerous there than I ever knew them to be at the front. These officers, many of whom won their positions by political wire-pulling at Washington, we privates thought the great bane of

the war; they ought to have been sent to the front rank of battle, to serve as privates until they had learned the duties of a soldier. Mingled with these gaudy, useless officers were citizens in search of fat contracts, privates, "non-com's" and officers whose uniforms were well worn and faded, showing that they were from encampments and active service. Occasionally a regiment passed through the streets, on the way to camp; all surged up and down wide Pennsylvania Avenue.

The soldiers of this period were eager to collect mementoes of the war. One of my acquaintances in another regiment made sketches of the different camps he had visited around Washington, including "Brightwood" and Camp Cameron; the latter he termed "a nursery for brigadier-generals." Another friend hoarded specimens of official signatures and passes issued in Washington, conspicuous among which was a pass with the well-known John-Hancock-like signature of Drake De Kay.

Before enlisting, and while on a visit to a neighboring town, I was one evening at the village store, when the talk turned upon the duration of the war. Jim Tinkham, the clerk of the grocery store, announced his belief in a sixty days' war. I modestly asked him for more time. The older ones agreed with Jim and argued, as was common at that time, that the Government would soon blockade all the rebel ports and starve them out. Tinkham proposed to wager a supper for those present, if the rebels did not surrender before snow came that year. I accepted.

JOHN N. OPIE
Joining the Army

John N. Opie, son of a prosperous Virginia farmer, was 17 when the war broke. His wartime experiences were many and varied. He served under Thomas "Stonewall" Jackson and later J. E. B. Stuart before being captured in late 1864, an experience from which he barely emerged alive. After the war he practiced law and served in the Virginia State Senate. His memoirs, A Rebel Cavalryman with Lee, Stuart, and Jackson *(Chicago, 1899), are lively and amusing, as can be seen from the following excerpts which cover the period from his enlistment through his initiation into military life to his first taste of action, in the now virtually forgotten combat at Hainesville on 2 July 1861.*

My father, Col. Hierome L. Opie, who was a well-to-do farmer, resided in the beautiful and fruitful County of Jefferson, now West Virginia, until 1856, when, anticipating the impending struggle between the States, he moved up the Valley of Virginia and purchased a farm one mile from the city of Staunton, where we were living at the outbreak of the war. On the 16th day of April, 1861, I, a boy of seventeen years of age, was seated in a school room vainly wrestling with a proposition in analytical geometry. Not being able to master my mathematical problem, I was revolving in my mind how I should cut the Gordian knot, when I was informed that my father wished to see me.

I went to the door, and, to my great surprise, he informed me that the volunteer companies were ordered into service, and that, in fulfillment of a promise made a year previous, I could go with them; but it was his wish that I would not go, on account of my youth. I desired very much to please my noble father; but two mighty influences actuated me: one my unsolved mathematical problem; the other, the effect of having just read *Charles O'Malley, the Irish Dragoon*, the reading of which induced me to believe that war was a glorious thing; and so I went, with many other thoughtless men and youths, and plunged heedlessly into a long and deadly war, without, at the time, being able to give a reasonable why or wherefore. . . .

It was [at Harper's Ferry] that the first Virginia army, which was composed of volunteer militia, assembled.

When we reached the place, where a Government armory and arsenal were located, we found that the small Union force had fled, first setting fire to the public buildings. We succeeded, however, in saving most of the machinery and some hundred stand of muskets. Our stay here was spent in organizing and drilling. I was detailed to assist Maj. John A. Harman, afterwards Jackson's quartermaster, my duty being to quarter the troops as they arrived. The Major at first gave me the countersign every evening, until, finally, he remarked to me, "Your father has asked me not to give you the countersign." I replied that, being an enlisted man, I was no longer under his authority. I had, that evening, an engagement, and must have the countersign, so I got my musket, and buckled on my belt, determined not to be circumvented. I took post at the mouth of an alley, and marched up and down as a sentinel, until, finally, hearing some one advancing, I brought my gun to a charge and gave the usual command, "Halt! Who comes there?" "Friend with the countersign." "Advance, friend, and give the countersign." The officer advanced and gave me the countersign, when, returning to the office and divesting myself of gun and accoutrements, I pursued the even tenor of my way. This I continued to do, for several nights, until, at last, one night I heard some one approach, and, upon going through the usual ceremony, I found that I had halted the Major himself, who, recognizing me, exclaimed, "You d—— little rascal!" After this he always gave me the countersign. This mode of procuring the countersign I used during the whole war, together with the following plan: When there was a cordon of sentinels around the camp, and there was no possibility of making a new post, I wedged in between two sentinels and walked the beat until I met one, when, having forgotten the countersign, I would ask him for it. He, supposing I was a sentinel, invariably gave it to me.

While we were at Harper's Ferry many leading citizens of Maryland, among them a delegation of the Maryland Legislature, visited us and entreated us to enter that State, but they were entirely disregarded by our authorities.

We had many false alarms, as our officers supposed that the enemy would enter the town on trains and disembark at the depot.

At last Gen. T. J. Jackson, afterwards known as "Stonewall" Jackson, arrived, took command, and soon produced order out of chaos. Finding that there were great quantities of liquor in the town, he ordered it to be poured out. The barrels were brought forth, the heads knocked in, and the contents poured into the gutter; but the men dipped it up in buckets, and there was a sound of revelry by night. Finally, he ordered the whiskey to be poured into the Potomac river; but still the soldiers, particularly the Kentuckians, gathered round, with buckets tied to the ends of ropes, and caught great quantities of the disturbing element as it poured into the waters below.

Finally, Gen. Jos. E. Johnson arrived and superseded General Jackson, who was assigned to the brigade afterwards made famous by the well-earned appellation of the "Stonewall Brigade," consisting of the Second, Fourth, Fifth, Twenty-seventh, and Thirty-third Virginia. I joined Company L, Fifth Virginia, a superb company from my town, known as the "West August Guards."

When [Union] General Patterson reached the Potomac river at Williamsport, thereby threatening our rear, we evacuated Harper's Ferry and marched across the country to meet him. Near a little hamlet known as Hainesville, in Berkeley County, West Virginia, about equally distant between Martinsburg and Williamsport, we came in sight of him; but so little did our men realize that we were going into battle, that they broke ranks and climbed upon the fences, that they might thereby obtain a better view. On they came in battle array, the first army we had ever beheld; and a grand sight it was—infantry, artillery, and mounted men; their arms and accoutrements glittering in the sunlight, their colors unfurled to the breeze, their bands playing and drums beating, the officers shouting the commands, as regiments, battalions and companies marched up and wheeled into position. Then a battery took position and commenced firing at us, when four of our guns, unlimbering, immediately returned their fire.

Regular Confederate troops.

The officer in command of our artillery was a pious old gentleman, an Episcopal preacher, Captain Pendleton, who subsequently became general of artillery. He named his cannon Matthew, Mark, Luke and John. When he wished a gun to be fired, he raised his hands towards the heavens and exclaimed aloud, "May the Lord have mercy on their wicked souls! Fire!" Our regiment, the Fifth Virginia, was deployed, and a fight immediately commenced with the enemy's sharpshooters. Just at the time when the firing commenced a mounted officer belonging to Patterson's army galloped up to our men in the road and gave some command, when, seeing his mistake, regardless of the many commands to halt and surrender, on our part, the gallant fellow wheeled about and, amidst a showerbath of bullets, rode safely back to his own people. That officer was evidently not related to Major André, the British officer who, although mounted, surrendered to three dismounted American militia armed with flint-lock muskets.

When the first shell exploded over us, one of our company threw away his gun and fled down the pike at breakneck speed, throwing the broken metal of the pike from his feet like balls from a Gatling gun.

I saw a soldier fall, slightly wounded in the neck and begging to be helped up, who, when assisted to his feet, made for the rear with lightning-like rapidity, although he would not rise until assisted.

After firing at each other for about two hours, we were withdrawn and marched to Martinsburg. Neither side suffered much loss, as we were all novices in the art of killing each other. We, however, captured between forty and fifty prisoners.

BÉLA ESTVÁN
A Troublesome Regiment

Béla Estván was a Hungarian officer. In 1848 he fought against the liberal revolutions in Hungary and Italy, serving as a Hapsburg officer. On the collapse of the revolution, he went abroad and, like so many others eventually found himself in America. On the outbreak of the Civil War he entered the Confederate Army. He served mostly in Virginia, rising to colonel of cavalry, before being discharged for ill health—some said he deserted—in 1862, where-upon he went to England—by way of New York! His account of his experiences, War Pictures from the South *(New York, 1863), is part memoir and part history, with a good sense of humor and detail. The following selection actually deals with an incident which occurred in early 1862, but illustrates a problem that plagued both armies in the early portion of the war, the numerous ill-disciplined militia and volunteer outfits which flocked to the colors.*

Troops of every possible description continued to arrive at Richmond to take part in the war in Virginia. It was a fine sight to see them arrive. The North Carolina troops, especially, attracted the attention of the citizens by their frank and courteous bearing. It is true they did not boast of the fine names of their Southern brethren, such as "Tigers," "Wildcats," "Alligators," &c., their regiments being simply designated by numbers, but they were fine-looking, brave fellows. Then came the Zouave regiment of Colonel C——, formerly a noted professional gambler at New Orleans, who when he found his trade spoilt, took to forming a regiment. With the sanction of the mayor of the city of New Orleans, he established recruiting booths in the different jails there. Each criminal was given the option to stay out the full time of his sentence, or join Colonel C——'s body guard. Hundreds took advantage of the offer to escape from prison, and in a short time the regiment was complete. The officer's staff consisted of noted gamblers of New Orleans, and this noble band started, not to fight for their country so much, perhaps, as in the hope of a little freebooting. In their wide red breeches, blue jackets, and capped with the Turkish fez, these men, bronzed by a Southern sun, made a warlike show and excited much attention whenever they made their appearance. It was a strange, heterogeneous corps, formed of daring men from every country; but whenever a Zouave had been seen, something or other was pretty sure to be missed shortly afterward. Never, at any previous period, were so many robberies committed in and about Richmond, as during the stay of these defenders of their country. They laid their hands upon everything that came within their reach, and were the dread of the farmers all round. The poultry of the peasantry was carried off at night; yet what were the poor Zouaves to do? the officers kept back their pay, so they revenged themselves upon the population. It soon became necessary to assign them a separate encampment, as the officers and men of the other regiments would not mix with them. Strife and bloodshed were the order of the day: no man's life was safe who showed himself within the precinct of their encampment. Among other cases of lawlessness attributed to these men, I may mention that of a poor German gardener who lived in the vicinity, and who was compelled to abandon his house and garden, which was all he had to depend upon for his livelihood, owing to the ill treatment he received. The Government was at last under the necessity of ordering the Zouaves to leave Richmond, and sent them to the Peninsula, where they were soon dispersed, either by the enemy's bullets or through desertion.

The Zouaves had a reputation.

War Songs of 1861

★★★

Through most of history armies got from place to place on foot, wearily marching mile after dusty mile. One result of this was that armies sang, an aspect of military life which has become a casualty of the machine age. During the Civil War a great many marches and songs were popular with the troops. Some of these have gained an enduring niche in American history.

Dixie

Perhaps the most popular of Civil War songs, the sprightly "Dixie" was written by a Northerner, Daniel Decatur Emmett, of Ohio. A popular tunesmith of the age, Emmett was one of the founders of the so-called Negro minstrel shows. He wrote "Dixie" in 1859 and it was first performed on Broadway. On the outbreak of the Civil War it rapidly became the unofficial anthem of the South, a status which it still retains. During the war, Emmett, a loyal Union man, wrote new words making reference to "the land of treason," but the original version retained its hold, both North and South. Indeed, at the end of the war, Lincoln himself requested it be played, remarking "now it belongs to us all."

I wish I was in de land ob cotton,
Old times dar am not forgotten,
　　Look away, look away, look away, Dixie Land!
In Dixie Land whar I was born in,
Early on one frosty mornin',
Look away, look away, look away, Dixie Land!

　　CHORUS—Den I wish I was in Dixie—
　　　　　　Horray, hooray!
　　　　　　In Dixie land I'll take my stan'!
　　　　　　To lib an' die in Dixie
　　　　　　Away, away,
　　　　　　Away down south in Dixie
　　　　　　Away, away,
　　　　　　Away down south in Dixie.

Ole Missus marry "Will-de-Weaber,"
William was a gay deceber
　　Look away, look away, look away, Dixie Land!
But when he put his arm around 'er
He smiled as fierce as a forty-pounder
　　Look away, look away, look away, Dixie Land!—
　　　CHORUS

His face was sharp as a butcher's cleaber,
But dat did not seem to grieb 'er,
　　Look away, look away, look away, Dixie Land!
Ole Missus acted de foolish part,
An' died for a man dat broke her heart,
　　Look away, look away, look away, Dixie Land!—
　　　CHORUS

Now, here's a health to de next ole Missus,
An' all de gals dat want to kiss us,
　　Look away, look away, look away, Dixie Land!
But if you want to drive 'way sorrow,
Come an' hear dis song to-morrow,
　　Look away, look away, look away, Dixie Land!—
　　　CHORUS

Dar's buckwheat cakes an' Injun batter,
Makes you fat, or a little fatter,
　　Look away, look away, look away, Dixie Land!
Den hoe it down and scratch your grabble,
To Dixie's Land I'm bound to trabble,
　　Look away, look away, look away, Dixie Land!—
　　　CHORUS

The Bonnie Blue Flag

In September of 1861 a New Orleans songwriter, Harry McCarthy, wrote "The Bonnie Blue Flag" in haste to fill a hole in a theatrical program which he was directing. The song was an instant hit, and was soon popular throughout the Confederacy. Unlike many other songs of the war, it was not popular in the North, due to its blatantly secessionist sentiments and its reference to slavery in the line "Fighting for the property we gained by honest toil."

General McGowan addresses volunteers in front of Charleston Hotel.

We are a band of brothers, and native to the soil,
Fighting for the property we gained by honest toil;
And when our rights were threatened, the cry rose
  near and far:
Hurrah for the bonnie Blue Flag that bears a single
  star!
  Hurrah! hurrah! for the bonnie Blue Flag
  That bears a single star.

As long as the Union was faithful to her trust,
Like friends and like brothers, kind were we and
  just;
But now when Northern treachery attempts our
  rights to mar,
We hoist on high the bonnie Blue Flag that bears a
  single star.

First, gallant South Carolina nobly made the stand;
Then came Alabama, who took her by the hand;
Next, quickly Mississippi, Georgia, and Florida—
All raised the flag, the bonnie Blue Flag that bears a
  single star.

Ye men of valor, gather round the banner of the
  right;
Texas and fair Louisiana join us in the fight.
Davis, our loved President, and Stephens,
  statesmen are;
Now rally round the bonnie Blue Flag that bears a
  single star.

And here's to brave Virginia! the Old Dominion
  State
With the young Confederacy at length has linked
  her fate.
Impelled by her example, now other States prepare
To hoist on high the bonnie Blue Flag that bears a
  single star.

Then here's to our Confederacy; strong we are and
  brave,
Like patriots of old we'll fight, our heritage to save;
And rather than submit to shame, to die we would
  prefer;
So cheer for the bonnie Blue Flag that bears a single
  star.

Then cheer, boys, cheer, raise the joyous shout,
For Arkansas and North Carolina now have both
  gone out;
And let another rousing cheer for Tennessee be
  given,
The single-star of the bonnie Blue Flag has grown
  to be eleven!
Hurrah! hurrah! for the bonnie Blue Flag
That bears a single star.

Maryland! My Maryland!

James Ryder Randall, an expatriate Baltimorean teaching in New Orleans, wrote "Maryland! My Maryland!" as a poem upon hearing of the clash between the 6th Massachusetts and a secessionist mob in Baltimore on 19 April 1861 [cf. Warren Lee Goss, "Going to the Front"]. Soon after the poem was published in a New Orleans newspaper it began to circulate widely throughout the South. Shortly afterwards it was set to the tune of the Christmas carol "O Tannenbaum" and became one of the most popular Southern marching songs. Later adopted as the Maryland state song, its avowedly secessionist sentiment remains a constant irritant to the state's black population.

The despot's heel is on thy shore,
  Maryland!
His torch is at thy temple door,
  Maryland!
Avenge the patriotic gore
That flecked the streets of Baltimore,
And be the battle queen of yore,
  Maryland! My Maryland!

Hark to an exiled son's appeal,
  Maryland!
My mother State! to thee I kneel,
  Maryland!
For life and death, for woe and weal,
Thy peerless chivalry reveal,
And gird thy beauteous limbs with steel,
  Maryland! My Maryland!

Thou wilt not cower in the dust,
  Maryland!
Thy beaming sword shall never rust,
  Maryland!
Remember Carroll's sacred trust,
Remember Howard's warlike thrust,—
And all thy slumberers with the just,
  Maryland! My Maryland!

Come! for thy shield is bright and strong,
  Maryland!
Come! for thy dalliance does thee wrong,
  Maryland!
Come to thine own heroic throng,
Stalking with Liberty along,
And chaunt thy dauntless slogan song,
  Maryland! My Maryland!

Dear Mother! burst the tyrant's chain,
  Maryland!
Virginia should not call in vain,
  Maryland!
She meets her sisters on the plain—
"Sic semper!" 'tis the proud refrain
That baffles minions back again,
  Maryland! My Maryland!

I hear the distant thunder-hum,
  Maryland!
The Old Line's bugle, fife, and drum,
  Maryland!
She is not dead, nor deaf, nor dumb—
Huzza! she spurns the Nothern scum!
She breathes! she burns! she'll come! she'll come!
  Maryland! My Maryland!

John Brown's Body

The origins of "John Brown's Body" are obscure. The tune derives from an old Negro spriritual, while the words seem to have been written by one Thomas B. Bishop. The music and words were combined soon after the war began, reputedly by two Massachusetts men, Messrs. Gilmore and Greenleaf. The song rapidly became a favorite Union march. As with all genuine folk songs, there were many variations to the original version, the most popular of which was "We'll Hang Jeff Davis to a Sour Apple Tree." In early 1862 the most enduring and powerful version was written, "The Battle Hymn of the Republic."

John Brown's body lies a-mould'ring in the grave,
John Brown's body lies a-mould'ring in the grave,
John Brown's body lies a-mould'ring in the grave,
  His soul is marching on.

  CHORUS: Glory! Glory Hallelujah!
          Glory! Glory Hallelujah!
          Glory! Glory Hallelujah!
          His soul is marching on.

He's gone to be a soldier in the army of the Lord!
  His soul is marching on.—CHORUS

John Brown's knapsack is strapped upon his back.
  His soul is marching on.—CHORUS

His pet lambs will meet him on the way,
  And they'll go marching on.—CHORUS

THE BULL RUN CAMPAIGN

THE FIRST MONTHS AFTER FORT SUMTER WERE A REMARKABLY QUIET TIME. SUCH fighting as did take place was largely a matter of skirmishes and little combats—some three dozen or so—involving at most three or four regiments. With few exceptions most people, most soldiers, and most politicians, both North and South, believed that the war would be decided in one glorious, smashing, decisive major battle. So both sides sought to improvise powerful forces in anticipation of an early and decisive clash. The focus of military attention was along the Potomac in the vicinity of Washington. And when the clash did come, along Bull Run Creek in late July, it was neither glorious, nor smashing, nor decisive, but merely the first of many major battles to come.

JAMES B. FRY
McDowell's Advance to Bull Run

James B. Fry, a West Pointer from Illinois, had a varied career in the Old Army, including service on the frontier and in Mexico, and took part in the capture of John Brown. In the spring of 1861 he was appointed chief of staff—technically Assistant Adjutant General—to Maj. Gen. Irvin McDowell, in which capacity he served during the Bull Run Campaign. Fry

subsequently served in a variety of important staff positions in the field—at Shiloh, Corinth, and Perryville—and in Washington. Continuing in the army after the war, he retired in 1881 as a brigadier general and major general by brevet. His account of Bull Run is taken from Battles and Leaders of the Civil War.

Northern forces had hastened to Washington upon the call of President Lincoln, but prior to May 24th they had been held rigidly on the north side of the Potomac. On the night of May 23d–24th, the Confederate pickets being then in sight of the Capitol, three columns were thrown across the river by General J. K. F. Mansfield, then commanding the Department of Washington, and a line from Alexandria below to chain-bridge above Washington was intrenched under guidance of able engineers. On the 27th Brigadier-General Irvin McDowell was placed in command south of the Potomac.

By the 1st of June the Southern Government had been transferred from Montgomery to Richmond, and the capitals of the Union and of the Confederacy stood defiantly confronting each other. General Scott was in chief command of the Union forces, with McDowell south of the Potomac, confronted by his old classmate, Beauregard, hot from the capture of Fort Sumter.

General Patterson, of Pennsylvania, a veteran of the war of 1812 and the war with Mexico, was in command near Harper's Ferry, opposed by General Joseph E. Johnston. The Confederate President, Davis, then in Richmond, with General R. E. Lee as military adviser, exercised in person general military control of the Southern forces. The enemy to be engaged by McDowell occupied what was called the "Alexandria line," with headquarters at Manassas, the junction of the Orange and Alexandria with the Manassas Gap railroad. The stream known as Bull Run, some three miles in front of Manassas, was the line of defense. On Beauregard's right, 30 miles away, at the mouth of Aquia Creek, there was a Confederate brigade of 3000 men and 6 guns under General Holmes. The approach to Richmond from the Lower Chesapeake, threatened by General B. F. Butler, was guarded by Confederates under Generals Huger and Magruder. On Beauregard's left, sixty miles distant, in the Lower Shenandoah Valley and separated from him by the Blue Ridge Mountains, was the Confederate army of the Shenandoah under

Irwin McDowell commanded troops at Bull Run.

command of General Johnston. Beauregard's authority did not extend over the forces of Johnston, Huger, Magruder, or Holmes, but Holmes was with him before the battle of Bull Run, and so was Johnston, who, as will appear more fully hereafter, joined at a decisive moment.

Early in June Patterson was pushing his column against Harper's Ferry, and on the 3d of that month

McDowell was called upon by General Scott to submit "an estimate of the number and composition of a column to be pushed toward Manassas Junction and perhaps the Gap, say in 4 or 5 days, to favor Patterson's attack upon Harper's Ferry." McDowell had then been in command at Arlington less than a week, his raw regiments south of the Potomac were not yet brigaded, and this was the first intimation he had of offensive operations. He reported, June 4th, that 12,000 infantry, 2 batteries, 6 or 8 companies of cavalry, and a reserve of 5000 ready to move from Alexandria would be required. Johnston, however, gave up Harper's Ferry to Patterson, and the diversion by McDowell was not ordered. But the public demand for an advance became imperative—stimulated perhaps by the successful dash of fifty men of the 2d United States Cavalry, under Lieutenant C. H. Tompkins, through the enemy's outposts at Fairfax Court House on the night of June 1st, and by the unfortunate result of the movement of a regiment under General Schenck toward Vienna, June 7th, as well as by a disaster to some of General Butler's troops on the 10th at Big Bethel, near Fort Monroe. On the 24th of June, in compliance with verbal instructions from General Scott, McDowell submitted a "plan of operations and the composition of the force required to carry it into effect." He estimated the Confederate force at Manassas Junction and its dependencies at 25,000 men, assumed that his movements could not be kept secret and that the enemy would call up additional forces from all quarters, and added: "If General J.E. Johnston's force is kept engaged by Major-General Patterson, and Major-General Butler occupies the force now in his vicinity, I think they will not be able to bring up more than 10,000 men, so we may calculate upon having to do with about 35,000 men." And as it turned out, that was about the number he "had to do with." For the advance, McDowell asked "a force of 30,000 of all arms, with a reserve of 10,000." He knew that Beauregard had batteries in position at several places in front of Bull Run and defensive works behind the Run and at Manassas Junction. The stream being fordable at many places, McDowell proposed in his plan of operations to turn the enemy's position and force him out of it by seizing or threatening his communications. Nevertheless, he said in his report:

Relieving the chances are greatly in favor of the enemy's accepting battle between this and the Junction and that the consequences of that battle will be of the greatest importance to the country, as establishing the prestige in this contest, on the one side or the other,—the more so as the two sections will be fairly represented by regiments from almost every State,—I think it of great consequence that, as for the most part our regiments are exceedingly raw and the best of them, with few exceptions, not over steady in line, they be organized into as many small fixed brigades as the number of regular colonels will admit,

. . . so that the men may have as fair a chance as the nature of things and the comparative inexperience of most will allow.

This remarkably sound report was approved, and McDowell was directed to carry his plan into effect July 8th. But the government machinery worked slowly and there was jealousy in the way, so that the troops to bring his army up to the strength agreed upon did not reach him until the 16th.

Beauregard's Army of the Potomac at Manassas consisted of the brigades of Holmes, Bonham, Ewell, D. R. Jones, Longstreet, Cocke and Early, and of 3 regiments of infantry, 1 regiment and 3 battalions of cavalry, and 6 batteries of artillery, containing in all 27 guns, making an aggregate available force on the field of Bull Run of about 23,000 men. Johnston's army from the Shenandoah consisted of the brigades of Jackson, Bee, Bartow, and Kirby Smith, 2 regiments of infantry not brigaded, 1 regiment of cavalry (12 companies), and 5 batteries (20 guns), making an aggregate at Bull Run of 8340.

McDowell's army consisted of 5 divisions, Tyler's First Division, containing 4 brigades (Keyes's, Schenck's, W. T. Sherman's, and Richardson's); Hunter's Second Division, containing 2 brigades (Andrew Porter's and Burnside's); Heintzelman's Third Division, containing 3 brigades (Franklin's, Willcox's, and Howard's); Runyon's Fourth Division (9 regiments not brigaded); and Miles's Fifth Division, containing 2 brigades (Blenker's and Davies's),—10 batteries of artillery, besides 2 guns attached to infantry regiments, 49 guns in all, and 7 companies of regular cavalry. Of the foregoing forces, 9 of the batteries and 8 companies of infantry were regulars, and 1 small battalion was marines. The aggregate force was about 35,000 men. Runyon's Fourth Division was 6 or 7 miles in the rear guarding the road to Alexandria, and, though counted in the aggregate, was not embraced in McDowell's order for battle.

There was an ill-suppressed feeling of sympathy with the Confederacy in the Southern element of Washington society; but the halls of Congress resounded with the eloquence of Union speakers. Martial music filled the air, and war was the topic wherever men met. By day and night the tramp of soldiers was heard, and staff-officers and orderlies galloped through the streets between the headquarters of Generals Scott and McDowell. Northern enthusiasm was unbounded. "On to Richmond" was the war-cry. Public sentiment was irresistible, and in response to it the army advanced. It was a glorious spectacle. The various regiments were brilliantly uniformed according to the aesthetic taste of peace, and the silken banners they flung to the breeze were unsoiled and untorn. The bitter realities of war were nearer than we knew.

McDowell marched on the afternoon of July 16, the men carrying three days' rations in their haversacks; provision wagons were to follow from Alexandria the next day. On the morning of the 18th his forces were concentrated at Centreville, a point about 20 miles west of the Potomac and 6 or 7 miles east of Manassas Junction. Beauregard's outposts fell back without resistance. Bull Run, flowing south-easterly, is about half-way between Centreville and Manassas Junction, and, owing to its abrupt banks, the timber with which it was fringed, and some artificial defenses at the fords, was a formidable obstacle. The stream was fordable, but all the cross-ings for eight miles, from Union Mills on the south to the Stone Bridge on the north, were defended by Beauregard's forces. The Warrenton Turnpike, pass-ing through Centreville, leads nearly due west, crossing Bull Run at the Stone Bridge. The direct road from Centreville to Manassas crosses Bull Run at Mitchell's Ford, half a mile or so above another crossing known as Blackburn's Ford. Union Mills was covered by Ewell's brigade, supported after the

Bull Run. A-A-A is line of Confederates from July 18 to morning of July 21. B-B-B is line of Confederates to repel McDowell's flank attack.

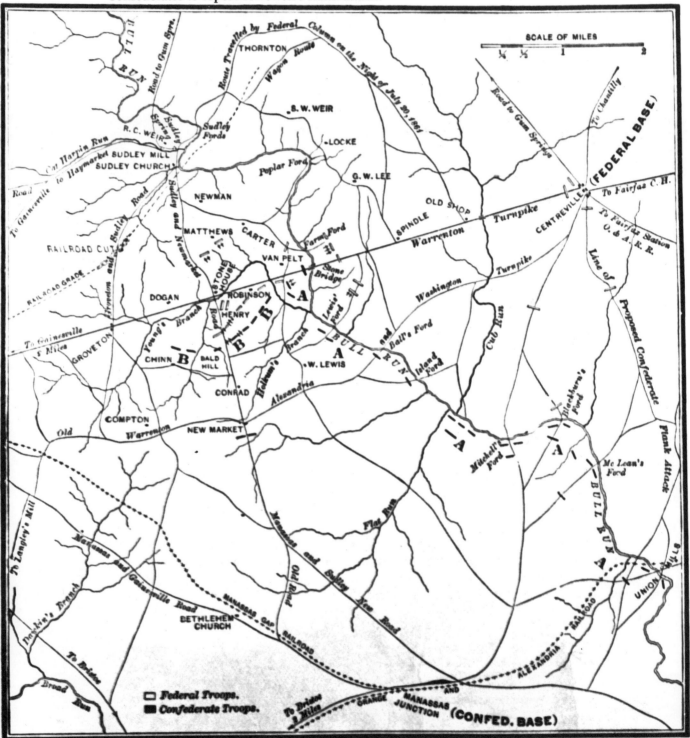

18th by Holmes's brigade; McLean's Ford, next to the north, was covered by D. R. Jones's brigade; Blackburn's Ford was defended by Longstreet's brigade, supported by Early's brigade; Mitchell's Ford was held by Bonham's brigade, with an outpost of two guns and an infantry support east of Bull Run; the stream between Mitchell's Ford and the Stone Bridge was covered by Cocke's brigade; the Stone Bridge on the Confederate left was held by Evans with 1 regiment and Wheat's special battalion of infantry, 1 battery of 4 guns, and 2 companies of cavalry.

McDowell was compelled to wait at Centreville until his provision wagons arrived and he could issue rations. His orders having carried his leading division under Tyler no farther than Centreville, he wrote that officer at 8:15 A.M. on the 18th, "Observe well the roads to Bull Run and to Warrenton. Do not bring on an engagement, but keep up the impression that we are moving on Manassas." McDowell then went to the extreme left of his line to examine the country with reference to a sudden movement of the army to turn the enemy's right flank. The reconnoissance showed him that the country was unfavorable to the movement, and he abandoned it. While he was gone to the left, Tyler, presumably to "keep up the impression that we were moving on Manassas," went forward from Centreville with a squadron of cavalry and two companies of infantry for the purpose of making a reconnoissance of Mitchell's and Blackburn's fords along the direct road to Manassas. The force of the enemy at these fords has just been given. Reaching the crest of the ridge overlooking the valley of Bull Run and a mile or so from the stream, the enemy was seen on the opposite bank, and Tyler brought up Benjamin's artillery, 2 20-pounder rifled guns, Ayres's field battery of 6 guns, and Richardson's brigade of infantry. The 20-pounders opened from the ridge and a few shots were exchanged with the enemy's batteries. Desiring more information than the long-range cannonade afforded, Tyler ordered Richardson's brigade and a section of Ayres's battery, supported by a squadron of cavalry, to move from the ridge across the open bottom of Bull Run and take position near the stream and have skirmishers "scour the thick woods" which skirted it. Two regiments of infantry, 2 pieces of artillery, and a squadron of cavalry moved down the slope into the woods and opened fire, driving Bonham's outpost to the cover of intrenchments across the stream. The brigades of Bonham and Longstreet, the latter being reënforced for the occasion by Early's brigade, responded at short range to the fire of the Federal reconnoitering force and drove it back in disorder. Tyler reported that having satisfied himself "that the enemy was in force," and ascertained "the position of his batteries," he withdrew. This unauthorized reconnoissance, called by the Federals the affair at Blackburn's Ford, was regarded at the time by the Confederates as a serious attack, and was dignified by the name of the "battle of Bull Run," the engagement of the 21st being called by them the battle of Manassas. The Confederates, feeling that they had repulsed a heavy and real attack, were encouraged by the result. The Federal troops, on the other hand, were greatly depressed. The regiment which suffered most was completely demoralized, and McDowell thought that the depression of the repulse was felt throughout his army and produced its effect upon the Pennsylvania regiment and the New York battery which insisted (their terms having expired) upon their discharge, and on the 21st, as he expressed it, "marched to the rear to the sound of the enemy's cannon." Even Tyler himself felt the depressing effect of his repulse, if we may judge by his cautious and feeble action on the 21st when dash was required.

The operations of the 18th confirmed McDowell in his opinion that with his raw troops the Confederate position should be turned instead of attacked in front. Careful examination had satisfied him that the country did not favor a movement to turn the enemy's right. On the night of the 18th the haversacks of his men were empty, and had to be replenished from the provision wagons, which were late in getting up. Nor had he yet determined upon his point or plan of attack. While resting and provisioning his men, he devoted the 19th and 20th to a careful examination by his engineers of the enemy's position and the intervening country. His men, not soldiers, but civilians in uniform, unused to marching, hot, weary, and footsore, dropped down as they had halted and bivouacked on the roads about Centreville. Notwithstanding Beauregard's elation over the affair at Blackburn's Ford on the 18th, he permitted the 19th and 20th to pass without a movement to follow up the advantage he had gained. During these two days, McDowell carefully examined the Confederate position, and made his plan to manoeuvre the enemy out of it. Beauregard ordered no aggressive movement until the 21st, and then, as appears from his own statement, through miscarriage of orders and lack of apprehension on the part of subordinates, the effort was a complete fiasco, with the comical result of frightening his own troops, who, late in the afternoon, mistook the return of one of their brigades for an attack by McDowell's left, and the serious result of interfering with the pursuit after he had gained the battle of the 21st.

But Beauregard, though not aggressive on the 19th and 20th, was not idle within his own lines. The Confederate President had authorized Johnston, Beauregard's senior, to use his discretion in moving to the support of Manassas, and Beauregard, urging Johnston to do so, sent railway transportation for the Shenandoah forces. But, as he states, "he at the same time submitted the alternative proposition to Johnston that, having passed the Blue Ridge, he should assemble his forces, press forward by way of Aldie, north-west of Manassas, and fall upon McDowell's right rear," while he, Beauregard, "prepared for the operation at the first sound of the conflict, should strenuously assume the offensive in front." "The situation and circumstances specially favored the signal success of such an operation," says Beauregard. An attack by two armies moving from opposite points upon an enemy, with the time of attack for one depending upon the sound of the other's cannon, is hazardous even with well-disciplined and well-seasoned troops, and is next to fatal with raw levies. Johnston chose the wiser course of moving by rail to Manassas, thus preserving the benefit of "interior lines," which, Beauregard says, was the "sole military advantage at the moment that the Confederates possessed."

The campaign which General Scott required McDowell to make was undertaken with the understanding that Johnston should be prevented from joining Beauregard. With no lack of confidence in himself, McDowell was dominated by the feeling of subordination and deference to General Scott which at that time pervaded the whole army, and General Scott, who controlled both McDowell and Patterson, assured McDowell that Johnston should not join Beauregard without having "Patterson on his heels." Yet Johnston's army, nearly nine thousand strong, joined Beauregard, Bee's brigade and Johnston in person arriving on the morning of the 20th, the remainder about noon on the 21st. Although the enforced delay at Centreville enabled McDowell to provision his troops and gain information upon which to base an excellent plan of attack, it proved fatal by affording time for a junction of the opposing forces. On the 21st of July General Scott addressed a dispatch to McDowell, saying: "It is known that a strong reënforcement left Winchester on the afternoon of the 18th, which you will also have to beat. Four new regiments will leave to-day to be at Fairfax

Station to-night. Others shall follow to-morrow—twice the number if necessary." When this dispatch was penned, McDowell was fighting the "strong re-ënforcement" which left Winchester on the 18th. General Scott's report that Beauregard had been re-ënforced, the information that four regiments had been sent to McDowell, and the promise that twice the number would be sent if necessary, all came too late—and Patterson came not at all.

During the 19th and 20th the bivouacs of McDowells' army at Centreville, almost within cannon range of the enemy, were thronged by visitors, official and unofficial, who came in carriages from Washington, bringing their own supplies. They were under no military restraint, and passed to and fro among the troops as they pleased, giving the scene the appearance of a monster military picnic. Among others, the venerable Secretary of War, Cameron,

called upon McDowell. Whether due to a naturally serious expression, to a sense of responsibility, to a premonition of the fate of his brother who fell upon the field on the 21st, or to other cause, his countenance showed apprehension of evil; but men generally were confident and jovial.

McDowell's plan of battle promulgated on the 20th, was to turn the enemy's left, force him from his defensive position, and, "if possible, destroy the railroad leading from Manassas to the Valley of Virginia, where the enemy has a large force." He did not know when he issued this order that Johnston had joined Beauregard, though he suspected it. Miles's Fifth Division, with Richardson's brigade of Tyler's division, and a strong force of artillery was to remain in reserve at Centreville, prepare defensive works there and threaten Blackburn's Ford. Tyler's First Division, which was on the turnpike in advance,

The Battle of Bull Run was July 21, 1861.

The 69th New York State Militia makes a gallant charge against a rebel battery.

was to move at 2:30 A.M., threaten the Stone Bridge and open fire upon it at daybreak. This demonstration was to be vigorous, its first purpose being to divert attention from the movements of the turning column. As soon as Tyler's troops cleared the way, Hunter's Second Division, followed by Heintzelman's Third Division, was to move to a point on the Warrenton Turnpike about 1 or 2 miles east of Stone Bridge and there take a country road to the right, cross the Run at Sudley Springs, come down upon the flank and rear of the enemy at the Stone Bridge, and force him to open the way for Tyler's division to cross there and attack, fresh and in full force.

Tyler's start was so late and his advance was so slow as to hold Hunter and Heintzelman 2 or 3 hours on the mile or two of the turnpike between their camps and the point at which they were to turn off for the flank march. This delay, and the fact that the flank march proved difficult and some 12 miles instead of about 6 as was expected, were of serious moment. The flanking column did not cross at Sudley Springs until 9:30 instead of 7, the long march, with its many interruptions, tired out the men, and the delay gave the enemy time to discover the turning movement. Tyler's operations against the Stone Bridge were feeble and ineffective. By 8 o'clock Evans was satisfied that he was in no danger in front, and perceived the movement to turn his position. He was on the left of the Confederate line, guarding the point where the Warrenton Turnpike, the great highway to the field, crossed Bull Run, the Confederate line of defense. He had no instructions to guide him in the emergency that had arisen. But he did not hesitate. Reporting his information and purpose to the adjoining commander, Cocke, and leaving 4 companies of infantry to deceive and hold Tyler at the bridge, Evans before 9 o'clock turned his back upon the point he was set to guard, marched a mile away, and, seizing the high ground to the north of Young's Branch of Bull Run, formed line of battle at right angles to his former line, his left resting near the Sudley Springs road, by which Burnside with the head of the turning column was approaching, thus covering the Warrenton Turnpike and opposing a determined front to the Federal advance upon the Confederate left and rear. In his rear to the south lay the valley of Young's Branch, and rising from that was the higher ridge or plateau on which the Robinson house and the Henry house were situated, and on which the main action took place in the afternoon. Burnside, finding Evans across his path, promptly formed line of battle and attacked about 9:45 A.M. Hunter, the division commander, who was at the head of Burnside's brigade directing the formation of the first skirmish line, was severely wounded and taken to the rear at the opening of the action. Evans not only repulsed but pursued the troops that made the attack upon him. Andrew Porter's brigade of Hunter's division followed Burnside closely and came to his support. In the mean time Bee had formed a Confederate line of battle with his and Bartow's brigades of Johnston's army on the Henry house plateau, a stronger position than the one held by Evans, and desired Evans to fall back to that line; but Evans, probably feeling bound to cover the Warrenton Turnpike and hold it against Tyler as well as against the flanking column, insisted that Bee should move across the valley to his support, which was done.

After Bee joined Evans, the preliminary battle continued to rage upon the ground chosen by the latter. The opposing forces were Burnside's and Porter's brigades, with one regiment of Heintzelman's division on the Federal side, and Evans's, Bee's, and Bartow's brigades on the Confederate side. The Confederates were dislodged and driven back to the Henry house plateau, where Bee had previously formed line and where what Beauregard called "the mingled remnants of Bee's, Bartow's, and Evans's commands" were re-formed under cover of Stonewall Jackson's brigade of Johnston's army.

The time of this repulse, as proved by so accurate an authority as Stonewall Jackson, was before 11:30 A.M., and this is substantially confirmed by Beauregard's official report made at the time. Sherman and Keyes had nothing to do with it. They did not begin to cross Bull Run until noon. Thus, after nearly two hours' stubborn fighting with the forces of Johnston, which General Scott had promised should be kept away, McDowell won the first advantage; but Johnston had cost him dearly.

During all this time Johnston and Beauregard had been waiting near Mitchell's Ford for the development of the attack they had ordered by their right upon McDowell at Centreville. The gravity of the situation upon their left had not yet dawned upon them. What might the result have been if the Union column had not been detained by Tyler's delay in moving out in the early morning, or if Johnston's army, to which Bee, Bartow, and Jackson belonged, had not arrived?

But the heavy firing on the left soon diverted Johnston and Beauregard from all thought of an offensive movement with their right, and decided them, as Beauregard has said, "to hurry up all available reënforcements, including the reserves that were to have moved upon Centreville, to our left, and fight the battle out in that quarter." Thereupon Beauregard ordered "Ewell, Jones, and Longstreet to make a strong demonstration all along their front on the other side of Bull Run, and orderd the reserves, Holmes's brigade with six guns, and Early's brigade, to move swiftly to the left," and he and Johnston set out at full speed for the point of conflict, which they reached while Bee was attempting to rally his men about Jackson's brigade on the Henry house plateau. McDowell had waited in the morning at the point on the Warrenton Turnpike where his flanking column turned to the right, until the troops, except Howard's brigade, which he halted at that point, had passed. He gazed silently and with evident pride upon the gay regiments as they filed briskly but quietly past in the freshness of the early morning, and then, remarking to his staff, "Gentlemen, that is a big force," he mounted and moved forward to the field by way of Sudley Springs. He reached the scene of actual conflict somewhat earlier than Johnston and Beauregard did, and, seeing the enemy driven across the valley of Young's Branch and behind the Warrenton Turnpike, at once sent a swift aide-de-camp to Tyler with orders to "press the attack" at the Stone Bridge. Tyler acknowledged that he received this order by 11 o'clock. It was Tyler's division upon which McDowell relied for the decisive fighting of the day. He knew that the march of the turning column would be fatiguing, and when by a sturdy fight it had cleared the Warrenton Turnpike for the advance of Tyler's division, it had, in fact, done more than its fair proportion of the work. But Tyler did not attempt to force the passage of the Stone Bridge, which, after about 8 o'clock, was defended by only four companies of infantry, though he admitted that by the plan of battle, when Hunter and Heintzelman had attacked the enemy in the vicinity of the Stone Bridge, "he was to force the passage of Bull Run at that point and attack the enemy in flank." Soon after McDowell's arrival at the front, Burnside rode up to him and said that his brigade had borne the brunt of the battle, that it was out of ammunition, and that he wanted permission to withdraw, refit and fill cartridge-boxes. McDowell in the excitement of the occasion gave reluctant consent, and the brigade, which certainly had done nobly, marched to the rear, stacked arms, and took no further part in the fight.

Having sent the order to Tyler to press his attack and orders to the rear of the turning column to hurry forward, McDowell, like Beauregard, rushed in person into the conflict, and by the force of circumstances became for the time the commander of the turning column and the force actually engaged, rather than the commander of his whole army. With the exception of sending his adjutant-general to find and hurry Tyler forward, his subsequent orders were mainly or wholly to the troops under his own observation. Unlike Beauregard, he had no Johnston in rear with full authority and knowledge of the situation to throw forward reserves and reënforcements. It was not until 12 o'clock that Sherman received orders from Tyler to cross the stream, which he did at a ford above the Stone Bridge, going to the assistance of Hunter. Sherman reported to McDowell on the field and joined in the pursuit of Bee's forces across the valley of Young's Branch. Keyes's brigade, accompanied by Tyler in person, followed across the stream where Sherman forded, but without uniting with the other forces on the field, made a feeble advance upon the slope of the plateau toward the Robinson house, and then about 2 o'clock filed off by flank to its left and, sheltered by the east front of the bluff that forms the plateau, marched down Young's Branch out of sight of the enemy and took no further part in the engagement. McDowell did not know where it was, nor did he then know that Schenck's brigade of Tyler's division did not cross the Run at all.

Men of Federal line charge Henry Hill.

The line taken up by Stonewall Jackson upon which Bee, Bartow, and Evans rallied on the southern part of the plateau was a very strong one. The ground was high and afforded the cover of a curvilinear wood with the concave side toward the Federal line of attack. According to Beauregard's official report made at the time, he had upon this part of the field, at the beginning, 6500 infantry, 13 pieces of artillery, and 2 companies of cavalry, and this line was continuously reënforced from Beauregard's own reserves and by the arrival of the troops from the Shenandoah Valley.

To carry this formidable position, McDowell had at hand the brigades of Franklin, Willcox, Sherman, and Porter, Palmer's battalion of regular cavalry, and Ricketts's and Griffin's regular batteries. Porter's brigade had been reduced and shaken by the morning

by the shortness of range." The short range was due to the Federal advance, and the several struggles for the plateau were at close quarters and gallant on both sides. The batteries of Ricketts and Griffin, by their fine discipline, wonderful daring, and matchless skill, were the prime features in the fight. The battle was not lost till they were lost. When in their advanced and perilous position, and just after their infantry supports had been driven over the slopes, a fatal mistake occurred. A regiment of infantry came out of the woods on Griffin's right, and as he was in the act of opening upon it with canister, he was deterred by the assurance of Major Barry, the chief of artillery, that it "was a regiment sent by Colonel Heintzelman to support the battery." A moment more and the doubtful regiment proved its identity by a deadly volley, and, as Griffin states in

Captain Charles Griffin.

Captain James B. Ricketts.

fight. Howard's brigade was in reserve and only came into action late in the afternoon. The men, unused to field service, and not yet over the hot and dusty march from the Potomac, had been under arms since midnight. The plateau, however, was promptly assaulted, the northern part of it was carried, the batteries of Ricketts and Griffin were planted near the Henry house, and McDowell clambered to the upper story of that structure to get a glance at the whole field. Upon the Henry house plateau, of which the Confederates held the southern and the Federals the northern part, the tide of battle ebbed and flowed as McDowell pushed in Franklin's, Willcox's, Sherman's, Porter's, and at last Howard's brigades, and as Beauregard put into action reserves which Johnston sent from the right and reënforcements which he hurried forward from the Shenandoah Valley as they arrived by cars. On the plateau, Beauregard says, the disadvantage of his "smooth-bore guns was reduced

his official report, "every cannoneer was cut down and a large number of horses killed, leaving the battery (which was without support excepting in name) perfectly helpless." The effect upon Ricketts was equally fatal. He, desperately wounded, and Ramsay, his lieutenant, killed, lay in the wreck of the battery. Beauregard speaks of his last advance on the plateau as "leaving in our final possession the Robinson and Henry houses, with most of Ricketts's and Griffin's batteries, the men of which were mostly shot down where they bravely stood by their guns." Having become separated from McDowell, I fell in with Barnard, his chief engineer, and while together we observed the New York Fire Zouaves, who had been supporting Griffin's battery, fleeing to the rear in their gaudy uniforms, in utter confusion. Thereupon I rode back to where I knew Burnside's brigade was at rest, and stated to Burnside the condition of affairs, with the suggestion that he form and move his brigade to the front. Returning, I again met Bernard, and as the battle seemed to him and me to be going against us, and not knowing where McDowell was, with the concurrence of Barnard, as stated in his official report, I immediately sent a note to Miles, telling him to move two brigades of his reserve up to the Stone Bridge and telegraph to Washington to send forward all the troops that could be spared.

After the arrival of Howard's brigade, McDowell for the last time pressed up the slope to the plateau, forced back the Confederate line, and regained possession of the Henry and Robinson houses and of the lost batteries. But there were no longer cannoneers to man or horses to move these guns that had done so much. By the arrival upon this part of the field of his own reserves and Kirby Smith's brigade of Johnston's army about half-past 3, Beauregard extended his left to outflank McDowell's shattered, shortened, and disconnected line, and the Federals left the field about half-past 4. Until then they had fought wonderfully well for raw troops. There were no fresh horses on the field to support or encourage them, and the men seemed to be seized simultaneously by the conviction that it was no use to do anything more and they might as well start home. Cohesion was lost, the organizations with some exceptions being disintegrated, and the men quietly walked off. There was no special excitement except that arising from the frantic efforts of officers to stop men who paid little or no attention to anything that was said. On the high ground by the Matthews house, about where Evans had taken position in the morning to check Burnside, McDowell and his staff, aided by other officers, made a desperate but futile effort to arrest the masses and form them into line. There I went to Arnold's battery as it came by, and advised that he unlimber and make a stand as a rallying-point, which he did, saying he was in fair condition and ready to fight as long as there was any fighting to be done. But all efforts failed. The stragglers moved past the guns, in spite of all that could be done, and, as stated in his report, Arnold at my direction joined Sykes's battalion of infantry of Porter's brigade and Palmer's battalion of cavalry, all of the regular army, to cover the rear, as the men trooped back in great disorder across Bull Run. There were some hours of daylight for the Confederates to gather the fruits of victory, but a few rounds of shell and canister checked all the pursuit that was attempted, and the occasion called for no sacrifices of valorous deeds by the stanch regulars of the rear-guard. There was no panic, in the ordinary meaning of the word, until the retiring soldiers, guns, wagons, congressmen, and carriages were fired upon, on the road east of Bull Run. Then the panic began, and the bridge over Cub Run being rendered impassable for vehicles by a wagon that was upset upon it, utter confusion set in: pleasure-carriages, gun-carriages, and ammunition wagons which could not be put across the Run were abandoned and blocked the way, and stragglers broke and threw

aside their muskets and cut horses from their harness and rode off upon them. In leaving the field the men took the same routes, in a general way, by which they had reached it. Hence when the men of Hunter's and Heintzelman's divisions got back to Centreville, they had walked about 25 miles. That night they walked back to the Potomac, an additional distance of 20 miles; so that these undisciplined and unseasoned men within 36 hours walked fully 45 miles, besides fighting from about 10 A.M. until 4 P.M. on a hot and dusty day in July. McDowell in person reached Centreville before sunset and found there Miles's division with Richardson's brigade and 3 regiments of Runyon's division, and Hunt's, Tidball's, Ayres's, and Greene's batteries and 1 or 2 fragments of batteries, making about 20 guns. It was a formidable force, but there was a lack of food and the mass of the army was completely demoralized. Beauregard had about an equal force which had not been in the fight, consisting of Ewell's, Jones's, and Longstreet's brigades and some troops of other brigades. McDowell consulted the division and brigade commanders who were at hand upon the question of making a stand or retreating. The verdict was in favor of the latter, but a decision of officers one way or the other was of no moment; the men had already decided for themselves and were streaming away to the rear, in spite of all that could be done. They had no interest or treasure in Centreville, and their hearts were not there. Their tents, provisions, baggage, and letters from home were upon the banks of the Potomac, and no power could have stopped them short of the camps they had left less than a week before. As before stated, most of them were sovereigns in uniform, not soldiers. McDowell accepted the situation, detailed Richardson's and Blenker's brigades to cover the retreat, and the army, a disorganized mass, with some creditable exceptions, drifted as the men pleased away from the scene of action. There was no pursuit, and the march from Centreville was as barren of opportunities for the rear-guard as the withdrawal from the field of battle had been. When McDowell reached Fairfax Court House in the night, he was in communication with Washington and exchanged telegrams with General Scott, in one of which the old hero said, "We are not discouraged"; but that dispatch did not lighten the gloom in which it was received. McDowell was so tired that while sitting on the ground writing a dispatch he fell asleep, pencil in hand, in the middle of a sentence. His adjutant-general aroused him; the dispatch was finished, and the weary ride to the Potomac resumed. When the unfortunate commander dismounted at Arlington next forenoon in a soaking rain, after 32 hours in the saddle, his disastrous campaign of 6 days was closed.

The first martial effervescence of the country was over. The three-months men went home, and the three-months chapter of the war ended—with the South trimphant and confidant; the North disappointed but determined.

Rebs say farewell as they leave for Manassas.

★★★

PIERRE G. T. BEAUREGARD
The First Battle of Bull Run

Pierre Gustave Tonnant Beauregard, a Loui-siana creole who looked every inch the beau sabeur, was one of the most prominent of Southern generals. A West Point graduate with a distinguished record as a combat engineer in Mexico, Beauregard's pre-war career was as a director of navigational improvements on the Mississippi. He went South in February of 1861 and was commissioned a brigadier general in Confederate service. Beauregard became the South's first war hero, commanding at the bom-bardment of Fort Sumter. At Bull Run he was directly in command of the forces engaged, though technically subordinate to General Joseph Johnston. Bull Run was the high point of

Beauregard's career. Although he subsequently served at Shiloh, where he assumed command on the death of General Albert Sidney Johnston, serious differences with Jefferson Davis relegated him to relatively minor posts. In 1864–65 he commanded with some distinction, but little reward, in the defense of Richmond, in the West, and in the Carolinas. After the war he became a successful railroad president, declined offers to command the Romanian and Egyptian armies, became involved in the crooked Loui-siana lottery, and wrote several volumes on a variety of subjects. His account of Bull Run is taken from Battles and Leaders of the Civil War.

Soon after the first conflict between the authorities of the Federal Union and those of the Confederate States had occurred in Charleston Harbor, by the bombardment of Fort Sumter,—which, beginning at 4:30 A.M. on the 12th of April 1861, forced the surrender of that fortress within thirty hours thereafter into my hands,—I was called to Richmond, which by that time had become the Confederate seat of government, and was directed to "assume command of the Confederate troops on the Alexandria line." Arriving at Manassas Junction, I took command on the 2d of June, forty-nine days after the evacuation of Fort Sumter.

Although the position at the time was strategically of commanding importance to the Confederates, the mere terrain was not only without natural defensive advantages, but, on the contrary, was absolutely unfavorable. Its strategic value was that, being close to the Federal capital, it held in observation the chief army then being assembled near Arlington by General McDowell, under the immediate eye of the commander-in-chief, General Scott, for an offensive movement against Richmond; and while it had a railway approach in its rear for the easy accumulation of reënforcements and all the necessary munitions of war from the southward, at the same time another (the Manassas Gap) railway, diverging laterally to the left from that point, gave rapid communications with the fertile valley of the Shenandoah, then teeming with live stock and cereal subsistence, as well as with other resources essential to the Confederates. There was this further value in the position to the Confederate army: that during the period of accumulation, seasoning, and training, it might be fed from the fat fields, pastures, and garners of Loudoun, Fauquier, and the Lower Shenandoah Valley counties, which otherwise must have fallen into the hands of the enemy. But, on the other hand, Bull Run, a petty stream, was of little or no defensive strength; for it abounded in fords, and although for the most part its banks were rocky and abrupt, the side from which it would be approached offensively in most places commanded the opposite ground.

At the time of my arrival at Manassas, a Confederate army under General Joseph E. Johnston was in occupation of the Lower Shenandoah Valley, along the line of the Upper Potomac, chiefly at Harper's Ferry, which was regarded as the gateway of the valley and of one of the possible approaches to Richmond; a position from which he was speedily forced to retire, however, by a flank movement of a Federal army, under the veteran General Patterson, thrown across the Potomac at or about Martinsburg. On my other or right flank, so to speak, a Confederate force of some 2500 men under General Holmes occupied the position of Aquia Creek of the lower Potomac, upon the line of approach to Richmond from that direction through Fredericksburg. The other approach, that by way of the James River, was held by Confederate troops under Generals Huger and Magruder. Establishing small outposts at Leesburg

to observe the crossings of the Potomac in that quarter, and at Fairfax Court House in observance of Arlington, with other detachments in advance of Manassas toward Alexandria on the south side of the railroad, from the very outset I was anxiously aware that the sole military advantage at the moment to the Confederates was that of holding the interior lines. On the Federal or hostile side were all material advantages, including superior numbers, largely drawn from the old militia organizations of the great cities of the North, decidedly better armed and equipped than the troops under men, and strengthened by a small but incomparable body of regular infantry as well as a number of batteries of regular field artillery of the highest class, and a very large and thoroughly organized staff corps, besides a numerous body of professionally educated officers on command of volunteer regiments, all precious military elements at such a juncture.

Happily, through the foresight of Colonel Thomas Jordan,—whom General Lee had placed as the adjutant-general of the forces there assembled before my arrival,—arrangements were made which enabled me to receive regularly, from private persons at the Federal capital, most accurate information, of which politicians high in council, as well as War Department clerks, were the unconscious ducts. On the 4th of July, my pickets happened upon and captured a soldier of the regulars, who proved to be a clerk in the adjutant-general's office of General McDowell, intrusted with the special duty of compiling returns of his army—a work which he confessed, without reluctance, he had just executed, showing the forces under McDowell about the 1st of July. His statement of the strength and composition of that force tallied so closely with that which had been acquired through my Washington agencies, already mentioned, as well as through the leading Northern newspapers (regular files of which were also transmitted to my headquarters from the Federal capital), that I could not doubt them.

In these several ways, therefore, I was almost as well advised of the strength of the hostile army in my front as its commander, who, I may mention, had been a classmate of mine at West Point. Under those circumstances I had become satisfied that a well-equipped, well-constituted Federal army at least 50,000 strong, of all arms, confronted me at or about Arlington, ready and on the very eve of an offensive operation against me, and to meet which I could muster barely 18,000 men with 29 field guns.

Previously,—indeed, as early as the middle of June,—it had become apparent to my mind that through only one course of action could there be a well-grounded hope of ability on the part of the Confederates to encounter successfully the offensive operations for which the Federal authorities were then vigorously preparing in my immediate front, with so consummate a strategist and military administrator as Lieutenant-General Scott in general command at Washington, aided by his accomplished heads of the large General Staff Corps of the

United States Army. This course was to make the most enterprising, warlike use of the interior lines which we possessed, for the swift concentration at the critical instant of every available Confederate force upon the menaced position, at the risk, if need were, of sacrificing all minor places to the one clearly of major military value—there to meet our adversary so offensively as to overwhelm him, under circumstances that must assure immediate ability to assume the general offensive even upon his territory, and thus conquer an early peace by a few well-delivered blows.

My views of such import had been already earnestly communicated to the proper authorities; but about the middle of July, satisfied that McDowell was on the eve of taking the offensive against me, I dispatched Colonel James Chesnut, of South Carolina, a volunteer aide-de-camp on my staff who had served on an intimate footing with Mr. Davis in the Senate of the United States, to urge in substance the necessity for the immediate concentration of the larger part of the forces of Johnston and Holmes at Manassas, so that the moment McDowell should be sufficiently far detached from Washington, I would be enabled to move rapidly round his more convenient flank upon his rear and his communications, and attack him in reverse, or get between his forces, then separated, thus cutting off his retreat upon Arlington in the event of his defeat, and insuring as an immediate consequence the crushing of Patterson, the liberation of Maryland, and the capture of Washington.

This plan was rejected by Mr. Davis and his military advisers (Adjutant-General Cooper and General Lee), who characterized it as "brilliant and comprehensive," but essentially impracticable. Furthermore, Colonel Chesnut came back impressed with the views entertained at Richmond,—as he communicated at once to my adjutant-general,—that should the Federal army soon move offensively upon my position, my best course would be to retire behind the Rappahannock and accept battle there instead of at Manassas. In effect, it was regarded as best to sever communications between the two chief Confederate armies, that of the Potomac and that of the Shenandoah, with the inevitable immediate result that Johnston would be forced to leave Patterson in possession of the Lower Shenandoah Valley, abandoning to the enemy so large a part of the most resourceful sections of Virginia, and to retreat southward by way of the Luray Valley, pass across the Blue Ridge at Thornton's Gap and unite with me after all, but at Fredericksburg, much nearer Richmond than Manassas. These views, however, were not made known to me at the time, and happily my mind was left free to the grave problem imposed upon me by the rejection of my plan for the immediate concentration of a materially larger force,—i. e., the problem of placing and using my resources for a successful encounter behind Bull Run with the Federal army, which I was not permitted to doubt was about to take the field against me.

It is almost needless to say that I had caused to be made a thorough reconnoissance of all the ground in my front and flanks, and had made myself personally acquainted with the most material points, including the region of Sudley's Church on my left, where a small detachment was posted in observation. Left now to my own resources, of course the contingency of defeat had to be considered and provided for. Among the measures of precaution for such a result, I orderd the destruction of the railroad bridge across Bull Run at Union Mills, on my right, in order that the enemy, in the event of my defeat, should not have the immediate use of the railroad in following up their movement against Richmond—a railroad which could have had no corresponding value to us eastward beyond Manassas in any operations on our side with Washington as the objective, inasmuch as any such operations must have been made by the way of the Upper Potomac and upon the rear of that city.

Just before Colonel Chesnut was dispatched on the mission of which I have spoken, a former clerk in one of the departments at Washington, well known to him, had volunteered to return thither and bring back the latest information of the military and political situation from our most trusted friends. His loyalty to our cause, his intelligence, and his desire to be of service being vouched for, he was at once sent across the Potomac below Alexandria, merely accredited by a small scrap of paper bearing in Colonel Jordan's cipher the two words, "Trust bearer," with which he was to call at a certain house in Washington within easy rifle-range of the White House, ask for the lady of the house, and present it only to her. This delicate mission was as fortunately as it was deftly executed. In the early morning, as the newsboys were crying in the empty streets of Washington the intelligence that the order was given for the Federal army to move at once upon my position, that scrap of paper reached the hands of the one person in all that city who could extract any meaning from it. With no more delay than was necessary for a hurried breakfast and the writing in cipher by Mrs. G——of the words, "Order issued for McDowell to march upon Manassas to-night," my agent was placed in communication with another friend, who carried him in a buggy with a relay of horses as swiftly as possible down the eastern shore of the Potomac to our regular ferry across that river. Without untoward incident the momentous dispatch was quickly delivered into the hands of a cavalry courier, and by means of relays it was in my hands between 8 and 9 o'clock that night. Within half an hour my outpost commanders, advised of what was impending, were directed, at the first evidence of the near presence of the enemy in their front, to fall back in the manner and to positions already prescribed in anticipation of such a contingency in an order confidentially communicated to them four weeks before, and the detachment at Leesburg was directed to join me by forced marches. Having thus cleared my decks for action, I next

Young Lieutenant Jackson.

acquainted Mr. Davis with the situation, and ventured once more to suggest that the Army of the Shenandoah, with the brigade at Fredericksburg or Aquia Creek, should be ordered to reënforce me,— suggestions that were at once heeded so far that General Holmes was ordered to carry his command to my aid, and General Johnston was given discretion to do likewise. After some telegraphic discussion with me, General Johnston was induced to exercise this discretion in favor of the swift march of the Army of the Shenandoah to my relief; and to facilitate that vital movement, I hastened to accumulate all possible means of railway transport at a designated point on the Manassas Gap railroad at the eastern foot of the Blue Ridge, to which Johnston's troops directed their march. However, at the same time, I had submitted the alternative proposition to General Johnston, that, having passed the Blue Ridge, he should assemble his forces, press forward by way of Aldie, north-west of Manassas, and fall upon McDowell's right rear; while I, prepared for the operation, at the first sound of the conflict, should strenuously assume the offensive in my front. The situation and circumstances specially favored the signal success of such an operation. The march to the point of attack could have been accomplished as soon as the forces were brought ultimately by rail to Manassas Junction; our enemy, thus attacked so nearly simultaneously on his right flank, his rear, and his front, naturally would suppose that I had been able to turn his flank while attacking him in front, and therefore, that I must have an overwhelming superiority of numbers; and his forces, being new troops, most of them under fire for the first time, must have soon fallen into a disastrous panic. Moreover, such an operation must have resulted advantageously to the Confederates, in the event that McDowell should, as might have been anticipated, attempt to strike the Manassas Gap railway to my left, and thus cut off railway communications between Johnston's forces and my own, instead of the mere effort to strike my left flank which he actually essayed.

It seemed, however, as though the deferred attempt at concentration was to go for naught, for on the morning of the 18th the Federal forces were massed around Centreville, but three miles from Mitchell's Ford, and soon were seen advancing upon the roads leading to that and Blackburn's Ford. My order of battle, issued in the night of the 17th, contemplated an offensive return, particularly from the strong brigades on the right and right center. The Federal artillery opened in front of both fords, and the infantry, while demonstrating in front of Mitchell's Ford, endeavored to force a passage at Blackburn's. Their column of attack, Tyler's division, was opposed by Longstreet's forces, to the reënforcement of which Early's brigade, the reserve line at McLean's Ford, was ordered up. The Federals, after several attempts to force a passage, met a final repulse and retreated. After their infantry attack had ceased, about 1 o'clock, the contest lapsed into an artillery duel, in which the Washington Artillery of New Orleans won credit against the renowned batteries of the United States regular army. A comical effect of this artillery fight was the destruction of the dinner of myself and staff by a Federal shell that fell into the fire-place of my headquarters at the McClean House.

Our success in this first limited collision was of special prestige to my army of new troops, and, moreover, of decisive importance by so increasing General McDowell's caution as to give time for the arrival of some of General Johnston's forces. But while on the 19th I was awaiting a renewed and general attack by the Federal army, I received a telegram from the Richmond military authorities, urging me to withdraw my call on General Johnston on account of the supposed impracticability of the concentration—an abiding conviction which had been but momentarily shaken by the alarm caused by McDowell's march upon Richmond. As this was not an order in terms, but an urgency which, notwithstanding its superioer source, left me technically free and could define me as responsible for any misevent, I preferred to keep both the situation and the responsibility, and continued every effort for the prompt arrival of the Shenandoah forces, being resolved, should they come before General McDowell again attacked, to take myself the offensive. General McDowell, fortunately for my plans, spent the 19th and 20th in reconnoissances; and, meanwhile, General Johnston brought 8340 men from the Shenandoah Valley, with 20 guns, and General Holmes 1265 rank and file, with 6 pieces of artillery, from Aquia Creek. As these forces arrived (most of them in the afternoon of the 20th) I placed them chiefly so as to strengthen my left center and left, the latter being weak from lack of available troops.

The disposition of the entire force was now as follows: At Union Mills Ford, Ewell's brigade, supported by Holmes's; at McLean's Ford, D. R. Jones's brigade, supported by Early's; at Blackburn's Ford, Longstreet's brigade; at Mitchell's Ford, Bonham's brigade. Cocke's brigade held the line in front and rear of Bull Run from Bonham's left, covering Lewis's, Ball's, and Island fords, to the right of Evans's demi-brigade, which covered the Stone Bridge and a farm ford about a mile above, and formed part also of Cocke's command. The Shenandoah forces were placed in reserve—Bee's and Bartow's brigades between McLean's and Blackburn's fords, and Jackson's between Blackburn's and Mitchell's fords. This force mustered 29,188 rank and file and 55 guns, of which 21,923 infantry, cavalry, and artillery, with 29 guns, belonged to my immediate forces, i. e., the Army of the Potomac.

The preparation, in front of an ever-threatening enemy, of a wholly volunteer army, composed of men very few of whom had ever belonged to any military organization, had been a work of many cares not incident to the command of a regular army. These were increased by the insufficiency of my staff organization, an inefficient management of the quartermaster's department at Richmond, and the preposterous mismanagement of the commissary-general, who not only failed to furnish rations, but caused the removal of the army commissaries, who, under my orders, procured food from the country in front of us to keep the army from absolute want—supplies that were otherwise exposed to be gathered by the enemy. So specially severe had been the recent duties at headquarters, aggravated not a little by night alarms arising from the enemy's immediate presence, that, in the evening of the 20th, I found my chief-of-staff sunken upon the papers that covered his table, asleep in sheer exhaustion from the over-straining and almost slumberless labor of the last days and nights. I covered his door with a guard to secure his rest against any interruption, after which the army had the benefit of his usual active and provident services.

There was much in this decisive conflict about to open, not involved in any after battle, which pervaded the two armies and the people behind them and colored the reponsibility of the respective commanders. The political hostilities of a generation were now face to face with weapons instead of words. Defeat to either side would be a deep mortification, but defeat to the South must turn its claim of independence into an empty vaunt; and the defeated commander on either side might expect, though not the personal fate awarded by the Carthaginians to an unfortunate commander, at least a moral fate quite similar. Though disappointed that the concentration I had sought had not been permitted at the moment and for the purpose preferred by me, and notwithstanding the non-arrival of some five thousand troops of the Shenandoah forces, my strength was now so increased that I had good hope of successfully meeting my adversary.

General Johnston was the ranking officer, and entitled, therefore, to assume command of the united forces; but as the extensive field of operations was one which I had occupied since the beginning of June, and with which I was thoroughly familiar in all its extent and military bearings, while he was wholly unacquainted with it, and, moreover, as I had made my plans and dispositions for the maintenance of the position, General Johnston, in view of the gravity of the impending issue, preferred not to assume the responsibilities of the chief direction of the forces during the battle, but to assist me upon the field. Thereupon, I explained my plans and purposes, to which he agreed.

Sunday, July 21st, bearing the fate of the new-born Confederacy, broke brightly over the fields and woods that held the hostile forces. My scouts, thrown out in the night toward Centreville along the Warrenton Turnpike, had reported that the enemy was concentrating along the latter. This fact, together with the failure of the Federals in their attack upon my center at Mitchell's and Blackburn's fords, had caused me to apprehend that they would attempt my left flank at the Stone Bridge, and orders were accordingly issued by half-past 4 o'clock to the brigade commanders to hold their forces in readiness to move at a moment's notice, together with the suggestion that the Federal attack might be expected in that quarter. Shortly afterward the enemy was reported to be advancing from Centreville on the Warrenton Turnpike, and at half-past 5 o'clock as deploying a force in front of Evans. As their movement against my left developed the opportunity I desired, I immediately sent orders to the brigade commanders, both front and reserves, on my right and center to advance and vigorously attack the Federal left flank and rear at Centreville, while my

Joseph E. Johnston, ranking officer, was unfamiliar with the field of operations.

left, under Cocke and Evans with their supports, would sustain the Federal attack in the quarter of the Stone Bridge, which they were directed to do to the last extremity. The center was likewise to advance and engage the enemy in front, and directions were given to the reserves, when without orders, to move toward the sound of the heaviest firing. The ground in our front on the other side of Bull Run afforded particular advantage for these tactics. Centreville was the apex of a triangle—its short side running by the Warrenton Turnpike to Stone Bridge, its base Bull Run, its long side a road that ran from Union Mills along the front of my other Bull Run positions and trended off to the rear of Centreville, where McDowell had massed his main forces; branch roads led up to this one from the fords between Union Mills and Mitchell's. My forces to the right of the latter ford were to advance, pivoting on that position; Bonham was in advance from Mitchell's Ford, Longstreet from Blackburn's, D. R. Jones from McLean's, and Ewell from Union Mills by the Centreville road. Ewell, as having the longest march, was to begin the movement, and each brigade was to be followed by its reserve. In anticipation of this method of attack, and to prevent accidents, the subordinate commanders had been carefully instructed in the movement by me, as they were all new to the responsibilities of command. They were to establish close communication with each other before making the attack. About half-past

Bernard E. Bee gave Jackson the name "Stonewall."

8 o'clock I set out with General Johnston for a convenient position,—a hill in rear of Mitchell's Ford,—where we waited for the opening of the attack on our right, from which I expected a decisive victory by midday, with the result of cutting off the Federal army from retreat upon Washington.

Meanwhile, about half-past 5 o'clock, the peal of a heavy rifled gun was heard in front of the Stone Bridge, its second shot striking through the tent of my signal-officer, Captain E. P. Alexander; and at 6 o'clock a full rifled battery opened against Evans and then against Cocke, to which our artillery remained dumb, as it had not sufficient range to reply. But later, as the Federal skirmish-line advanced, it was engaged by ours, thrown well forward on the other side of the Run. A scattering musketry fire followed, and meanwhile, about 7 o'clock, I ordered Jackson's brigade, with Imboden's and five guns of Walton's battery, to the left, with orders to support Cocke as well as Bonham; and the brigades of Bee and Bartow, under the command of the former, were also sent to the support of the left.

At half-past 8 o'clock Evans, seeing that the Federal attack did not increase in boldness and vigor, and observing a lengthening line of dust above the trees to the left of the Warrenton Turnpike, became satisfied that the attack in his front was but a feint, and that a column of the enemy was moving around through the woods to fall on his flank from the direction of Sudley Ford. Informing his immediate commander, Cocke, of the enemy's movement, and of his own dispositions to meet it, he left 4 companies under cover at the Stone Bridge, and led the remainder of his force, 6 companies of Sloan's 4th South Carolina and Wheat's battalion of Louisiana Tigers, with 2 6-pounder howitzers, across the valley of Young's Branch to the high ground beyond it. Resting his left on the Sudley road, he distributed his troops on each side of a small copse, with such cover as the ground afforded, and looking over the open fields and a reach of the Sudley road which the Federals must cover in their approach. His two howitzers were placed one at each end of his position, and here he silently awaited the enemy now drawing near.

The Federal turning column, about 18,000 strong, with 24 pieces of artillery, had moved down from Centreville by the Warrenton Turnpike, and after passing Cub Run had struck to the right by a forest road to cross Bull Run at Sudley Ford, about 3 miles above the Stone Bridge, moving by a long circuit for the purpose of attacking my left flank. The head of the column, Burnside's brigade of Hunter's division, at about 9:45 A.M. debouched from the woods into the open fields, in front of Evans. Wheat at once engaged their skirmishers, and as the Second Rhode Island regiment advanced, supported by its splendid battery of 6 rifled guns, the fronting thicket held by Evans's South Carolinians poured forth its sudden volleys, while the 2 howitzers flung their grape-shot upon the attacking line, which was soon shattered and driven back into the woods behind. Major Wheat, after handling his battalion with the utmost determination, had fallen severely wounded in the lungs. Burnside's entire brigade was now sent forward in a second charge, supported by 8 guns; but they encountered again the unflinching fire of Evans's line, and were once more driven back to the woods, from the cover of which they continued the attack, reënforced after a time by the arrival of 8 companies of United States regular infantry, under Major Sykes, with 6 pieces of artillery, quickly followed by the remaining regiments of Andrew Porter's brigade of the same division. The contest here lasted fully an hour; meanwhile Wheat's battalion, having lost its leader, had gradually lost its organization, and Evans, though still opposing these heavy odds with undiminished firmness, sought reënforcement from the troops in his rear.

General Bee, of South Carolina, a man of marked character, whose command lay in reserve in rear of Cocke, near the Stone Bridge, intelligently applying the general order given to the reserves, had already moved toward the neighboring point of conflict, and taken a position with his own and Bartow's brigades on the high plateau which stands in rear of Bull Run in the quarter of the Stone Bridge, and overlooking the scene of engagement upon the stretch of high ground from which it was separated by the valley of Young's Branch. This plateau is inclosed on three sides by two small watercourses, which empty into Bull Run within a few yards of each other, a half mile to the south of the Stone Bridge. Rising to an elevation of quite 100 feet above the level of Bull Run at the bridge, it falls off on three sides to the level of the inclosing streams in gentle slopes, but furrowed by ravines of irregular directions and length, and studded with clumps and patches of young pine and oaks. The general direction of the crest of the plateau is oblique to the course of Bull Run in that quarter and to the Sudley and turnpike roads, which intersect each other at right angles. On the northwestern brow, overlooking Young's Branch, and near the Sudley road, as the latter climbs over the plateau, stood the house of the widow Henry, while to its right and forward on a projecting spur stood the house and sheds of the free negro Robinson, just behind the turnpike, densely embowered in trees and shrubbery and environed by a double row of fences on two sides. Around the eastern and southern brow of the plateau an almost unbroken fringe of second-growth pines gave excellent shelter for our marksmen, who availed themselves of it with the most satisfactory skill. To the west, adjoining the fields that surrounded the houses mentioned, a broad belt of oaks extends directly across the crest on both sides of the Sudley road, in which, during the battle, the hostile forces contended for the mastery. General Bee, with a soldier's eye to the situation, skillfully disposed his forces. His two brigades on either side of Imboden's battery—which he had borrowed from his neighboring reserve, Jackson's brigade—were placed in a small depression of the plateau in advance of the Henry house, whence he had a full view of the contest on the opposite height across the valley of Young's Branch. Opening with his artillery upon the Federal batteries, he answered Evans's request by advising him to withdraw to his own position on the height; but Evans, full of the spirit that would not retreat, renewed his appeal that the forces in rear would come to help him hold his ground. The newly arrived forces had given the Federals such superiority at this point as to dwarf Evans's means of resistance, and General Bee, generously yielding his own better judgment to Evans's persistence, led the two brigades across the valley under the fire of the enemy's artillery, and threw them into action—1 regiment in the copse held by Colonel Evans, 2 along a fence on the right, and 2 under General Bartow on the prolonged right of this line, but extended forward at a right angle and along the edge of a wood not more than 100 yards from that held by the enemy's left, where the contest at short range became sharp and deadly, bringing many casualties to both sides. The Federal infantry, though still in superior numbers, failed to make any headway against this sturdy van, notwithstanding Bee's whole line was hammered also by the enemy's powerful batteries, until Heintzelman's division of 2

P.S. Bartow.

strong brigades, arriving from Sudley Ford, extended the fire on the Federal right, while its battery of 6 10-pounder rifled guns took an immediately effective part from a position behind the Sudley road. Against these odds the Confederate force was still endeavoring to hold its ground, when a new enemy came into the field upon its right. Major Wheat, with characteristic daring and restlessness, had crossed Bull Run alone by a small ford above the Stone Bridge, in order to reconnoiter, when he and Evans had first moved to the left, and, falling on some Federal scouts, had shouted a taunting defiance and withdrawn, not, however, without his place of crossing having been observed. This disclosure was now utilized by Sherman's (W. T.) and Keyes's brigades of Tyler's division; crossing at this point, they appeared over the high bank of the stream and moved into position on the Federal left. There was no choice now for Bee but to retire—a movement, however, to be accomplished under different circumstances than when urged by him upon Evans. The three leaders endeavored to preserve the steadiness of the ranks as they withdrew over the open fields, aided by the fire of Imboden's guns on the plateau and the retiring howitzers; but the troops were thrown into confusion, and the greater part soon fell into rout across Young's Branch and around the base of the height in the rear of the Stone Bridge.

Meanwhile, in rear of Mitchell's Ford, I had been waiting with General Johnston for the sound of conflict to open in the quarter of Centreville upon the Federal left flank and rear (making allowance, however, for the delays possible to commands unused to battle), when I was chagrined to hear from General D. R. Jones that, while he had been long ready for the movement upon Centreville, General Ewell had not come up to form on his right, though he had sent him between 7 and 8 o'clock a copy of his own order which recited that Ewell had been already ordered to begin the movement. I dispatched an immediate order to Ewell to advance; but within a quarter of an hour, just as I received a dispatch from him informing me that he had received no order to advance in the morning, the firing on the left began to increase so intensely as to indicate a severe attack, where-upon General Johnston said that he would go personally to that quarter.

After weighing attentively the firing, which seemed rapidly and heavily increasing, it appeared to me that the troops on the right would be unable to get into position before the Federal offensive should have made too much progress on our left, and that it would be better to abandon it altogether, maintaining only a strong demonstration so as to detain the enemy in front of our right and center, and hurry up all available reënforcements—including the reserves

Troops rally behind the Robinson House.

that were to have moved upon Centreville—to our left and fight the battle out in that quarter. Communicating this view to General Johnston, who approved it (giving his advice, as he said, for what it was worth, as he was not acquainted with the country), I ordered Ewell, Jones, and Longstreet to make a strong demonstration all along their front on the other side of the Run, and ordered the reserves below our position, Holmes's brigade with 6 guns, and Early's brigade, also 2 regiments of Bonham's brigade, near at hand, to move swiftly to the left. General Johnston and I now set out at full speed for the point of conflict. We arrived there just as Bee's troops, after giving way, were fleeing in disorder behind the height in rear of the Stone Bridge. They had come around between the base of the hill and the Stone Bridge into a shallow ravine which ran up to a point on the crest where Jackson had already formed his brigade along the edge of the woods. We found the commanders resolutely stemming the further flight of the routed forces, but vainly endeavoring to restore order, and our own efforts were as futile. Every segment of line we succeeded in forming was again dissolved while another was being formed; more than two thousand men were shouting each some suggestion to his neighbor; their voices mingling with the noise of the shells hurtling through the trees overhead, and all word of command drowned in the confusion and uproar. It was at this moment that General Bee used the famous expression, "Look at Jackson's brigade! It stands there like a stone wall"—a name that passed from the brigade to its immortal commander. The disorder seemed irretrievable, but happily the thought came to me that if their colors were planted out to the front the men might rally on them, and I gave the order to carry the standards forward some forty yards, which was promptly executed by the regimental officers, thus drawing the common eye of the troops. They now received easily the orders to ad-.vance and form on the line of their colors, which they obeyed with a general movement; and as General Johnston and myself rode forward shortly after with the colors of the 4th Alabama by our side, the line that had fought all morning, and had fled, routed and disorderd, now advanced again into position as steadily as veterans. The 4th Alabama had previously lost all its field-officers; and noticing Colonel S. R. Gist, an aide to General Bee, a young man whom I had known as adjutant-general of South Carolina, and whom I greatly esteemed, I presented him as an able and brave commander to the stricken regiment, who cheered their new leader, and maintained under him, to the end of the day, their previous gallant behavior. We had come none too soon, as the enemy's forces, flushed with the belief of accomplished victory, were already advancing across the valley of Young's Branch and up the slope, where they had encountered for a while the fire of the Hampton Legion, which had been led forward toward the Robinson house and the turn-pike in front, covering the retreat and helping materially to check the panic of Bee's routed forces.

As soon as order was restored I requested General Johnston to go back to Portici (the Lewis house), and from that point—which I considered most favorable for the purpose—forward me the reënforcements as they would come from the Bull Run lines below and those that were expected to arrive from Manassas, while I should direct the field. General Johnston was disinclined to leave the battle-field for that position. As I had been compelled to leave my chief-of-staff, Colonel Jordan, at Manassas to forward any troops arriving there, I felt it was a necessity that one of us should go to this duty, and that it was his place to do so, as I felt I was responsible for the battle. He considerately yielded to my urgency, and we had the benefit of his energy and sagacity in so directing the reënforcements toward the field, as to be readily and effectively assistant to my pressing needs and insure the success of the day.

As General Johnston departed for Portici, I hastened to form our line of battle against the on-coming enemy. I ordered up the 49th and 8th Virginia regiments from Cocke's neighboring brigade in the Bull Run lines. Gartrell's 7th Georgia I placed in position on the left of Jackson's brigade, along the belt of pines occupied by the latter on the eastern rim of the plateau. As the 49th Virginia rapidly came up, its colonel, ex-Governor William Smith, was encouraging them with cheery word and manner, and, as they approached, indicated to them the immediate presence of the commander. As the regiment raised a loud cheer, the name was caught by some of the troops of Jackson's brigade in the immediate wood, who rushed out, calling for General Beauregard. Hastily acknowledging these happy signs of sympathy and confidence, which reënforce alike the capacity of commander and troops, I placed the 49th Virginia in position on the extreme left next to Gartrell, and as I paused to say a few words to Jackson, while hurrying back to the right, my horse was killed under me by a bursting shell, a fragment of which carried away part of the heel of my boot. The Hampton Legion, which had suffered greatly, was placed on the right of Jackson's brigade, and Hunton's 8th Virginia, as it arrived, upon the right of Hampton; the two latter being drawn somewhat to the rear so as to form with Jackson's right regiment a reserve, and be ready likewise to make defense against any advance from the direction of the Stone Bridge, whence there was imminent peril from the enemy's heavy forces, as I had just stripped that position almost entirely of troops to meet the active crisis on the plateau, leaving this quarter now covered only by a few men, whose defense was otherwise assisted solely by the obstruction of an abatis.

With 6500 men and 13 pieces of artillery, I now awaited the onset of the enemy, who were pressing foward 20,000 strong, with 24 pieces of superior artillery and 7 companies of regular cavalry. They soon appeared over the farther rim of the plateau, seizing the Robinson house on my right and the Henry house opposite my left center. Near the latter they placed in position the two powerful batteries of Ricketts and Griffin of the regular army, and pushed forward up the Sudley road, the slope of which was cut so deep below the adjacent ground as to afford a covered way up to the plateau. Supported by the formidable lines of Federal musketry, these 2 batteries lost no time in making themselves felt, while 3 more batteries in rear on the high ground beyond the Sudley and Warrenton cross-roads swelled the shower of shell that fell among our ranks.

Our own batteries, Imboden's, Stanard's, five of Walton's guns, reënforced later by Pendleton's and Alburtis's (their disadvantage being reduced by the shortness of range), swept the surface of the plateau from their position on the eastern rim. I felt that, after the accidents of the morning, much depended on maintaining the steadiness of the troops against the first heavy onslaught, and rode along the lines encouraging the men to unflinching behavior, meeting, as I passed each command, a cheering response. The steady fire of their musketry told severely on the Federal ranks, and the splendid action of our batteries was a fit preface to the marked skill exhibited by our artillerists during the war. The enemy suffered particularly from the musketry on our left, now further reënforced by the 2d Mississippi—the troops in this quarter confronting each other at very short range. Here two companies of Stuart's cavalry charged through the Federal ranks that filled the Sudley road, increasing the disorder wrought upon that flank of the enemy. But with superior numbers the Federals were pushing on new regiments in the attempt to flank my position, and several guns, in the effort to enfilade ours, were thrust forward so near the 33d Virginia that some of its men sprang forward and captured them, but were driven back by an overpowering force of Federal musketry. Although the enemy were held well at bay, their pressure became so strong that I resolved to take the offensive, and ordered a charge on my right for the purpose of recovering the plateau. The movement, made with alacrity and force by the commands of Bee, Bartow, Evans, and Hampton, thrilled the entire line, Jackson's brigade piercing the enemy's center, and the left of the line under Gartrell and Smith following up the charge, also, in that quarter, so that the whole of the open surface of the plateau was swept clear of the Federals.

Apart from its impressions on the enemy, the effect of this brilliant onset was to give a short breathing-spell to our troops from the immediate strain of conflict, and encourage them in withstanding the still more strenuous offensive that was soon to bear upon them. Reorganizing our line of battle under the unremitting fire of the Federal batteries opposite, I prepared to meet the new attack which the enemy were about to make, largely reënforced by the troops of Howard's brigade, newly arrived on the field. The Federals again pushed up the slope, the

face of which partly afforded good cover by the numerous ravines that scored it and the clumps of young pines and oaks with which it was studded, while the sunken Sudley road formed a good ditch and parapet for their aggressive advance upon my left flank and rear. Gradually they pressed our lines back and regained possession of their lost ground and guns. With the Henry and Robinson houses once more in their possession, they resumed the offensive, urged forward by their commanders with conspicuous gallantry.

The conflict now became very severe for the final possession of this position, which was the key to victory. The Federal numbers enabled them so to extend their lines through the woods beyond the Sudley road as to outreach my left flank, which I was compelled partly to throw back, so as to meet the attack from that quarter; meanwhile their numbers equally enabled them to outflank my right in the direction of the Stone Bridge, imposing anxious watchfulness in that direction. I knew that I was safe if I could hold out till the arrival of reënforcements, which was but a matter of time; and, with the full sense of my own responsibility, I was determined to hold the line of the plateau, even if surrounded on all sides, until assistance should come, unless my forces were sooner overtaken by annihilation.

It was now between half-past 2 and 3 o'clock; a scorching sun increased the oppression of the troops, exhausted from incessant fighting, many of them having been engaged since the morning. Fearing lest the Federal offensive should secure too firm a grip, and knowing the fatal result that might spring from any grave infraction of my line, I determined to make another effort for the recovery of the plateau, and ordered a charge of the entire line of battle, including the reserves, which at this crisis I myself led into action. The movement was made with such keeping and dash that the whole plateau was swept clear of the enemy, who were driven down the slope and across the turnpike on our right and the valley of Young's Branch on our left, leaving in our final possession the Robinson and Henry houses, with most of Ricketts's and Griffin's batteries, the men of which were mostly shot down where they bravely stood by their guns. Fisher's 6th North Carolina, directed to the Lewis house by Colonel Jordan from Manassas, where it had just arrived, and thence to the field by General Johnston, came up in happy time to join in this charge on the left. Withers's 18th Virginia, which I had ordered up from Cocke's brigade, was also on hand in time to follow and give additional effect to the charge, capturing, by aid of the Hampton Legion, several guns, which were immediately turned and served upon the broken ranks of the enemy by some of our officers. This handsome work, which broke the Federal fortunes of the day, was done, however, at severe cost. The soldierly Bee, and the gallant, impetuous Bartow, whose day of strong deeds was about to close with such credit, fell a few rods back of the Henry house, near the

Confederate cavalry charges the Fire Zouaves at
Bull Run.

very spot whence in the morning they had first looked forth upon Evans's struggle with the enemy. Colonel Fisher also fell at the very head of his troops. Seeing Captain Ricketts, who was badly wounded in the leg, and having known him in the old army, I paused from my anxious duties to ask him whether I could do anything for him. He answered that he wanted to be sent back to Washington. As some of our prisoners were there held under threats of not being treated as prisoners of war, I replied that that must depend upon how our prisoners were treated, and ordered him to be carried to the rear. I mention this, because the report of the Federal Committee on the Conduct of the War exhibits Captain Ricketts as testifying that I only approached him to say that he would be treated as our prisoners might be treated. I sent my own surgeons to care for him, and allowed his wife to cross the lines and accompany him to Richmond; and my adjutant-general, Colonel Jordan, escorting her to the car that carried them to that city, personally attended to the comfortable placing of the wounded enemy for the journey.

That part of the enemy who occupied the woods beyond our left and across the Sudley road had not been reached by the headlong charge which had swept their comrades from the plateau; but the now arriving reënforcements (Kershaw's 2d and Cash's 8th South Carolina) were led into that quarter. Kemper's battery also came up, preceded by its commander, who, while alone, fell into the hands of a number of the enemy, who took him prisoner, until a few moments later, when he handed them over to some of our own troops accompanying his battery. A small plateau, within the south-west angle of the Sudley and turnpike cross-roads, was still held by a strong Federal brigade—Howard's troops, together with Sykes's battalion of regulars; and while Kershaw and Cash, after passing through the skirts of the oak wood along the Sudley road, engaged this force, Kemper's battery was sent forward by Kershaw along the same road, into position near where a hostile battery had been captured, and whence it played upon the enemy in the open field.

Quickly following these regiments came Preston's 28th Virginia, which, passing through the woods, encountered and drove back some Michigan troops, capturing Brigadier-General Willcox. It was now about 3 o'clock, when another important reënforcement came to our aid—Elzey's brigade, 1700 strong, of the Army of the Shenandoah, which, coming from Piedmont by railroad, had arrived at Manassas station, 6 miles in rear of the battle-field, at noon, and had been without delay directed thence toward the field by Colonel Jordan, aided by Major T. G. Rhett, who that morning had passed from General Bonham's to General Johnston's staff. Upon nearing the vicinity of the Lewis house, the brigade was directed by a staff-officer sent by General Johnston toward the left of the field. As it reached the oak wood, just across the Sudley road, led by General Kirby Smith, the latter fell severely wounded; but

the command devolved upon Colonel Elzey, an excellent officer, who was now guided by Captain D. B. Harris of the Engineers, a highly accomplished officer of my staff, still farther to the left and through the woods, so as to form in extension of the line of the preceding reënforcements. Beckham's battery, of the same command, was hurried forward by the Sudley road and around the woods into position near the Chinn house; from a well-selected point of action, in full view of the enemy that filled the open fields west of the Sudley road, it played with deadly and decisive effect upon their ranks, already under the fire of Elzey's brigade. Keyes's Federal brigade, which had made its way across the turnpike in rear of the Stone Bridge, was lurking along under cover of the ridges and a wood in order to turn my line on the right, but was easily repulsed by Latham's battery, already placed in position over that approach by Captain Harris, aided by Alburtis's battery, opportunely sent to Latham's left by General Jackson, and supported by fragments of troops collected by staff-officers. Meanwhile, the enemy had formed a line of battle of formidable proportions on the opposite height, and stretching in crescent outline, with flanks advanced, from the Pittsylvania (Carter) mansion on their left across the Sudley road in rear of Dogan's and reaching toward the Chinn house. They offered a fine spectacle as they threw forward a cloud of skirmishers down the opposite slope, preparatory to a new assault against the line on the plateau. But their right was now severely pressed by the troops that had successively arrived; the force in the southwest angle of the Sudley and Warrenton cross-roads were driven from their position, and, as Early's brigade, which, by direction of General Johnston, had swept around by the rear of the woods through which Elzey had passed, appeared on the field, his line of march bore upon the flank of the enemy, now retiring in that quarter.

This movement by my extreme left was masked by the trend of the woods from many of our forces on the plateau; and bidding those of my staff and escort around me raise a loud cheer, I dispatched the information to the several commands, with orders to go forward in a common charge. Before the full advance of the Confederate ranks the enemy's whole line, whose right was already yielding, irretrievably broke, fleeing across Bull Run by every available direction. Major Sykes's regulars, aided by Sherman's brigade, made a steady and handsome withdrawal, protecting the rear of the routed forces, and enabling many to escape by the Stone Bridge. Having ordered in pursuit all the troops on the field, I went to the Lewis house, and, the battle being ended, turned over the command to General Johnston. Mounting a fresh horse,—the fourth on that day,—I started to press the pursuit which was being made by our infantry and cavalry, some of the latter having been sent by General Johnston from Lewis's Ford to intercept the enemy on the turnpike. I was soon overtaken, however, by a courier bearing a message from Major T. G. Rhett, General Johnston's chief-of-staff on duty at Manassas railroad station, informing me of a report that a large Federal force, having pierced our lower line on Bull Run, was moving upon Camp Pickens, my depot of supplies near Manassas. I returned, and communicated this important news to General Johnston. Upon consultation it was deemed best that I should take Ewell's and Holmes's brigades, which were hastening up to the battle-field, but too late for the action, and fall on this force of the enemy, while reënforcements should be sent me from the pursuing forces, who were to be re-called for that purpose. To head off the danger and gain time, I hastily mounted a force of infantry be-hind the cavalrymen then present, but, on approach-ing the line of march near McLean's Ford, which the Federals must have taken, I learned that the news was a false alarm caught from the return of General Jones's forces to this side of the Run, the similarity of the uniforms and the direction of their march having convinced some nervous person that they were a force of the enemy. It was now almost dark, and too late to resume the broken pursuit; on my return I met the coming forces, and, as they were very tired, I ordered them to halt and bivouac for the night where they were. After giving such attention as I could to the troops, I started for Manassas, where I arrived about 10 o'clock, and found Mr. Davis at my headquarters with General Johnston. Arriving from Richmond late in the afternoon, Mr. Davis had immediately galloped to the field, accom-panied by Colonel Jordan. They had met between Manassas and the battle-field the usual number of stragglers to the rear, whose appearance belied the determined array then sweeping the enemy before it, but Mr. Davis had the happiness to arrive in time to witness the last of the Federals disappearing beyond Bull Run. The next morning I received from his hand at our breakfast-table my commission, dated July 21st, as General in the Army of the Confederate States, and after his return to Richmond the kind congratulations of the Secretary of War and of Gen-eral Lee, then acting as military adviser to the Presi-dent.

It was a point made at the time at the North that, just as the Confederate troops were about to break and flee, the Federal troops anticipated them by doing so, being struck into this precipitation by the arrival upon their flank of the Shenandoah forces marching from railroad trains halted *en route* with that aim—errors that have been repeated by a number of writers, and by an ambitious but super-ficial French author.

There were certain sentiments of a personal character clustering about this first battle, and per-sonal anxiety as to its issue, that gladly accepted this theory. To this may be added the general readiness to accept a sentimental or ultra-dramatic explana-tion—a sorcery wrought by the delay or arrival of some force, or the death or coming of somebody, or any other single magical event—whereby history is easily caught, rather than to seek an understanding of that which is but the gradual result of the opera-tion of many forces, both of opposing design and actual collision, modified more or less by the falls of chance. The personal sentiment, though natural enough at the time, has no place in any military estimate, or place of any kind at this day. The battle of Manassas was, like any other battle, a progression and development from the deliberate counter-em-ployment of the military resources in hand, affected by accidents, as always, but of a kind very different from those referred to. My line of battle, which twice had not only withstood the enemy's attack, but had taken the offensive and driven him back in disorder, was becoming momentarily stronger from the arrival, at last, of the reënforcements provided for; and if the enemy had remained on the field till the arrival of Ewell and Holmes, they would have been so strongly outflanked that many who escaped would have been destroyed or captured.

Though my adversary's plan of battle was a good one as against a passive defensive opponent, such as he may have deemed I must be from the respective numbers and positions of our forces, it would, in my judgment, have been much better if, with more dash, the flank attack had been made by the Stone Bridge itself and the ford immediately above it. The plan adopted, however, favored above all things the easy execution of the offensive operations I had designed and ordered against his left flank and rear at Cen-treville. His turning column—18,000 strong, and presumably his best troops—was thrown off by a long ellipse through a narrow forest road to Sudley Ford, from which it moved down upon my left flank, and was thus dislocated from his main body. This severed movement of his foces not only left his exposed left and rear at Centreville weak against the simultaneous offensive of my heaviest forces upon it, which I had ordered, but the movement of his returning column would have been disconcerted and paralyzed by the early sound of this heavy conflict in its rear, and it could not even have made its way back so as to be available for manoeuvre before the Centreville fraction had been thrown back upon it in disorder. A new army is very liable to panic, and, in view of the actual result of the battle, the conclusion can hardly be resisted that the panic which fell on the Federal army would thus have seized it early in the day, and with my forces in such a position as wholly to cut off its retreat upon Washington. But the commander of the front line on my right, who had been ordered to hold himself in readiness to initiate the offensive at a moment's notice, did not make the move expected of him because through accident he failed to receive his own immediate order to advance. The Federal commander's flanking movement, being thus uninterrupted by such a counter-movement as I had projected, was further assisted through the rawness and inadequacy of our staff organization through which I was left unac-quainted with the actual state of affairs on my left. The Federal attack, already thus greatly favored, and encouraged, moreover, by the rout of General Bee's advanced line, failed for two reasons: their forces

were not handled with concert of masses (a fault often made later on both sides), and the individual action of the Confederate troops was superior, and for a very palpable reason. That one army was fighting for a union and the other for disunion is a political expression; the actual fact on the battle-field, in the face of cannon and musket, was that the Federal troops came as invaders, and the Southern troops stood as defenders of their homes, and further than this we need not go. The armies were vastly greater than had ever before fought on this continent, and were the largest volunteer armies ever assembled since the era of regular armies. The personal material on both sides was of exceptionally good character, and collectively superior to that of any subsequent period of the war. The Confederate army was filled with generous youths who had answered the first call to arms. For certain kinds of field duty they were not as yet adapted, many of them having at first come with their baggage and servants; these they had to dispense with, but, not to offend their susceptibilities, I then exacted the least work from them, apart from military drills, even to the prejudice of important fieldworks, when I could not get sufficient negro labor; they "had come to fight, and not to handle the pick and shovel," and their fighting redeemed well their shortcomings as intrenchers. Before I left that gallant army, however, it had learned how readily the humbler could aid the nobler duty.

Rebel sympathizers at Richmond celebrate the news of Bull Run.

A Yankee Zouave veteran of Bull Run embellishes his experiences.

V

THE STRUGGLE FOR THE BORDER STATES

ALTHOUGH BOTH BEFORE AND AFTER BULL RUN THE FOCUS OF ATTENTION IN THE FIRST year of the Civil War was on the East, most of the action was elsewhere, along the frontier between the loyal states and Secessia, a long, ill-defined zone which included Missouri, Kentucky, and northwestern Virginia, the counties which would later become West Virginia. These were areas in which loyalties were sharply divided, yet areas of critical importance. Won for the Confederacy, they might well tip the balance decisively against the Union; held to the Union they might tell with equal decision against the Confederacy. From the spring of 1861 into that of the following year, a series of small, often bitter actions were fought which in the end secured this strategic zone for the Union.

THOMAS L. SNEAD
The First Year of War in Missouri

Thomas L. Snead held a variety of staff positions in the Confederate Army for most of the war, being variously aide-de-camp to the Governor of Missouri, Acting Adjutant General of the Missouri State Guard, and Chief of Staff in the Army of the West, during which period he fought in the early battles for Missouri, at Shiloh, and in the struggle for Arkansas. At the end of the war he was serving in the Confederate Congress. He afterwards dabbled in politics and business. His account of the struggle for control of Missouri is highly partisan, but generally accurate and is taken from Battles and Leaders of the Civil War.

South Carolina had just seceded and the whole country was in the wildest excitement when the General Assembly of Missouri met at Jefferson City on the last day of the year 1860. Responding to the recommendations of Governor Jackson and to the manifest will of the people of the State, it forthwith initiated measures for ranging Missouri with the South in the impending conflict. A State Convention was called; bills to organize, arm, and equip the militia were introduced; and the Federal Government was solemnly warned that if it sent an army into South Carolina, or into any other slaveholding State, in order to coerce it to remain in the Union, or to force its people to obey the laws of the United States, "the people of Missouri would instantly rally on the side of such State to resist the invaders at all hazards and to the last extremity."

The most conspicuous leader of this movement was Claiborne F. Jackson, who had just been inaugurated Governor. He had for many years been one of the foremost leaders of the Democrats of Missouri, and had been elected Governor in August. In the late canvass he had supported Douglas for President, not because he either liked him or approved his policy on the slavery question, but because Douglas was the choice of the Missouri Democrats, and to have opposed him would have defeated his own election; for in August, 1860, the people of Missouri were sincerely desirous that the questions at issue between the North and the South should be compromised and settled upon some fair basis, and were opposed to the election to the Presidency of any man—whether Lincoln or Breckinridge—whose success might intensify sectional antipathies and imperil the integrity of the Union.

But while loyally supporting the candidacy of Douglas, Jackson abated none of his devotion to the political principles which had been the constant guide of his life. He was a true son of the south, warmly attached to the land that had given him birth, and to her people, who were his own kindred. He was now nearly fifty-five years of age, tall, erect, and good-looking; kind-hearted, brave, and courteous; a thoughtful, earnest, upright man; a political leader, but not a soldier.

The Governor urged the people of Missouri to elect to the Convention men who would place Missouri unequivocally on the side of the South. He was disappointed. Francis P. Blair, Jr., banded together the unconditional Union men of the State; while the St. Louis *Republican*, Sterling Price, Hamilton R. Gamble, James S. Rollins, William A. Hall, and John B. Clark consolidated the conservatives, and together these elected on the 18th of February a Convention not one member of which would say that he was in favor of the secession of Missouri. To the courage, moderation, and tact of Francis P. Blair this result was greatly due.

Blair was just forty years of age. His father, the trusted friend of Andrew Jackson, had taken him to Washington City when he was about seven years old, and there he had been bred in politics. In 1843 he had come to St. Louis, where his brother Montgomery was already practicing law. For that profession, to which he too had been educated, Frank had no taste, and having in it no success, quickly turned his attention to politics. In 1852 he was elected to the Legislature as a Benton Democrat. Shortly afterward he and B. Gratz Brown established the St. Louis *Democrat*. When the Kansas conflict broke out in 1854, he identified himself with the Free-soil party, and in 1856 supported Frémont for the Presidency, though Senator Benton, Frémont's father-in-law, refused to do this. He was elected to Congress that year, for the first time. In the presidential canvass of 1860 he had been the leader of the Republicans of Missouri, and it was through him chiefly that Lincoln received 17,000 votes in the State. Immediately after the secession of South Carolina, he had begun to organize his adherents as Home Guards and had armed some of them, and was drilling the rest for the field, when the election of delegates to the State Convention took place. To complete the arming of these men was his first aim. In the city of St. Louis the United States had an arsenal within which were more than enough arms for this purpose—60,000 stand of arms and a great abundance of other munitions of war. So long as Buchanan was President, Blair could not get them, but the 4th of March was near at hand and he could well wait till then, for the Southern-rights men had been so demoralized by the defeat which they had sustained in the election of delegates to the Convention, that they were in no condition to attack the arsenal, as they had intended to do if the election had gone in their favor. It was, indeed, more than a month after the inauguration of Lincoln before the Southern-rights men ventured to make any move in that direction. The Governor then came to St. Louis to concert with General D. M. Frost (who commanded a small brigade of volunteer militia) measures for seizing the arsenal in the name of the State. While the matter was still under consideration the bombardment of Fort Sumter took place, and the President called for 75,000 troops to support the Government. To his call upon Missouri for her quota of such troops, the Governor replied that the requisition was, in his opinion, "illegal, unconstitutional, and revolutionary in its object, inhuman and diabolical," and that Missouri would not furnish one man "to carry on such an unholy crusade." A few days later he convened the General Assembly, to adopt measures for the defense of the State.

In the consultation with Frost it had been decided that the Governor, in pursuance of an existing law of the State, should order all its militia into encampment for the purpose of drill and discipline; and that, under cover of this order, Frost should camp his brigade upon the hills adjacent to and commanding the arsenal, so that when the opportunity occurred he might seize it and all its stores. A great difficulty in the way of the execution of this plan was the want of siege-guns and mortars. To remove this difficulty the Governor sent Captains Colton Greene and Basil W. Duke to Montgomery, Alabama, and Judge Cooke to Virginia to obtain these things. By Mr. Davis's order the arms were turned over to Duke and Greene at Baton Rouge, and were by them taken to St. Louis. Before they arrived there, however, the scheme to seize the arsenal had been completely frustrated by its commandant, Captain Nathaniel Lyon, who distributed a part of the coveted arms to Blair's Home Guards and removed the rest to Illinois, and then occupied with his own troops the hills around the arsenal. Frost consequently established Camp Jackson in a grove in the western part of the city, remote from the arsenal, and was drilling and disciplining his men there in conformity to the laws of the State and under the flag of the Union, when Jefferson Davis's gift to Missouri was taken into the camp.

Blair and Lyon, to whom every detail of the Governor's scheme had been made known, had been waiting for this opportunity. They had made up their minds to capture the camp and to hold the officers and men as prisoners of war. Frost went into camp on the 6th of May. The arms from the Confederacy were taken thither on the 8th. On Saturday, the 11th, the camp was to break up. Lyon had no time to lose.

Francis P. Blair prevented the secession of Missouri.

On Thursday he attired himself in a dress and shawl and other apparel of Blair's mother-in-law, Mrs. Alexander, and having completed his disguise by hiding his red beard and weather-beaten features under a thickly veiled sun-bonnet, took on his arm a basket, filled, not with eggs, but with loaded revolvers, got into a barouche belonging to Blair's brother-in-law, Franklin A. Dick, and was driven out to Camp Jackson and through it. Returning to the city, he called the Union Safety Committee together, and informed them that he intended to capture the camp the next day. Some of the committee objected, but Blair and James O. Broadhead sustained him, and he ordered his men to be in readiness to move in the morning. Just as they were about to march, Colonel John S. Bowen came to Lyon with a protest from Frost. Lyon refused to receive it, and marching out to the camp with about 7000 men, surrounded it and demanded its surrender. Frost, who had only 635 men, was obliged to comply.

While the surrender was taking place a great crowd of people, among whom were U. S. Grant and W. T. Sherman, hurried to the scene. Most of the crowd sympathized with the prisoners, and some gave expression to their indignation. One of Lyon's German regiments thereupon opened fire upon them, and twenty-eight men, women, and children were killed. The prisoners were then marched to the arsenal, and paroled the next day.

Nathaniel Lyon scouted the pro-secession garrison at St. Louis disguised as a woman.

The capture of Camp Jackson and the bloody scenes that followed—the shooting down then and the next day of unoffending men, women, and children—aroused the State.[1] The General Assembly, which had reconvened in extra session, enacted instantly a law for organizing, arming, and equipping the Missouri State Guard, created a military fund, and conferred dictatorial power upon the Governor.

Hardly less important than these things—for it was what gave effect to them all—was the fact that the capture of the camp caused ex-Governor Sterling Price, President of the State Convention, and up to that time a Union man, to tender his services to the Governor. The General Assembly forthwith authorized the Governor to appoint a major-general to command all the forces which the State might put into the field, and Price was appointed to that position.

In the Convention Price had been opposed under all circumstances to the secession of Missouri, but just as earnestly opposed to the invasion and conquest of the South by the Federal Government. To

that position he still adhered even when Mr. Lincoln, after the bombardment of Fort Sumter, had called for troops with which to repossess the Federal forts and enforce the laws of the Union within the seceded States. But considering Lyon's attack upon the State militia and his killing peaceable citizens an "unparalleled insult and wrong to the State," he believed it was the duty of Missouri to resent such wrongs.

The State now sprang to arms. Volunteers began to crowd the streets of Jefferson City, and everything indicated the opening of hostilities. Blair and Lyon would have met these demonstrations with force, would have driven Jackson and Price from the capital, would have dispersed the militia wherever it dared to show itself, would have occupied the State with Federal garrisons, and would have held her in unresisting obedience to the Union; but, unfortunately for the execution of their plans, General William S. Harney, who commanded the Military Department of the West, of which Missouri was part, had returned to St. Louis the day after the capture of Camp Jackson, and had resumed command there. Instead of using force Harney used conciliation. Instead of making war he made a truce with Price.

Blair now caused Harney to be relieved of the command of the Federal troops in Missouri, and on the 31st of May he was superseded by Lyon. As soon as this was made known to the Governor and General Price, they ordered the militia to be gotten in readiness for the field, for they knew that Blair and Lyon would quickly attack them. Some well-meaning gentlemen, who vainly imagined that Missouri could maintain her neutrality in the midst of war, now sought to establish a truce between Price and Lyon. Through them a conference was agreed upon, and the Governor and General Price came to St. Louis under Lyon's safe conduct. They met him and Blair at the Planters' House. Lyon was accompanied by his aide-de-camp, Major Horace A. Conant, and I was present as the Governor's aide. The interview, which lasted several hours, was at last terminated by Lyon's saying that he would see every man, woman, and child in Missouri under the sod before he would consent that the State should dictate to "his Government" as to the movement of its troops within her limits, or as to any other matter however unimportant. "This," said he, "means war. One of my officers will conduct you out of my lines in an hour." So saying, he left without another word, without even a salutation.

He had hardly left us when he was issuing orders for the movement of his troops. Sweeny and Sigel were sent with about 3000 men to the south-west to intercept the retreat of Jackson and Price if they should undertake to effect a junction with General Ben. McCulloch, who was believed to be concentrat-

---

1. Lyon officially stated that on both days the firing was in response to attacks by mobs.

ing a Confederate army in north-western Arkansas for the invasion of Missouri. Lyon would himself move up the Missouri after Jackson.

The conference was held on the 11th of June. On the 13th Lyon was on his way to Jefferson City with about 2000 men. Arriving there the next day, he found that the Governor had fled to Boonville. Leaving a garrison at Jefferson City, he pushed on to Boonville, where some 1300 militia had rendezvoused. Attacking these on the 17th, he dispersed them and drove the Governor southward with some two or three hundred men who still adhered to him and to the cause which he represented. General Price had meanwhile gone to Lexington, where several thousand militia had assembled.

From a military standpoint the affair at Boonville was a very insignificant thing, but it did in fact deal a stunning blow to the Southern-rights men of Missouri, and one which weakened the Confederacy during all of its brief existence. It was indeed the consummation of Blair's statesmanlike scheme to make it impossible for Missouri to secede, or out of her great resources to contribute liberally of men and material to the South, as she would have done could her people have had their own way. It was also the most brilliant achievement of Lyon's well-conceived campaign. The capture of Camp Jackson had disarmed the State, and completed the conquest of St. Louis and all the adjacent counties. The advance upon Jefferson City had put the State government to flight and taken away from the Governor the prestige which sustains established and acknowledged authority. The dispersion of the volunteers that were flocking to Boonville to fight under Price for Missouri and the South extended Lyon's conquest at once to the borders of Iowa, closed all the avenues by which the Southern men of North Missouri could get to Price and Jackson, made the Missouri River a Federal highway from its source to its mouth, and put an end to Price's hope of holding the rich and friendly counties in the vicinity of Lexington till the Confederacy could send an army to his support, and arms and supplies for the men whom he was concentrating there.

Price had, indeed, no alternative now but to retreat in all haste to the south-western part of the State, so as to organize his army within supporting distance of the force which McCulloch was assembling in western Arkansas for the protection of that State and the Indian Territory. He accordingly ordered Brigadier-General James S. Rains to take command of the militia at and near Lexington, and to move southward so as to effect a junction with the Governor in the vicinity of Lamar, toward which place the latter was retreating with Generals M. M. Parsons and John B. Clark and what was left of their commands. General Price himself, accompanied by his staff and a small escort, hastened rapidly toward Arkansas in order to bring McCulloch to the rescue of both the Governor and Rains. On the way he was joined, almost daily, by squads or companies, and by the time he reached Cowskin Prairie, in the extreme

Franz Sigel was known more for boldness than discretion.

south-western corner of the State, he had collected about 1200 men.

On the 3d of July Rains reached Lamar, near which place the Governor and his followers were already encamped. The combined force amounted to about 6000 men, of whom 4000 were armed, and they had seven pieces of artillery. Halting until the 5th in order to rest and organize, they pushed on that morning toward Carthage, having heard that a Federal force had occupied that place, which lay in their line of retreat. They had marched but a few miles when, as they were passing through the open prairie, they descried, some three miles away, on the declivity of a hill over which they had themselves to pass, a long line of soldiers with glistening bayonets and bright guns. These were part of the force which Lyon, on marching against Jefferson City, had sent under General Sweeny and Colonel Sigel to the south-west to intercept the Governor's retreat toward Arkansas. Sigel, in executing this plan, had first attempted to intercept Price. Failing in that, he had now, with more boldness than discretion, thrown himself, with about 1100 men and eight pieces of artillery, in front of the Governor, hoping either to defeat him or to hold him in check till Lyon could arrive and destroy him. Halting his column in the prairie, and deploying his armed men (about 4000), the Governor awaited Sigel's attack. The fight (known as the battle of Carthage) did not last long, for Sigel was outnumbered four to one, and the Missourians quickly put him to flight. He retreated, however, in perfect order, carrying off almost everything that he had brought with him. But he did not stop running till he had made forty miles. That night the State troops rested in Carthage. The next day they resumed their southward march, and soon met Price and McCulloch. Price now assumed command of the Missourians and led them to Cowskin Prairie, in the south-western corner of the State, while McCulloch went into camp near Maysville in Arkansas.

Lyon left Boonville in pursuit of the Governor, on the 3d of July, with about 2350 men, and directed his course toward Clinton in Henry county, where he had ordered Major Sturgis, who was following Rains with about 2500 regulars and Kansas troops, to unite with him. The two columns came together near Clinton on the 7th of July and pushed on after the Missourians. Lyon did not learn till the 9th that they had defeated Sigel and effected a junction with McCulloch. He then made in all haste for Springfield, fearing that the Confederates would attack that place. Arriving there on the 13th of July, he made it his headquarters.

Lyon, on the one hand, and Price on the other now began to get their armies in readiness for active operations. For Lyon this was a simple undertaking; for Price it was one of great complexity and great difficulty. Of the 7000 or 8000 men that he had, only a few had been organized into regiments. Several thousand of them had no arms of any kind. The rest were for the most part armed with the shot-guns and rifles which they had brought from their homes. Of powder and lead they had an abundance, but no fixed ammunition for either their seven pieces of artillery or for their small-arms. Tents they had none, nor camp equipage of any kind. There were no quartermasters' supplies, nor subsistence; and neither the quartermaster-general nor the chief commissary had a dollar of funds. The men were not fighting for pay, they wanted none, nor did they get any; but they and their thousands of horses and mules had to be fed. For their animals there was nothing but the grass of the prairies, and for themselves nothing but a scant supply of lean beef and coarse corn-meal. There were enough good officers to organize and command the men; but it would have puzzled almost any one to drill a company of raw recruits, armed, some with shot-guns, some with rifles, a few with old-fashioned flint-lock muskets, and here and there a man with a percussion musket. No better proof could be given of the dearth of material for the Staff, than the fact that I was myself assigned to duty by General Price as chief of ordnance of the army, though I told him at the time that I did not know the difference between a howitzer and a siege-gun, and had never seen a musket-cartridge in all my life; and a few days later I was assigned to the still more important position of acting Adjutant-General of the State Guard, though I had never then heard of a "morning report," and did not know the right of a company from its

left. Had Hardee or any other West Pointer been in command, he would have kept us in camp six months, drilling and disciplining us, getting together wagons and teams, tents and cartridge-boxes, uniforms and haversacks, quartermasters and red tape, and all the other equipments and *impedimenta* of an army in the field, and then we would have gone into winter quarters; Lyon would have had his own way in Missouri, and the Federal armies that were sent thither to whip us would have been sent to fight in Virginia or in Tennessee instead, and the Confederacy might have been vanquished sooner than it was. But Price had us all ready for the field in less than three weeks. We had no tents, it is true, but tents would only have been in our way; we had no uniforms, but a bit of flannel or calico fastened to the shoulder of an officer designated his rank sufficiently for all practical purposes; the ripening corn-fields were our depots of subsistence; the prairies furnished forage, and the people in defense of whose homes we were eager to fight gladly gave us of all their stores.

McCulloch, one of the bravest of men and best of scouts, looking at us through the eyes of the young army officers whom Mr. Davis had sent to teach him how to organize, equip and fight an army scientifically, saw in the Missourians nothing but a half-armed mob, led by an ignorant old militia general, but he consented to go with Price in search of Lyon, who was at Springfield and not hard to find. General N. B. Pearce, commanding a brigade of Arkansas State troops, agreed to go along with them.

Hardee, who was at Pitman's Ferry, Arkansas, within a few hundred yards of the Missouri line, and almost as near to Springfield as were Price and McCulloch, and who had with him several thousand good soldiers, was begged by both Price and McCulloch to coöperate in the movement against Lyon, but he replied that he "did not wish to march to their assistance with less than 5000 men, well appointed, and a full complement of artillery"!

By order of General Polk, made at the earnest personal solicitation of Governor Jackson, who had gone to Memphis for that purpose, General Pillow moved into Missouri from Tennessee, with twelve thousand men, and occupied New Madrid on the 28th of July, with the intent to unite in the effort to repossess the State.

On the same day, Price, McCulloch, and Pearce, relying upon the coöperation of both Hardee and Pillow, concentrated their forces at Cassville, within about fifty miles of Springfield. There Price was reënforced by General McBride's command, consisting of two regiments of foot and three companies of mounted men, about 700 in all. They had come from the hill country lying to the south and south-east of Springfield, and were a unique body of soldiers. Very few of the officers had any knowledge whatever of military principles or practices, and only the most superficial experience in company tactics. The staff was composed chiefly of country lawyers who took the ways of the court-room with them into the field.

Ben McCulloch was recognized for his bravery and scouting ability.

Colonels could not drill their regiments, nor captains their companies; a drum and a fife—the only ones in the entire command—sounded all the calls, and companies were paraded by the sergeant's calling out, "Oh, yes! Oh, yes! all you who belong to Captain Brown's company fall in here." Officers and men messed together, and all approached McBride without a salute, lounged around his quarters, listened to all that was said, and when they spoke to him called him "Jedge." Their only arms were the rifles with which they hunted the squirrels and other small game that abounded in their woods, but these they knew how to use. A powder-horn, a cap-pouch, "a string of patchin'," and a hunter's knife completed their equipment. I doubt whether among them all there was a man that had ever seen a piece of artillery. But, for all this, they were brave and intelligent. Like all frontiersmen, they were shrewd, quick-witted, wary, cunning, and ready for all emergencies, and like all backwoodsmen, their courage was serene, steady, unconscious. While there was no attempt at military discipline, and no pretense of it,

The siege of Lexington resulted in the surrender of Federal forces.

the most perfect order was maintained by McBride's mere force of character, by his great good sense, and by the kindness with which he exercised his patriarchal authority.

Leaving Cassville on the 31st of July, the com- bined Southern armies, nearly 11,000 strong, advanced toward Springfield. On the way they encountered Lyon, who had come out to meet them. McCulloch, who could not comprehend the Missourians or the able soldier who commanded them,

refused to attack unless Price and Pearce would confer upon him the chief command. Price had been a brigadier-general in Mexico, when McCulloch was but a captain of scouts, and had won more battles there than McCulloch had ever witnessed; he was now a major-general with more than 5000 men, and McCulloch had barely 3000; and in intellect, in experience, and in generalship he was worth a dozen McCullochs; nevertheless, he cheerfully placed himself and his army under the Texan's command.

The order to advance was then given. Lyon had been encamped six miles in front with between 5000 and 6000 men. McCulloch moved at midnight, hoping to fall upon him unexpectedly, and to defeat him. To his amazement he learned, on approaching the spot,

Union troops are besieged at Battle of Lexington.

that Lyon had left twenty hours before, and must now be almost in sight of Springfield. The Confederates kept on, and on the 6th of August went into camp on Wilson's Creek, within ten miles of Springfield. They were still lying there on the morning of the 10th of August, when they were surprised and suddenly attacked on the north by Lyon, and on the south by Sigel.

One of the stubbornest and bloodiest battles of the war now took place. Lyon's main attack was met by Price with about 3200 Missourians, and Churchill's regiment and Woodruff's battery, both from Arkansas. His left was met and driven back by McIntosh with a part of McCulloch's brigade (the Third Louisiana and McIntosh's regiment). McCulloch then took some companies of the Third Louisiana and parts of other commands, and with them attacked and routed Sigel (who had been sent to attack the rear), capturing five of his guns. This done, Pearce's Arkansas brigade, which up to this time had not fired a gun, was sent to reënforce Price. Lyon, seeing that the supreme moment had come, and that the day would be surely lost if he did not overwhelm Price before the Arkansans could reënforce him, now brought forward every available man, and was putting them into the fight, when his horse was killed, and himself wounded in the head. Dazed by the blow, dazed and stunned, his heart gave way for a moment under the sudden shock, but quickly coming to his sense he mounted another horse, and, swinging his hat in the air, called on his men to follow. Closing around him they dashed with him into the thick of the fight. But a moment later a bullet pierced his heart, and he fell from his horse into the arms of his orderly, and in an instant was dead. It was vain that Federals tried to prolong the battle. Sturgis, on whom the command devolved, ordered a retreat, and before the Confederates knew that the battle was ended he was a mile away, having withdrawn his men unseen through the dense undergrowth of the woods in which the battle mainly was fought. In the haste of their retreat, the Federals left Lyon's dead body on the field. I delivered it myself an hour or two later to a flag-of-truce party that had been sent to ask for it. I saw it again the next day in Springfield, where it had been again abandoned by his men.

Rarely have I met so extraordinary a man as Lyon, or one that has interested me so deeply. Coming to St. Louis from Kansas on the 6th of February, this mere captain of infantry, this little, rough-visaged, red-bearded, weather-beaten Connecticut captain, by his intelligence, his ability, his energy, and his zeal, had at once acquired the confidence of all the Union men of Missouri, and had made himself respected, if not feared, by his enemies. In less than five months he had risen to the command of the Union armies in Missouri, had dispersed the State government, had driven the Governor and his adherents into the extremest corner of the State, had almost conquered the State, and would have completely conquered it had he been supported by his

Government; and now he had given his life willingly for the Union which he revered, and to the cause of Human Freedom to which he was fanatically devoted.

The Federal force in the battle amounted to about 5400 officers and men. The Confederates had over 10,000 armed men on the ground, but 3000 of them took little or no part in the fight. The Confederates lost 279 killed and 951 wounded. The Federal loss was 258 killed, 873 wounded, and 186 captured or missing.

McCulloch refused to pursue, and Price resumed command of the Missouri troops. The next day he took possession of Springfield, and sent Rains with a mounted force to clear the western counties of the State of the marauding bands that had come into them from Kansas. On the 25th of August he moved northward with his army. On the 2d of September he met a part of Lane's Kansas Brigade under Colonel Montgomery on the banks of the Big Dry Wood. Montgomery had about 500 men and gave battle, but was forced to retreat before Price's superior force. The loss on either side was trifling.

Price now hastened toward Lexington, joined at every step by recruits. Reaching the city on the 12th of September with his mounted men, he drove Colonel Mulligan within his intrenchments, and as soon as his main body came up, completed the investment of the place. On the 20th he caused a number of hemp-bales saturated with water to be rolled to the front and converted them into movable breastworks, behind which his men advanced unharmed against the enemy. Colonel Mulligan was forced to surrender the next day. Price's loss was 25 killed and 72 wounded. Frémont reported to the War Department that the Union loss was 39 killed and 120 wounded. The Missourians captured about 3500 prisoners, five pieces of artillery, two mortars, 3000 stand of small-arms, a large number of sabers, about 750 horses, many sets of cavalry equipments, ammunition, many wagons and teams, more than $100,000 worth of commissary stores, and a large amount of other property. Price also recovered $900,000 that had been taken by the enemy from the Bank at Lexington, and restored it to the Bank. His force amounted to about 18,000 men, Mulligan's to about 3600.

In order to obtain the coöperation of the Confederate armies, the Governor and General Price sent me to Richmond, after the capture of Lexington, as a special commissioner to explain to President Davis the condition of affairs in Missouri, and to negotiate a treaty of alliance with the Confederate States, inasmuch as Missouri had not seceded nor been admitted into the Confederacy. By their direction I went by way of McCulloch's headquarters, in order to make one more effort to secure his coöperation, and failing in that, to get from him certain supplies which General Price greatly needed, particularly caps for the muskets which we had captured at Lexington. To all my entreaties McCulloch replied that Price had gone to the Missouri against his advice; that the movement was unwise and would result in disaster, and that he would not endanger his own army by going to his assistance; and that as for musket-caps, he had none to spare.

General John C. Frémont, who had assumed command of the Union armies in the West on the 25th of July, now began to concentrate his forces against Price. Sending about 40,000 men, with 100 pieces of artillery, to attack him in front, and others to cut off his retreat, he took the field himself. His plan was magnificent—to capture or disperse Price's army; march to Little Rock and occupy the place; turn the Confederates under Polk, Pillow, Thompson, and Hardee, and compel them to fall back southward; push on to Memphis with his army and Foote's flotilla; capture that city; and *then* make straight for New Orleans.

Price left Lexington on the 29th of September, after advising his unarmed men to return to their homes, and to wait for a more convenient time to rise. Marching as rapidly as his long train would permit, he reached the Osage on the 8th of October with about 7000 men. To cross his troops and trains over that difficult river on a single flat-boat was a tedious operation, but Frémont gave him all the time that he needed, and he got them safely over.

After crossing the Osage, Price marched quickly to Neosho, where the General Assembly had been summoned by Governor Jackson to meet. Frémont continued to follow till the 2d of November, when he was superseded by Major-General David Hunter, who immediately stopped the pursuit and turned the army back to St. Louis. On the 19th of November Major-General Halleck assumed command of the Federal Department.

When I returned from Richmond, Price had gone into winter quarters on the Sac River near Osceola. Many of his men had been furloughed so that they might go to their homes, where they could subsist themselves during the winter and provide for their families. McCulloch's brigade was on the Arkansas River, and Pearce's had been disbanded. Under the treaty which had been negotiated at Richmond, the enlistment of Missourians in the Confederate army was at once begun and was continued at Springfield, whither Price moved his army just before Christmas. Before the end of January, 1862, two regiments of infantry (Burbridge's and Rives's), one regiment of cavalry (Gates's), and two batteries (Wade's and Clark's) had been mustered into the Confederate service, and on the 28th I started to Richmond to deliver the muster-rolls to the Secretary of War, and to inform the President as to the strength and condition of the army in Missouri, and to communicate to him Price's views as to the future conduct of the war in that State.

On the way I met Major-General Earl Van Dorn at Jacksonport in Arkansas. He had just assumed command (January 29th) of the District of the Trans-Mississippi, constituting a part of General Albert Sidney Johnston's extensive department. He was a dashing soldier, and a very handsome man, and his manners were graceful and fascinating. He was slight of stature and his features were almost too delicately refined for a soldier, but this defect, if it was a defect, was converted into a charm by the martial aspect of his mustache and imperial, and by an exuberant growth of brownish hair. Quitting the United States army when Mississippi seceded, he first entered her service, and was afterward appointed to that of the Confederacy and placed in command of Texas. Transferred thence to Virginia in September, 1861, he was commissioned major-general and ordered to report to General J. E. Johnston, commanding the Army of the Potomac. Johnston ordered him to Beauregard, and Beauregard assigned him to the command of a division, October 4th, 1861. He was assigned to the command of the Trans-Mississippi District, January 10th, 1862. We Missourians were delighted; for he was known to be a fighting man, and we felt sure he would help us to regain our State. I explained to him the condition of affairs in Missouri, and General Price's views.

Van Dorn had already decided upon a plan of campaign, and in execution of it ordered General Albert Pike, a few days afterward, to Lawrence county, Missouri, with a mixed command of whites and Indians estimated at 7000 men; ordered McIntosh to report to Price at Springfield with McCulloch's infantry; ordered McCulloch to Pocahontas with his mounted men; and called upon Louisiana, Arkansas, and Texas to send reënforcements. Hopeful and enthusiastic by nature, he believed that Price would have 15,000 effective men at Springfield by the last of March, and himself 18,000 at Pocahontas, and that they could then march against St. Louis. The two columns were to effect a junction north of Ironton, and, moving thence rapidly without tents or baggage, take the city by assault. Possession of the city would give him possession of the State, and the enemy would supply the arms for the thousands of volunteers that would flock to his standard.

From this day-dream he was rudely awakened a few days later by news that Price had been driven from Springfield on the 12th of February, and was hotly pursued by a Federal army which Halleck had sent against him under General S. R. Curtis. With this army was Captain P. H. Sheridan, doing duty as quartermaster. Price sought refuge in the mountains of Arkansas, and February 21st was within thirty miles of Van Buren, near which place was Mc-Culloch.

On learning all this Van Dorn hastened to Van Buren and thence to Price's headquarters, which he reached on the 1st of March. After a hurried consultation with Price and McCulloch, he decided to instantly attack Curtis, who had taken a strong position among the mountains near Bentonville. He moved on the 4th of March with about 16,000 men, of whom 6800 were Missourians under Price, and the rest Confederates under McCulloch and Pike. When almost within reach of Curtis (who reported his own strength at 10,500 infantry and cavalry and forty-nine pieces of artillery) Van Dorn unwisely divided his army, and leaving McCulloch with his own command and Pike's to attack Curtis in front, himself made with Price and the Missourians a long circuit to the rear of Curtis, and out of communication with McCulloch. Both columns attacked about the same time on the 7th. Price was completely successful and carried everything before him, taking during the afternoon seven pieces of cannon and about 200 prisoners, and at night bivouacked near Elkhorn Tavern. But morning revealed the enemy in

Governor Jackson addresses troops after the surrender at Lexington.

a new and strong position, their forces united and offering battle. The Confederates soon learned that McCulloch and McIntosh had been killed the day before and their force routed and dispersed. The battle was renewed nevertheless, and the Missourians fought desperately and were still holding their ground when about 10 o'clock Van Dorn ordered a retreat, and the army leaving Missouri to her fate began to fall back toward Van Buren.

In this battle, sometimes called the battle of Pea Ridge, and at other times the battle of Elkhorn, the Federal general reported his losses at 203 killed, 980 wounded, and 201 missing. Van Dorn's were probably greater, and he lost heavily in good officers. McCulloch and McIntosh were killed; General Price was again wounded and narrowly escaped death; General W. Y. Slack, whom his men idolized and whom the whole army held in honor, was fatally wounded; and Colonel B. A. Rives, one of the knightliest of soldiers and bravest of gentlemen, and Churchill Clark, a heroic boy, were killed.

Halleck, who had determined to make the Tennessee "the great strategic line of the Western campaign," now began to concentrate all of his forces on

Federal troops make final advance at Pea Ridge

that river and the Mississippi, in order "to fight a great battle on the Tennessee," one which would "settle the campaign in the West." He consequently ordered Curtis not to advance any farther into Arkansas; and sent out of Missouri all the troops that could be safely taken thence, some of them to Pope on the Mississippi, and others to Grant on the Tennessee.

The concentration of Federal armies on the Mississippi portended such danger to Beauregard, who had lately assumed command of the defenses of that river, that General Albert Sidney Johnston ordered Van Dorn to move his army to within supporting distance of Beauregard. This Van Dorn began to do on the 17th of March, on which day he wrote to General Johnston that he would soon "relieve Beauregard by giving battle to the enemy near New Madrid," or, by marching "boldly and rapidly toward St. Louis, between Ironton and the enemy's grand depot at Rolla."

While he was executing this plan, and while the greater part of the army that had survived Elkhorn was on the march across the mountains of North Arkansas toward Jacksonport, Van Dorn was suddenly ordered by General Johnston on the 23d of March to move his entire command by "the best and most expeditious route" to Memphis. His forces, to which he had given the name of "the Army of the West," were accordingly concentrated in all haste at Des Arc, on the White River, whence they were to take boats for Memphis. The first division of this army, to the command of which General Price had been assigned, was the first to move, Little's Missouri Brigade embarking on the 8th of April for Memphis, just as Pope was taking possession of Island No. 10, and Beauregard was leading Johnston's army back to Corinth from the fateful field of Shiloh.

$$\star\star\star$$

WILLIAM M. WHERRY
Wilson's Creek and the Death of Lyon

William M. Wherry, a native Missourian, abandoned his business to join the Unionist faction of the state militia as a 1st lieutenant in May of 1861. During the fighting for control of the state that summer he served as an aide-de-camp to Nathaniel Lyon, one of the principal Unionist men in the state, and was with Lyon when the latter was killed at Wilson's Creek; his conduct during the battle earned him a belated Medal of Honor in 1895. Wherry subsequently trans-ferred to the Regular Army and served at Atlanta, Franklin, and Nashville with considerable distinction, ending the war as a brevet brigadier general. He remained in the service after the war, rising to brigadier general of Volunteers during the Spanish American War—during which he saw no service—and retired as a Regular Army brigadier in 1899. Wherry's account of Wilson's Creek is drawn from Battles and Leaders of the Civil War.

About the middle of July, 1861, the Army of the Union in south-west Missouri, under General Nathaniel Lyon, was encamped in and near the town of Springfield, and numbered approximately 6200 men, of whom about 500 were ill-armed and undisciplined "Home Guards." The organized troops were in all 5868, in four brigades. By the 9th of August these were reduced to an aggregate of about 5300 men, with the 500 Home Guards additional. Of these troops, the 1st Iowa regiment was entitled to discharge on the 14th of August, and the 3d and 5th Missouri, Sigel's and Salomon's, at different periods, by companies, from the 9th to the 18th of August. All except the regulars had been enrolled since the attack on Sumter in April, and but little time had been possible for drill and instruction. They had been moved and marched from St. Louis and points in Kansas, taking part in several spirited but minor engagements, and were ill-provided with clothing and food, but their spirits were undaunted, and they were devoted to their leader.

The latter part of July was spent by Lyon in drilling his troops and procuring supplies, the mills in the neighborhood having been seized and employed in grinding flour for the troops. He continued to send urgent appeals to St. Louis for reënforcements.

On the 1st of August, however, having received information of an advance by the enemy, in superior numbers, Lyon moved down the Fayetteville road (also known as the Cassville road) to meet and attack the largest and most advanced force, hoping to drive it back and then strike the others in detail. A lively skirmish with Price's advance-guard, under Rains, took place at Dug Springs on the 2d of August; and on the 3d a more insignificant affair occurred with the rear-guard of Rains's forces at McCullah's farm, which had been his headquarters, but from which he retired without resistance. Here Lyon became convinced he was being drawn farther and farther from his base, without supplies, and he determined to fall back to Springfield, which place he reached on the 5th. During those blistering August days the men marched with bleeding feet and parched lips, Lyon himself urging forward the weary and footsore stragglers.

On the 8th a march in force was planned for the following night, to make an attack on the enemy's front at Wilson's Creek at daylight. From this intention General Lyon was dissuaded, after having called together the principal officers to receive their instructions. Many of the troops were exhausted, and all were tired; moreover, some supplies having arrived from Rolla, it was deemed wise to clothe and shoe the men as far as practicable, and to give them another day for recuperation.

On the 9th it was intended to march that evening with the whole force united, as agreed upon the 8th, and attack the enemy's left at daylight, and Lyon's staff were busied in visiting the troops and seeing that all things were in order. During the morning Colonel Sigel visited Lyon's headquarters, and had a prolonged conference, the result of which was that Colonel Sigel was ordered to detach his brigade, the 3d and 5th Missouri, one six-gun battery, one company of the 1st U.S. Cavalry, under Captain Eugene A. Carr, and one company of the 2d Dragoons, under Lieutenant Charles E. Farrand, for an attack upon the enemy from the south, while Lyon with the remainder of his available force should attack on the north.

The troops were put in march in the evening; those about Springfield immediately under General Lyon moving out to the west on the Little York road until joined by Sturgis's command from their camps, when they turned to the south across the prairie. The head of the main column reached the point where the enemy's pickets were expected to be found, about 1 A.M., and went into bivouac. Sigel's force, consisting of 1200 men and six pieces of artillery, moved four miles down the Fayetteville road, and then, making a long détour to the left by a by-road, arrived within a mile of the enemy's camp and rear at daylight.

In the vicinity of the Fayetteville road crossing, the creek acquires considerable depth, and in most places has rough, steep, and rather high banks, rendering fording difficult. On the left side the hills assume the proportion of bluffs; on the right or western bank the ground is a succession of broken ridges, at that time covered for the most part with trees and a stunted growth of scrub oaks with dense foliage, which in places became an almost impenetrable tangle. Rough ravines and deep gullies cut up the surface.

The Confederates were under command of General Ben. McCulloch. On the west side of the stream, "Old Pap" Price, with his sturdy Missourians, men who in many battles bore themselves with a valor and determination that won the plaudits of their comrades and the admiration of their foes, was holding the point south of Wilson's Creek, selected by Lyon for attack. Price's command consisted of five bodies of Missourians, under Slack, Clark, Parsons, McBride, and Rains, the last-named being encamped farther up the stream. On the bluffs on the east side of the creek were Hébert's 3d Louisiana and McIntosh's Arkansas regiment, and, father south, Pearce's brigade and two batteries, while other troops, under Greer, Churchill, and Major, were in the valley along the Fayetteville road, holding the extreme of the Confederate position.

Lyon put his troops in motion at early dawn on the 10th, and about 4 o'clock struck Rains's most advanced picket, which escaped and gave warning of the attack of which General Price was informed just as he was about to breakfast. Captain Plummer's battalion of regular infantry was the advance, followed by Osterhaus's two companies of the 2d Missouri Volunteers, and Totten's battery. A body of 200 mounted Home Guards was on Plummer's left. Having reached the enemy's pickets, the infantry was deployed as skirmishers, Plummer to the left and Osterhaus to the right, and Lieutenant-Colonel Andrews, with the 1st Missouri Infantry, was brought up in support of the battery. Advancing a mile and a half and crossing a brook tributary to the creek, the Union skirmishers met and pushed the Confederate skirmishers up the slope. This disclosed a considerable force of the enemy, along a ridge perpendicular to the line of march and to the valley of the creek, which was attacked by the 1st Missouri and the 1st Kansas, assisted by Totten's battery, who drove back the Confederates on the right to the foot of the slope beyond.

Plummer on the left early became separated from the main body by a deep ravine terminating in a swampy piece of ground, beyond which lay a cornfield which he entered, encountering a large force, the main part of which was the Louisiana regiment. These troops fought with determined valor and checked Plummer's progress. DuBois's battery was moved up to a hill on the left, supported by Osterhaus's battalion, the 1st Iowa, and the 2d Kansas, and opened a deadly fire with shells upon the cornfield, with such marked effect as to throw the Confederates into disorder and enable Plummer to draw off his command in good order across the ravine.

A momentary lull occurred at this time, except on our extreme right, where Price's Missourians opposed the 1st Missouri and attempted to turn that flank, but the 2d Kansas by its timely arrival and gallant attack bore back Price's overwhelming numbers and saved the flank. Meanwhile Totten's battery, which had been brought into action by section and by piece as the conformation of the ground would admit, performed extraordinary service. Steele's regular infantry was added to its support. Price's troops had fought with great bravery and determination, advancing and retiring two or three times before they were compelled to give way on the lower slope of the ridge they had occupied. Many times the firing was one continuous roar.

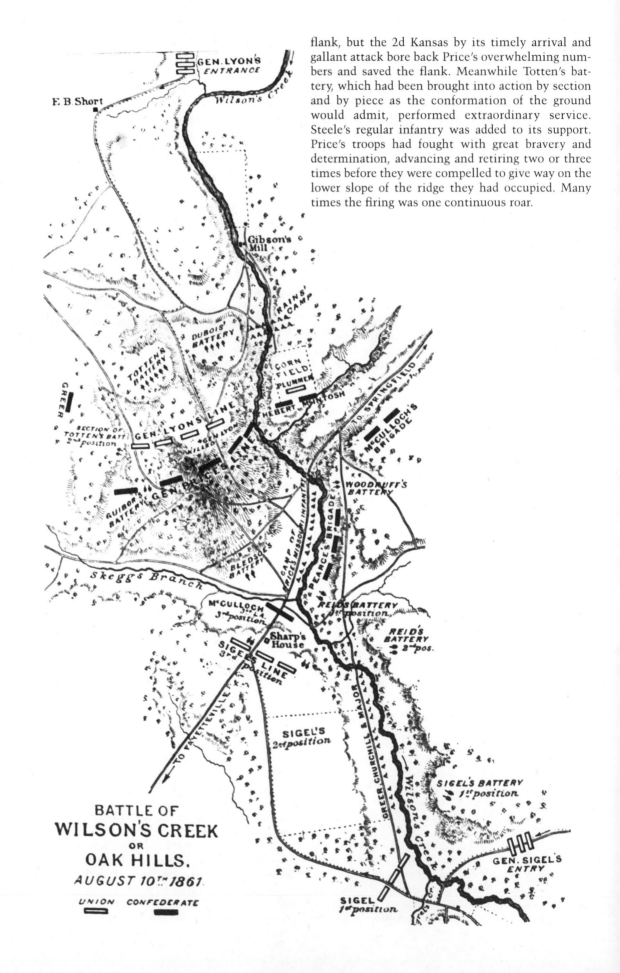

BATTLE OF
WILSON'S CREEK
OR
OAK HILLS.
AUGUST 10TH 1861.

UNION   CONFEDERATE

The lull enabled the enemy to re-adjust his lines and bring up fresh troops, having accomplished which, Price made a determined advance along nearly the whole of Lyon's front. He charged fiercely in lines of three or four ranks, to within thirty or forty yards pouring in a galling fire and directing his most determined efforts against Totten's battery, for which Woodruff's, which was pitted against it, was no match at all.

Every available man of Lyon's was now brought into action and the battle raged with redoubled energy on both sides. For more than an hour the balance was about even, one side gaining ground only to give way in its turn to the advance of the other, till at last the Confederates seemed to yield, and a suspension of the fury took place.

General Lyon had bivouacked near the head of his column on the night of the 9th, sharing a rubber-coat with Major (now Major-General) John M. Schofield, his chief of staff, between two rows of corn in a field by the roadside, his other staff-officers near by. He did not seem hopeful, but was oppressed with the responsibility of his situation, with anxiety for the cause, and with sympathy for the union people in that section, when he should retreat and leave to their fate those who could not forsake their homes. He repeatedly expressed himself as having been abandoned by his superiors. When the troops were put in motion, he went at the head of the column, and when the action opened he kept his place at the front, entering the heat of the engagement with the line, near Totten's battery. He maintained an imperturbable coolness, and his eye shone with the ardor of conflict. He directed, encouraged, and rallied his troops in person, sending his staff in all directions, and was frequently without an attendant except one or two faithful orderlies. Early in the attack while on the line to the left of Totten's battery, rallying a part of the 1st Missouri Infantry, his horse, which he was leading, was killed and he received a slight wound in the leg. Shortly afterward he was wounded in the head. He continued dismounted during the contest above described, and walking a few paces toward the rear with his chief of staff, Major Schofield, who had also lost his horse, shot under him, Lyon said, "I fear the day is lost." Schofield encouraged him to take a more hopeful view of the case, assuring him that the troops were easily rallied and were gaining confidence, and that the disorder was only temporary, and then proceeded to another part of the line in search of a mount.

About 9 o'clock, during a brief cessation in the firing, Lyon started toward the top of the ridge, accompanied by an aide, who was urging him to accept his horse, when they met Major Sturgis and a few troopers. One of these was dismounted, and his horse was given to General Lyon. Lyon also expressed himself despondingly to Sturgis, and was by him encouraged. Sturgis proceeded to another quarter, and Lyon toward DuBois's battery.

About this time great anxiety began to be felt for the fate of Sigel's command. Shortly after Lyon's attack the sound of battle had been heard in the rear of the enemy's line. It continued but a short time, and was renewed shortly afterward for a very brief period only, when it ceased altogether. Sigel had proceeded to within a mile of the camps, and his cavalry had cut off the enemy's small parties and thus suppressed information of his coming. He then advanced his infantry toward the point where the by-road crosses the creek, his flanks supported by the cavalry on the right and dragoons on the left, four guns being placed on a hill overlooking the tents. At about 5:30 A.M., hearing the musketry on Lyon's front, he opened fire with his guns, pushing his infantry across the creek and into the lower camp, whence they had fled, overwhelmed by the suddenness of the attack. Sigel crossed his guns and pushed with infantry and artillery forward a short distance in pursuit, meeting with slight resistance. He advanced from his first position near the creek, by a road west of the deserted camp, and formed line of battle in a field between the road and the camp. Afterward he advanced to Sharp's house. The Arkansans and Texans retired to the northward, fell in with Price's Missouri line, and assisted in the fight against Lyon. Meanwhile McCulloch called upon a battalion of mounted Missourians, and upon a part of the Louisiana regiment which had been confronting Plummer in the corn-field, and with these attacked Sigel's men, who were in line at Sharp's farm, and drove them from the field. When the attack by the Confederates, from the direction of Lyon's front, was made, the confusion of Sigel's men was brought about by the enfilading fire of Reid's battery east of the creek, and by the belief that the infantry in their front were friends. Sigel went back the way he came with a part of his command, including Carr's cavalry. All but the cavalry, who were ahead, were ambuscaded and, for the most part, killed or captured; Sigel narrowly escaped capture. Colonel Salomon with 450 of the troops retreated, by a détour to the west, to the Little York road, as did also Lieutenant Farrand, with the dragoons. The latter, finding himself with his company alone, forcibly detained a guide, and made up teams for one gun and one caisson of the abandoned artillery. He was finally compelled to unhorse and leave the caisson, in order to put the animals to the gun. Thus by 10 o'clock Sigel was out of the fight, and the enemy could turn his whole force upon Lyon.

Meantime a body of troops was observed moving down the hill on the east bank of Wilson's Creek toward Lyon's left, and an attack by other troops from that direction was anticipated. Schofield deployed eight companies of the 1st Iowa and led them in person to repel this. They did so most gallantly after a sanguinary contest, effectually assisted by the fire from DuBois's battery, which alone drove back the column on the opposite side of the stream before it began a crossing.

Lyon, accompanied by [the writer] and his six or eight orderlies, followed closely the right of the Iowa regiment. After proceeding a short distance, his at-

General Lyon leads the charge of 1st Iowa at Wilson's Creek.

tention was called by the aide to a line of men drawn up on the prolongation of the left of our main line and nearly perpendicular to the 1st Iowa as it moved to the eastward. A party of horsemen came out in front of this line of the enemy and proceeded to reconnoiter. General Price and Major Emmett Mac Donald (who had sworn that he would not cut his hair till the Confederacy was acknowledged) were easily recognized. General Lyon started as if to confront them, ordering his party to "draw pistols and follow" him, when the aide protested against his exposing himself to the fire of the line, which was partly concealed by the mass of dense underbrush, and asked if he should not bring up some other troops. To this Lyon assented, and directed the aide to order up the 2d Kansas. The general advanced a short distance, joining two companies of the 1st Iowa, left to protect an exposed position.

Colonel Mitchell of the 2d Kansas, near DuBois's battery, sent his lieutenant-colonel, Blair, to Lyon to

ask to be put in action, and the two messengers passed each other without meeting. Lyon repeated his order for the regiment to come forward. The regiment moved promptly by the flank, and as it approached Lyon he directed the two companies of Iowa troops to go forward with it, himself leading the column, swinging his hat. A murderous fire was opened from the thick brush, the 2d Kansas deployed rapidly to the front and with the two companies of the 1st Iowa swept over the hill, dislodging the enemy and driving them back into the next ravine; but while he was at the head of the column, and pretty nearly in the first fire, a ball penetrated Lyon's left breast, inflicting a mortal wound. He slowly dismounted, and as he fell into the arms of his faithful orderly, Lehmann, he exclaimed, "Lehmann, I am killed," and almost immediately expired. Colonel Mitchell was also severely wounded about the same time and removed to the rear.

Lieutenant Gustavus Schreyer and two of his men of the 2d Kansas bore the body of Lyon through the ranks, Lehmann bearing the hat and loudly bemoaning the death of his chief. In the line of file-closers the returning aide was met, who, apprehensive of the effect upon the troops, stopped the clamor of the orderly, covered the general's features with his coat, and had the body carried to a sheltered spot near DuBois's battery. Surgeon Florence M. Cornyn was found and called upon to examine the lifeless body of the dead general, and having pronounced life extinct, the aide went to seek Schofield and inform him of the calamity. He was met returning from the successful charge he had led, and at once announced that Major Sturgis should assume command, but visited the remains of Lyon on his way to find Sturgis. These were taken charge of by the aide, and conveyed to the field-hospital, where the body was placed in a wagon and carefully covered. Strict orders were given that under no circumstances was the body to be removed till the army returned to Springfield, after which the aide returned to the front to report to Major Sturgis for duty.

The engagement on different parts of the line lasted about half an hour after Lyon's death, when the Confederates gave way, and silence reigned for nearly the same length of time. Many of the senior officers having been disabled, Sturgis assumed command, and the principal officers were summoned for consultation. This council and the suspended hostilities were soon abruptly terminated by the appearance of the Confederates along our entire front, where the troops had been readjusted in more compact form and were now more determined and cooler than ever. A battery planted on a hill in the front began to use shrapnel and canister, a species of ammunition which, so far as I know, the enemy had not fired before at the troops who were with General Lyon.

DuBois's battery continued on the left supported by Osterhaus's battalion and the 1st Missouri; the

Lyon lies mortally wounded at Wilson's Creek.

1st Iowa, 1st Kansas, and the regular infantry supported Totten's battery in the center, and the 2d Kansas held the extreme right. With unabated ardor and impetuosity the Confederates assailed this front and endeavored to gain the rear of the right flank, but Totten's battery in the center was the main point of assault. For the first time during this bloody day, the entire line maintained its position without flinching, the inexperienced volunteers vieing with the seasoned regulars in tenacity and coolness. The flash and roar were incessant, and the determined Southrons repeatedly advanced nearly to the muzzles of the pieces of their foes, only to be hurled back before the withering fire as from the blast of a furnace and to charge again with a like result.

At a moment when the contest seemed evenly balanced, except for the overwhelming numbers of the Confederates on the field, Captain Gordon Granger, noted for his daring and intrepidity, rushed to the rear and brought up the supports of DuBois's battery, hurling them upon the enemy's right flank, into which they poured a murderous, deadly volley, which created a perfect rout along the whole front. Our troops continued to send a galling fire into the disorganized masses as they fled, until they disappeared, and the battle was ended.

The order to withdraw was then given, and Du-Bois's battery with its supports was moved to a hill and ridge in rear to cover the movement. Before the withdrawal of the main body took place, Captain Granger and others urged remaining on the ground, but Sturgis had received information of Sigel's rout, and in view of his depleted, worn-out forces and exhausted ammunition, persisted in a return to Springfield. The infantry and artillery, as soon as Totten's disabled horses were replaced, left the scene of conflict, and, passing through the troops placed in rear, took up the march for Springfield. On reaching the Little York road, a body of horsemen was seen to the west, which proved to be Lieutenant Farrand with his dragoons, leading in a remnant of Sigel's brigade, with the one piece of artillery he had saved. In his hand he carried a captured flag, which he trailed by his side. He was received with vociferous cheering, and became for the time the admiration of all, having marched around both armies and brought his command in safe.

On reaching Springfield, Sturgis found that Sigel had arrived there half an hour earlier. Regarding him as the senior, the command was given over to him. On the following morning the army withdrew.

★★★

JACOB D. COX
McClellan in West Virginia

Jacob D. Cox (whom we have met before in "Ohio Goes to War") commanded a brigade during the Union campaign in West Virginia in mid- and late-1861, a series of operations which met with considerable success and helped propel George B. McClellan to prominence, but in which Robert E. Lee failed to demonstrate the tactical genius for which he is justly famed. Cox's account is taken from Battle and Leaders of the Civil War.

The reasons which made it important to occupy West Virginia with National troops were twofold—political and strategic. The people were strongly attached to the Union, and had opposed the secession of Virginia, of which State they were then a part. But few slaves were owned by them, and all their interests bound them more to Ohio and Pennsylvania than to eastern Virginia. Under the influence of Lincoln's administration, strongly backed, and, indeed, chiefly represented, by Governor Dennison of Ohio, a movement was on foot to organize a loyal Virginia government, repudiating that of Governor Letcher and the State convention as self-destroyed by the act of secession. Governor Dennison had been urging McClellan to cross the Ohio to protect and encour-age the loyal men when, on the 26th of May, news came that the Confederates had taken the initiative, and that some bridges had been burned on the Baltimore and Ohio railroad a little west of Grafton, the crossing of the Monongahela River, where the two western branches of the railroad unite, viz., the line from Wheeling and that from Parkersburg. The great line of communication between Washington and the west had thus been cut, and action on our part was made necessary. Governor Dennison had anticipated the need of more troops than the thirteen regiments which had been organized as Ohio's quota under the President's first call. He had organized nine other regiments, numbering them consecutively with those mustered into the national service, and had put them in camps near the Ohio River, where they could occupy Wheeling, Parkersburg, and the mouth of the Great Kanawha at a moment's notice. Two Union regiments were also organizing in West Virginia itself, at Wheeling and Parkersburg, of which the first was commanded by Colonel (afterward General) B. F. Kelley. West Virginia was in McClellan's department, and the formal authority to act had come from Washington on the 24th, in the shape of an inquiry from General Scott whether the enemy's force at Grafton could be counteracted. The dispatch directed McClellan to "act promptly." On the 27th Colonel Kelley was sent by rail from Wheeling to drive off the enemy and protect the railroad. The hostile parties withdrew at Kelley's approach, and the bridges were quickly rebuilt. At the same time several of the Ohio regiments were ordered across the river, and a brigade of Indiana volunteers under Brigadier-General Thomas A. Morris was sent forward by rail from Indianapolis. Morris reached Grafton on the 1st of June, and was intrusted with the command of all the troops in West Virginia. He found that Colonel Kelley had already planned an expedition against the enemy, who had retired southward to Philippi, about thirty miles from Grafton. Morris approved the plan, but enlarged it by sending another column under Colonel Ebenezer Dumont of the 7th Indiana to coöperate with Kelley. Both columns were directed to make a night march, starting from points on the railroad about twelve miles apart, and converging on Philippi, which they were to attack at daybreak of June 3d. Each column consisted of about 1500 men, and Dumont's had with it 2 field-pieces of artillery, smooth 6-pounders.

The Confederate force was commanded by Colonel G. A. Porterfield, of the Virginia volunteers, and was something less than a thousand strong, about one-fourth cavalry.

The night was dark and stormy, and Porterfield's raw troops had not learned picket duty. The concerted movement against them was more successful than such marches commonly are, and Porterfield's first notice of danger was the opening of the artillery upon his sleeping troops. It had been expected that the two columns would inclose the enemy's camp and capture the whole; but, though in disorderly rout, Porterfield succeeded, by personal coolness and courage, in getting them off with but few casualties and the loss of a few arms. The camp equipage and supplies were, of course, captured. Colonel Kelley was wounded by a pistol-shot in the breast, which was the only injury reported on the National side; no prisoners were taken, nor did any dead or wounded fall into our hands. Porterfield retreated to Beverly, some thirty miles farther to the south-east, and the National forces occupied Philippi. The telegraphic reports had put the Confederate force at 2000 and their loss at 15 killed. This implied a considerable list of wounded and prisoners also, and the newspapers gave it the air of a considerable victory. The campaign thus opened with apparent *éclat* for

McClellan, and the "Philippi races," as they were locally called, greatly encouraged the Union men of West Virginia and correspondingly depressed the secessionists.

McClellan, however, was still of the opinion that his most promising line of operations would be by the Great Kanawha Valley, and he retained in their camp of instruction the Ohio regiments which were mustered into the service of the United States, sending into Virginia only those known as the State forces. Another reason for this was that the older regiments were now nearly at the end of their three-months' enlistment, and were trying to reorganize under the President's second call, which required enlistment for "three years or the war." Nearly a month elapsed, when, having received reports that forces of the enemy were gathering at Beverly, McClellan determined to proceed in person to that region with his best-prepared troops, postponing his Kanawha plan till north-western Virginia should be cleared of hostile forces.

As the Potomac route was usually in the hands of the Northern forces, a Confederate occupation of West Virginia [had to] be made either by the Staunton and Beverly road, or by the Kanawha route, of which the key-point west of the mountains was Gauley Bridge.

General Lee determined to send columns upon both these lines—General Henry A. Wise upon the Kanawha route, and General Robert S. Garnett to Beverly. Upon Porterfield's retreat to Beverly after the "Philippi races," Garnett, who had been an officer in the United States army, was ordered to Beverly to assume command and to stimulate the recruiting and organization of regiments from the secession element of the population. Some Virginia regiments, raised on the eastern slope of the mountains, were sent with him, and to those was soon added the 1st Georgia. On the 1st of July he reported his force as 4500 men, but declared that his efforts to recruit had proven a complete failure, only 23 having joined. The West Virginians, he says, "are thoroughly imbued with an ignorant and bigoted Union sentiment." Other reënforcements were promised Garnett, but none reached him except the 44th Virginia regiment, which arrived at Beverly the very day of the action, but which did not take part in the fighting.

Tygart's Valley, in which Beverly lies, is between Cheat Mountain on the east, and Rich Mountain on the west. The river, of the same name as the valley, flows northward about fifteen miles, then turns westward, breaking through the ridge, passes by Philippi, and afterward crosses the railroad at Grafton. The Staunton and Parkersburg Turnpike divides at Beverly, the Parkersburg route passing over a saddle in Rich Mountain, and the Wheeling route following the river to Philippi. The ridge north of the river at the gap is known as Laurel Mountain, and the road passes over a spur of it. Garnett regarded the two positions at Rich Mountain and Laurel Mountain as the gates to all the region beyond, and to the West. A

rough mountain road, barely passable, connected the Laurel Mountain position with Cheat River on the east, and it was possible to go by this way northward through St. George to the Northwestern Turnpike, turning the mountain ranges.

Garnett thought the pass over Rich Mountain much the stronger and more easily held, and he therefore intrenched there about 1300 of his men and 4 cannon, under command of Lieutenant-Colonel Pegram. The position chosen was on a spur of the mountain near its western base, and it was rudely fortified with breastworks of logs covered with an abattis of slashed timber along its front. The remainder of his force he placed in a similar fortified position on the road at Laurel mountain, where he also had four guns, of which one was rifled. Here he commanded in person. His depot of supplies was at Beverly, which was 16 miles from the Laurel Mountain position and 5 from that at Rich Mountain. He was pretty accurately informed of McClellan's forces and movements, and his preparations had barely been completed by the 9th of July, when the Union general appeared in his front.

McClellan entered West Virginia in person on the 22d of June, and on the 23d issued from Grafton a proclamation to the inhabitants. He had gradually collected his forces along the Baltimore and Ohio railroad, which, at the time of the affair at Rich Mountain, consisted of 16 Ohio regiments, 9 from Indiana and 2 from West Virginia; in all, 27 regiments with 4 batteries of artillery of 6 guns each, 2 troops of cavalry, and an independent company of riflemen. Of his batteries, one was of the regular army, and another, a company of regulars (Company I, 4th U.S. Artillery), was with him awaiting mountain howitzers, which arrived a little later. The regiments varied somewhat in strength, but all were recently organized, and must have averaged at least 700 men each, making the whole force about 20,000. Of these, about 5000 were guarding the railroad and its bridges for some 200 miles, under the command of Brigadier-General C. W. Hill, of the Ohio Militia; a strong brigade under Brigadier-General Morris, of Indiana, was at Philippi, and the rest were in three brigades forming the immediate command of McClellan, the brigadiers being General W. S. Rosecrans, U.S.A., General Newton Schleich, of Ohio, and Colonel Robert L. McCook, of Ohio. On the date of his proclamation McClellan intended, as he informed General Scott, to move his principal column to Buckhannon on June 25th, and thence at once

upon Beverly; but delays occurred, and it was not till July 2d that he reached Buckhannon, which is 24 miles west of Beverly, on the Parkersburg branch of the turnpike. Before leaving Grafton the rumors he heard had made him estimate Garnett's force at 6000 or 7000 men, of which the larger part were at Laurel Mountain in front of General Morris. On the 6th of July he moved McCook with two regiments to Middle Fork Bridge, about half-way to Beverly, and on the same day ordered Morris to march with his brigade from Philippi to a position one and a half miles in front of Garnett's principal camp, which was promptly done. Three days later, McClellan concentrated the three brigades of his own column at Roaring Creek, about two miles from Colonel Pegram's position at the base of Rich Mountain. The advance on both lines had been made with only a skirmishing resistance, the Confederates being aware of McClellan's great superiority in numbers, and choosing to await his attack on their fortified positions. The National commander was now convinced that his opponent was 10,000 strong, of which about 2000 were before him at Rich Mountain. A reconnoissance made on the 10th showed that Pegram's position would be difficult to assail in front, but preparations were made to attack the next day, while Morris was directed to hold firmly his position before Garnett, watching for the effect of the attack at Rich Mountain. In the evening Rosecrans took to McClellan a young man named Hart, whose father lived on the top of the mountain two miles in rear of Pegram, and who thought he could guide a column of infantry to his father's farm by a circuit around Pegram's left flank south of the turnpike. The paths were so difficult that cannon could not go by them, but Rosecrans offered to lead a column of infantry and seize the road at the Hart farm. After some discussion McClellan adopted the suggestion, and it was arranged that Rosecrans should march at daybreak of the 11th with about two thousand men, including a troop of horse, and that upon the sound of his engagement in the rear of Pegram, McClellan would attack in force in front. By a blunder in one of the regimental camps, the reveille and assembly were sounded at midnight, and Pegram was put on the *qui vive.* He, however, believed that the attempt to turn his position would be by a path or country road passing round his right, between him and Garnett (of which the latter had warned him), and his attention was diverted from Rosecran's actual route, which he thought imprac-

Robert E. Lee, as he appeared before the war.

Troops gather on the north side of the Rappahannock.

ticable. The alert which had occurred at midnight made Rosecrans think it best to make a longer circuit than he at first intended, and it took ten hours of severe marching and mountain climbing to reach the Hart farm. The turning movement was made, but he found an enemy opposing him. Pegram had detached about 350 men from the 1300 which he had, and had ordered them to guard the road at the mountain summit. He sent with them a single cannon from the four which constituted his only battery, and they threw together a breastwork of logs. The turnpike at Hart's runs in a depression of the summit, and as Rosencrans, early in the afternoon, came out upon the road, he was warmly received by both musketry and cannon. The ground was rough, the men were for the first time under fire, and the skirmishing combat varied through two or three hours, when a charge by part of Rosecrans's line, aided by a few heavy volleys from another portion of his forces which had secured a good position, broke the enemy's line. Reënforcements from Pegram were nearly at hand, with another cannon, but they did not come into action, and the runaway team of the caisson on the hill-top, dashing into the gun that was coming up, capsized it down the mountain-side where the descending road was scarped diagonally along it. Both guns fell into Rosecrans's hands, and he was in possession of the field. The march and the assault had been made in rain and storm. Nothing was heard from McClellan, and the enemy, rallying on their reënforcements, made such show of resistance on the crest a little farther on, that Rosecrans directed his men to rest upon their arms till next morning. When day broke on the 12th, the enemy had disappeared from the mountain-top, and Rosecrans, feeling his way down to the rear of Pegram's position, found it also abandoned, the two remaining cannon being spiked, and a few sick and wounded being left in charge of a surgeon. Still nothing was seen of McClellan and Rosecrans sent word to him, in his camp beyond Roaring Creek, that he was in possession of the enemy's position. Rosecrans's loss had been 12 killed and 49 wounded. The Confederates left 20 wounded on the field, and 63 were surrendered at the lower camp, including the sick. No trustworthy report of their dead was made.

The noise of the engagement had been heard in McClellan's camp, and he formed his troops for attack, but the long continuance of the cannonade and some signs of exultation in Pegram's camp seem to have made him think Rosecrans had been repulsed. The failure to attack in accordance with the plan has never been explained. Rosecrans's messengers had failed to reach McClellan during the 11th, but the sound of the battle was sufficient notice that he had gained the summit and was engaged; and he was, in fact, left to win his own battle or to get out of his embarrassment as he could. Toward evening McClellan began to cut a road for artillery to a neighboring height, from which he hoped his twelve guns

General Rosecrans advances with troops to attack Confederates at Rich Mountain.

Federal troops attack Confederate positions on Rich Mountain.

would make Pegram's position untenable; but his lines were withdrawn again beyond Roaring Creek at nightfall, and further action was postponed to the next day.

About half of Pegram's men had succeeded in passing around Rosecrans's right flank during the night and had gained Beverly. These, with the newly arrived Confederate regiment, fled southward on the Staunton road. Garnett had learned in the evening by messenger from Beverly that Rich Mountain summit was carried, and evacuated his camp in front of Morris about midnight. He first marched toward Beverly, and was within five miles of that place when he received information (false at the time) that the National forces already occupied it. He then retraced his steps near to his camp, and, leaving the turnpike at Leadsville, he turned off upon a country road over Cheat Mountain into Cheat River Valley, following the stream northward toward St. George and West Union, in the forlorn hope of turning the mountains at the north end of the ridges and regaining his communications by a very long detour. He might have continued southward through Beverly almost at leisure, for McClellan did not enter the town till past noon on the 12th.

Morris learned of Garnett's retreat at dawn, and started in pursuit as soon as rations could be issued. He marched first to Leadsville, where he halted to communicate with McClellan at Beverly and get further orders. These reached him in the night, and at daybreak of the 13th he resumed the pursuit. His advance-guard of three regiments, accompanied by Captain H. W. Benham of the Engineers, overtook the rear of the Confederate column about noon and continued a skirmishing pursuit for some two hours. Garnett himself handled his rear-guard with skill, and at Carrick's Ford a lively encounter was had. A mile or two farther, at another ford and when the skirmishing was very slight, he was killed while withdrawing his skirmishers from behind a pile of driftwood which he had used as a barricade. One of his cannon had become stalled in the ford, and, with about forty wagons, fell into Morris's hands. The direct pursuit was here discontinued, but McClellan had sent a dispatch to General Hill at Grafton, to collect the garrisons along the railway and block the way of the Confederates where they must pass around the northern spurs of the mountains.

His military telegraph terminated at the Roaring Creek camp, and the dispatch written in the evening of the 12th was not forwarded to Hill till near noon of the 13th. This officer immediately ordered the collection of the greater part of his detachments at Oakland and called upon the railway officials for special trains to hurry them to the rendezvous. About one thousand men under Colonel James Irvine of the 16th Ohio were at West Union where the St. George road reaches the Northwestern Turnpike, and Hill's information was that a detachment of these held Red House, a crossing several miles in advance by which the retreating enemy might go.

The 13th Indiana captures a gun on Rich Mountain.

Irvine was directed to hold his positions at all hazards till he could be reënforced. Hill himself hastened with the first train from Grafton to Oakland with about 500 men and 3 cannon, reached his destination at nightfall, and hurried his detachment forward by a night march to Irvine, 10 or 12 miles over rough roads. It turned out that Irvine did not occupy Red House, and the prevalent belief that the enemy was about eight thousand in number, with the uncertainty of the road he would take, made it proper to keep the little force concentrated till reënforcements should come. The first of these reached Irvine about 6 o'clock on the morning of the 14th, raising his command to 1500, but a few moments after their arrival he learned that the enemy had passed Red House soon after daylight. He gave chase, but did not overtake them.

Meanwhile, General Hill had spent the night in trying to hasten forward the railway trains, but none were able to reach Oakland till morning, and Garnett's forces had now more than twenty miles the start, and were on fairly good roads, moving southward on the eastern side of the mountains. McClellan still telegraphed that Hill had the one opportunity of a lifetime to capture the fleeing army, and that officer hastened in pursuit, though unprovided with wagons or extra rations. When, however, the Union commander learned that the enemy had fairly turned the mountains, he ordered the pursuit stopped. Hill had used both intelligence and energy in his attempt to concentrate his troops, but it proved simply impossible for the railroad to carry them to Oakland before the enemy had passed the turning-point twenty miles to the southward.

During the 12th Pegram's situation and movements were unknown. He had intended, when he evacuated his camp, to follow the retreat taken by the detachment already near the mountain-top, but, in the darkness of the night and in the tangled woods and thickets of the mountain-side, his column got divided, and, with the rear portion of it, he wandered all day on the 12th, seeking to make his way to Garnett. He halted at evening at the Tygart Valley River, six miles north of Beverly, and learned from some country people of Garnett's retreat. It was still possible to reach the mountains east of the valley, but beyond was a hundred miles of wilderness and half a dozen mountain ridges on which little, if any, food could be found for his men. He called a council of war, and, by advice of his officers, sent to McClellan, at Beverly, an offer of surrender. This was received on the 13th, and Pegram brought in 30 officers and 525 men. McClellan then moved southward himself, following the Staunton road, by which the remnant of Pegram's little force had escaped, and on the 14th occupied Huttonsville. Two regiments of Confederate troops were hastening from Staunton to reënforce Garnett. These were halted at Monterey, east of the principal ridge of the Alleghanies, and upon them the retreating forces rallied. Brigadier-General H. R. Jackson was assigned to command in Garnett's place, and both Governor Letcher and General Lee made strenuous efforts to increase this army to a force sufficient to resume aggressive operations. On McClellan's part nothing further was attempted, till, on the 22d, he was summoned to Washington to assume command of the army which had retreated to the capital after the panic of the first Bull Run battle.

The affair at Rich Mountain and the subsequent movements were among the minor events of a great war, and would not warrant a detailed description, were it not for the momentous effect they had upon the conduct of the war, by being the occasion of McClellan's promotion to the command of the Potomac army. The narrative which has been given contains the "unvarnished tale," as nearly as official records of both sides can give it, and it is a curious task to compare it with the picture of the campaign and its results which was then given to the world in the series of proclamations and dispatches of the young general, beginning with his first occupation of the country and ending with his congratulations to his troops, in which he announced that they had "annihilated two armies, commanded by educated and experienced soldiers, intrenched in mountain fastnesses fortified at their leisure." The country was eager for good news, and took it as literally true. McClellan was the hero of the moment, and when, but a week later, his success was followed by the disaster to McDowell at Bull Run, he seemed pointed out by Providence as the ideal chieftain, who could repair the misfortune and lead our armies to certain victory. His personal intercourse with those about him was so kindly, and his bearing so modest, that his dispatches, proclamations, and correspondence are a psychological study, more puzzling to those who knew him well than to strangers. Their turgid rhetoric and exaggerated pretense did not seem natural to him. In them he seemed to be composing for stage effect, something to be spoken in character by a quite different person from the sensible and genial man we knew in daily life and conversation. The career of the great Napoleon had been the study and the absorbing admiration of young American soldiers, and it was, perhaps, not strange that when real war came they should copy his bulletins and even his personal bearing. It was, for the moment, the bent of the people to be pleased with McClellan's rendering of the rôle; they dubbed him the young Napoleon, and the photographers got him to stand with folded arms, in the historic pose. For two or three weeks his dispatches and letters were all on fire with enthusiastic energy. He appeared to be in a morbid condition of mental exaltation. When he came out of it, he was an genial as ever, as can be seen by the contrast between his official communications and that private letter to General Burnside, written just after the evacuation of Yorktown, which, oddly enough, has found its way into the official records of the war. The assumed dash and energy of his first campaign made the disappointment and the reaction more painful, when the excessive caution of his conduct in command of the Army of the Potomac was seen. But the Rich Mountain affair, when analyzed, shows the same characteristics which became well known later. There was the same overestimate of the enemy, the same tendency to interpret unfavorably the sights and sounds in front, the same hesitancy to throw in his whole force when he knew that his subordinate was engaged. If Garnett had been as strong as McClellan believed him, he had abundant time and means to overwhelm Morris, who lay four days in easy striking distance, while the National commander delayed attacking Pegram; and had Morris been beaten, Garnett would have been as near Clarksburg as his opponent, and there would have been a race for the railroad. But, happily, Garnett was less strong and less enterprising than he was credited with being. Pegram was dislodged, and the Confederates made a precipitate retreat.

THE KANAWHA VALLEY

When McClellan reached Buckhannon, on the 2d of July, the rumors he heard of Garnett's strength, and the news of the presence of General Wise with a considerable force in the Great Kanawha Valley, made him conclude to order a brigade to that region for the purpose of holding the lower part of the valley defensively till he might try to cut off Wise's army after Garnett should be disposed of. This duty was assigned to me. The brigade which I had organized had all been taken for his own campaign, except the 11th Ohio (only five companies present), but the 12th Ohio, which was still at Camp Dennison, was ordered to report to me, and these two regiments were to be sent by rail to Gallipolis as soon as the railways could furnish transportation. At Gallipolis we should find the 21st Ohio militia, and the 1st and 2nd Kentucky volunteers were also to join me there, coming by steamboat from Cincinnati. The two Kentucky regiments had been organized in Cincinnati, and were made up chiefly of steamboat crews and "longshoremen" thrown out of employment by the stoppage of commerce on the river. There were in them some companies of other material, but these gave the distinctive character to the regiments as a whole. The colonels and part of the field-officers were Kentuckians, but the organizations were Ohio regiments in nearly everything but the name. The men were mostly of a rough and reckless class, and gave a good deal of trouble by insubordination; but they did not lack courage, and, after they had been under discipline for a while, became good fighting regiments.

The troops moved the moment transportation could be furnished, and those going by rail were at Gallipolis and Point Pleasant (the mouth of the Great Kanawha) on the 10th. My only artillery was a section of 2 bronze rifles, altered from smooth 6-pounders, and my only cavalry some 30 raw recruits, useful only as messengers. Meanwhile, my orders had been changed, and in accordance with them I directed the 2d Kentucky to land at Guyandotte, on the Ohio, about 70 miles below the Kanawha, the

William S. Rosecrans later commanded the Federal forces in Western Virginia.

1st Kentucky to proceed to Ripley, landing at Ravenswood, about 50 miles above, while with two and a half regiments I myself should move up the Kanawha Valley. The two detachments would join me after a time by lateral roads. My total force, when assembled, would be a little over three thousand men, the regiments having the same average strength as those with McClellan. The opposing force under General Wise was four thousand by the time the campaign was fully opened, though somewhat less at the beginning.

The Kanawha River was navigable for small steamboats about 70 miles, to a point 10 or 12 miles above Charleston, the only important town of the region and lying at the confluence of the Kanawha and Elk rivers. Steamboats were plenty, owing to the interruption of trade, and wagons were wholly lacking, so that my column was accompanied and partly carried by a fleet of stern-wheel steamers.

On the 11th of July the movement from Point Pleasant began. An advance-guard was sent out on each side of the river, marching upon the roads

which were near its banks. The few horsemen were divided and sent with them as messengers, and the boats followed, steaming slowly along in rear of the marching men. Most of two regiments were carried on the steamers, to save fatigue to the men, who were as yet unused to their work, and many of

Light artillery pauses during a march.

whom were footsore from their first long march of 25 miles to Gallipolis, from the station where they left the railway. The arrangement was also a good one in a military point of view, for if an enemy were met on either bank of the stream, the boats could land in a moment and the troops disembark without delay.

Our first day's sail was thirteen miles up the river, and it was the very romance of campaigning. I took my station on top of the pilot-house of the leading boat, so that I might see over the banks of the stream and across the bottom-lands which bounded the valley. The afternoon was a lovely one. Summer clouds lazily drifted across the sky, the boats were dressed in their colors, and swarmed with men as a hive with bees. The bands played national tunes, and as we passed the houses of Union citizens, the inmates would wave their handkerchiefs to us and were answered by cheers from the troops. The scenery was picturesque, the gently winding river making beautiful reaches that opened new scenes upon us at every turn. On either side the advance-guard could be seen in the distance, the main body in the road, with skirmishers exploring the way in front and flankers on the sides. Now and then a horseman would bring some message to the shore from the front, and a small boat would be sent to receive it, giving us the rumors with which the country was rife, and which gave just enough of excitement and of the spice of possible danger to make this our first day in the enemy's country key everybody to a pitch that doubled the vividness of every sensation. The landscape seemed more beautiful, the sunshine more bright, and the exhilaration of outdoor life more joyous than any we had ever before known.

Our first night's camp was in a picturesque spot in keeping with the beauties of the day's progress, and was enlivened by a report that the enemy was advancing to attack us in force. It was only a rumor, based upon the approach of a reconnoitering party of cavalry, and the camp was not allowed to be disturbed except to send a small reconnoissance forward on our own part. Two more days' advance, in the face of a slight skirmishing resistance, brought us to the Pocotaligo, a stream entering the Kanawha from the north.

Wise had placed his principal camp at Tyler Mountain, a bold spur which reaches the river on the northern side (on which is also the turnpike road) about 12 miles above my position, while he occupied the south side with a detachment above Scary Creek some 3 miles from us. The hills closing in nearer to the river make it necessary to halt a little and await the arrival of the wagons which had not yet been sent me, and of the 2d Kentucky regiment, which was marching to me from Barboursville, where one wing of it, commanded by Lieutenant-Colonel Neff, had a brilliant little affair with a body of Confederate recruits occupying the place. On the afternoon of the 17th, the Kentuckians having arrived, and a reconnoissance having been made of the Scary Creek position, which was found to be held by about 500 of the enemy with 1 or 2 cannon, Colonel John W. Lowe of the 12th Ohio was ferried over the river with his own regiment and 2 companies of the 21st Ohio with our 2 cannon, and directed to occupy the attention of the enemy in front at the creek, which was unfordable at its mouth, while he tried to turn the position with part of his command. The enemy at first retreated, leaving one cannon disabled, but, being reënforced, they rallied, and, no good crossing of the creek being found, Lowe was foiled in his effort to dislodge them after a sharp engagement across the stream.

The wagons reached us a few at a time, but by the 24th I was able to move from our strong position behind Pocotaligo, and, taking circuitous country roads among the hills, to come upon the rear of Wise's camp at Tyler Mountain. The march was a long and difficult one, but was successful. As soon as his outposts were driven in, the enemy decamped in a panic, leaving his campkettles and supper over the fires. We had also cut off a steamboat with troops which was just below us as we came to the bluff, and which, under the fire of our cannon, was run ashore and burned, while the detachment on the other side of the river hastened by country roads to rejoin Wise at Charleston. It was now nightfall, and we bivouacked upon the mountain-side. Wise abandoned Charleston in the night and retreated toward Gauley Bridge. On the 25th I occupied Charleston without resistance, and moved on, ordering the 1st Kentucky up from Ripley to garrison the place and establish my depot there.

At every mile above Charleston the scenery grows wilder, the mountains crowding in upon the river, often with high, beetling cliffs overhanging it, and offering numerous positions where a small detachment might hold an army in check. Wise, however, made no resistance worth naming, except to fell timber into the road, and he passed the Gauley, burning the important bridge there and continuing his hasty retreat to the White Sulphur Springs, hurried, no doubt, by the fear that McClellan might intercept him by way of Huntersville and Lewisburg. McClellan had recognized the fact that he was asking me to face the enemy with no odds in my favor, and as soon as he heard that Wise was disposed to make a stand, he had directed me not to risk attacking him in front, but rather to await the result of his own movement toward the Upper Kanawha. Rosecrans did the same when he assumed command; but I knew the hope had been that I could reach Gauley Bridge, and I felt warranted, as soon as the wagons reached me, in attempting the turning movement which seems to have thrown Wise into a panic from which he did not recover till he got out of the valley. Rosecrans ordered me to remain on the defensive at Charleston, but his dispatches did not reach me, fortunately, till I was close to Gauley Bridge, some forty miles above Charleston, and I was quite sure of my ability to take possession of that defile, as I did on the 29th of July. Another reason for haste was that the time of enlistment of the 21st Ohio had expired, and I was ordered by the governor to send it back to Ohio for reorganization, which would make a reduction of one-fourth of my numbers.

At my first night's encampment above Charleston, in a lovely nook between spurs of the hills, I was treated to a little surprise on the part of three of my subordinates which was an unexpected enlargement of my military experience, and which is worth preserving to show some of the conditions attending the beginning of a war with undisciplined troops. The camp was nicely organized for the night and supper was over, when I was waited upon at my tent by these gentlemen. Their spokesman informed me that after consultation they had concluded that it was foolhardy to follow the Confederates into the gorge we were traveling, and, unless, I could show them satisfactory reasons for changing their opinion, they would not lead their commands farther into it. I dryly asked if he was quite sure he understood the nature of his communication. There was probably something in the tone of my question which was not altogether expected, and his companions began to look a little uneasy. He then protested that they meant no disrespect, but, as their military experience was about as extensive as my own, they thought I ought to make no movement but on consultation with them and by their consent. The others seemed better pleased with this way of putting it. My answer was that whether they meant it or not, their action was mutinous, and only their ignorance of military law could palliate it. The responsibility for the movement of the army was with me, and, while glad to confer freely with them, I should call no council of war and submit nothing to vote till I felt incompetent to decide for myself. If they apologized for their conduct and showed earnestness in military obedience, what they had now said would be overlooked, but on any recurrence of insubordination I should enforce my power by arresting the offender at once. I dismissed them with this, and immediately sent out orders through my adjutant-general to march early next morning. Before they slept, one of the three had come to me with an earnest apology for his part in the matter, and a short time made them all as subordinate as I could wish. The incident could not have occurred in the brigade which had been under my command at Camp Dennison, and was the natural result of the sudden assembling of inexperienced men under a brigade commander of whom they knew nothing except that at the beginning of the war he had been a civilian like themselves.

The same march enabled me to make the acquaintance of another army "institution,"—the newspaper correspondent. At Charleston I was joined by two men representing influential newspapers, who wished to know on what terms they might accompany the column. The answer was that the quartermaster would furnish them with a tent and with transportation, and that their letters should be submitted to one of the staff to protect us from the publication of facts which might aid the enemy. This seemed unsatisfactory, and they intimated that they expected to be taken into my mess, and to be announced as volunteer aids with military rank. They were told that military position or rank could only be given by authority much higher than mine, and that they could be more honestly independent if free from personal obligation and from temptation to repay favors with flattery. My only purpose was to put the matter upon the foundation of public right and of mutual self-respect. The day before we reached Gauley Bridge they opened the matter again to my adjutant-general, but were informed that I had decided it upon a principle by which I meant to abide. Their reply was, "Very well; General Cox thinks he can get along without us. We will show him. We will write him down!" They left the camp the same evening and wrote letters to their papers, describing the army as a rabble of ruffians, burning houses, ravishing women, robbing and destroying property, and the commander as totally incompetent. As to the troops, more baseless slander was never uttered. Their march had been orderly, no willful injury had been done to private property, and no case of personal violence to any non-combatant, man or woman, had been even charged. Yet the publication of such communications in widely read journals was likely to be as damaging as if it were true. My nomination as brigadier-general was then before the Senate for confirmation, and "the pen" would probably have proved "mightier than the sword" but for McClellan's knowledge of the nature of the task we had accomplished as he was then in the flood-tide of power at Washington, and had expressed his satisfaction at the performance of our part of the campaign which he had planned.

ROSECRANS IN COMMAND

General Rosecrans had succeeded McClellan as ranking officer in West Virginia, but it was not until the beginning of November, 1861, that the region was made a department and he was regularly assigned to command. Meanwhile the three-months' enlistments were expiring, many regiments were sent home, new ones were received, and a complete reorganization of his forces took place. Besides holding the railroad, he fortified the Cheat Mountain Pass looking toward Staunton, and the pass at Elkwater on the mountain summit between Huttonsville and Huntersville. In similar manner I was directed to fortify the camp at Gauley Bridge, and to cover the front in every direction with active detachments, constantly moving from the central position. By the middle of August, Rosecrans had established a chain of posts, with a regiment or two at each, on a line upon which he afterward marched from Weston, by way of Bulltown, Sutton, and Summersville, to Gauley Bridge.

The Confederates had also been straining every nerve to collect a force that might give us an effective return blow, and Robert E. Lee was expected to lead their forces in person. After ten days' quiet occupation of Gauley Bridge, in which I had reconnoitered the country nearly forty miles in front and on each flank, we learned that General John B. Floyd had joined Wise with a brigade, and that both were moving toward the Kanawha. At the same time the militia of Raleigh, Mercer, and Fayette counties were called out, making a force of two thousand men under General Chapman. The total force confronting us was thus about eighty thousand. To resist these I kept 2 regiments at Gauley Bridge, an advance-guard of 8 companies vigorously skirmishing

toward Sewell Mountain, a regiment distributed on the Kanawha to cover the steamboat communications, and some West Virginia recruits organizing at the mouth of the river. By extreme activity these were able to baffle the enemy and impose upon him the belief that our numbers were more than double our actual force. Rosecrans had informed me of his purpose to march a strong column to join me as soon as Lee's plans were fully developed, and I accumulated supplies and munitions at Gauley Bridge, de-

General Rosecrans meets with staff at headquarters in Clarksburg.

termined to stand a siege if necessary. On the 13th of August the 7th Ohio, Colonel E. B. Tyler was ordered by Rosecrans to Cross Lanes, covering Carnifex Ferry on the Gauley River about twenty miles above us, where a road from Lewisburg meets that going up the Gauley to Summersville. I was authorized to call Tyler to me if seriously attacked. On the 20th Wise made a strong demonstration in front, but was met at Pig Creek, three miles up the New River and easily repulsed. On the 26th Floyd, having raised two flat-boats which Tyler had sunk, crossed the Gauley at Carnifex Ferry with 2000 or 3000 men, and surprised him, routing the regiment with a loss to us of 15 killed and about 100 captured, of which 50 were wounded. The greater part of the regiment was rallied by Major Casement, and led over the mountains to Elk River, and thence to Charleston. Floyd intrenched his position, and built a foot-bridge to connect it with the eastern side of the wild gorge. Wise's failure to coöperate was Floyd's reason for abandoning his announced purpose of marching upon my rear; but he was on my northern line of communication with Rosecrans, and the latter hastened his preparations to come to my relief.

On the 3rd of September, Wise and Chapman attempted a concerted attack upon Gauley Bridge, the first pushing in upon the turnpike, while Chapman advanced from Fayette by Cotton Hill and a road to the river a little below Kanawha Falls. Wise was again met at Pig Creek and driven back; Chapman reached the bluffs overlooking the river in rear of us, driving in our outposts, but did us little mischief, except to throw a few shells into our lower camp, and on Wise's repulse he also withdrew. Our detachments followed them up on both lines with daily warm skirmishes, and the advance-guard ambushed and punished the enemy's cavalry in a very demoralizing way. Efforts to reach the river and stop our steamboats, kept the posts and detachments below us on the alert, and an expedition of half the 1st Kentucky, under Lieutenant-Colonel D. A. Enyart, sent to break up a Confederate militia encampment at Boone Court House, 40 miles southward, routed the enemy, who left 25 dead upon the field. The march and attack had been swift and vigorous, and the terror of the blow kept that region quiet for some time afterward.

I was puzzled at Floyd's inaction at Carnifex Ferry, but the mystery is partly solved by the publication of the Confederate records. There was no coöperation between the commanders, and Wise refused the assistance Floyd demanded, nor could even the authority of Lee reduce the ex-governor of Virginia to real subordination. The letters of Wise show a capacity for keeping a command in hot water which was unique. If he had been half as troublesome to me as he was to Floyd, I should, indeed, have had a hot time of it. But he did me royal service by preventing anything approaching unity of action between the two principal Confederate columns.

Rosecrans now began his march from Clarksburg with three brigades, having left the Upper Potomac line in command of General Kelley, and the Cheat Mountain region in command of General J. J. Reynolds. His route (already indicated) was a rough one, and the portion of it between Sutton and Summersville, over Birch Mountain, was very wild and difficult. He left his bivouac on the morning of the 10th of September, before daybreak, and, marching through Summersville, reached Cross Lanes about 2 o'clock in the afternoon. Floyd's position was now about two miles distant, and waiting only for his column to close up, he again pressed forward. General Benham's brigade was in front, and soon met the enemy's pickets. Getting the impression that Floyd was in retreat, Benham pressed forward rather rashly, deploying to the left, and coming under a sharp fire from the right of the enemy's works. The woods were dense and tangled, it was too late for a proper reconnoissance, and Rosecrans could only hasten the advance and deployment of the other brigades under Colonels McCook and Scrammon. Benham had sent a howitzer battery and two rifled cannon with his head of column at the left, and these soon got a position, from which, in fact, they enfiladed part of Floyd's line, though it was impossible to see much of the situation. Charges were made by portions of Benham's and McCook's brigades as they came up, but they lacked unity, and Rosecrans was dissatisfied that his head of column should be engaged before he had time to plan an attack. Colonel Lowe, of the 12th Ohio, had been killed at the head of his regiment, and Colonel W. H. Lytle, of the 10th, had been severely wounded; darkness was rapidly coming on, and Rosecrans ordered the troops withdrawn from fire, till positions could be rectified, and the attack renewed in the morning. Seventeen had been killed and 141 had been wounded in the sharp but irregular combat. Floyd, however, had learned that his position could be subjected to a destructive cannonade; he was himself slightly wounded, and his officers and men were discouraged. He therefore retreated across the Gauley in the night, having great difficulty in carrying his artillery down the cliffs by a wretched road in the darkness. He had built a slight foot-bridge for infantry, in the bit of smooth water known as the Ferry, though both above and below the stream is an impassable mountain torrent. Once over, the bridge was broken up and the flat-boats were destroyed. He reported but twenty casualties, and threw much of the responsibility upon Wise, who had not obeyed orders to reënforce him. His hospital, containing the wounded prisoners taken from Tyler, fell into Rosecrans's hands.

On the 12th of September we first heard, at Gauley Bridge, of the engagement at Carnifex Ferry, and I at once moved with two regiments to attack Wise, who retired as we advanced, till I occupied the junction of the turnpike with the Sunday road. The whole hostile force had retreated to Sewell Mountain, and Rosecrans halted me until he could create means of crossing the Gauley.

McCook's brigade joined me on the 16th of September, and my own command was increased by bringing up another of my regiments from below. With the two brigades I advanced to Spy Rock, a strong position overlooking a valley several miles broad, beyond which was Big Sewell Mountain, the crest of which we occupied with an advance-guard on the 20th and in force on the 24th. Before the 1st of October Rosecrans had concentrated his force at the mountain, the four brigades being so reduced by sickness and by detachments that he reported the whole as making only 5200 effective men. Immediately in front, across a deep gorge, lay the united forces of Floyd and Wise, commanded by Lee in person. The autumn rains set in upon the very day of Rosecrans's arrival, and continued without intermission. The roads became so difficult that the animals of the wagon trains were being destroyed in the effort to supply the command. The camp was 35 miles from Gauley Bridge, and our stores were landed from steamboats 25 miles below that post, making 60 miles of wagoning. The enemy was as badly off, and no aggressive operations were possible on either side. This became so evident that on the 5th of October Rosecrans withdrew his forces to camps within 3 or 4 miles of Gauley Bridge.

Lee had directed an effort to be made by General Loing, his subordinate on the Staunton line to test the strength of the posts under Reynolds at Cheat Mountain and Elkwater, and lively combats had resulted on the 12th and 14th of September. Reynolds held firm, and Rosecrans had not been diverted from his own plans. On October 3d Reynolds delivered a return blow upon the Confederate position at Greenbrier, but found it too strong to be carried. Both parties now remained in observation till the end of October. Floyd reported to his Government that the eleven days of cold storms at Sewell Mountain had "cost more men, sick and dead, than the battle of Manassas Plains." More enterprising in plans than resolute or skillful in carrying them out, he deter-

mined upon another effort, with Lee's consent. Taking advantage of Rosencrans's neglect to occupy Fayette Court House and Cotton Hill, a mountainous mass in the angle of the Kanawha and New rivers, he moved with a column of about five thousand men across New River and down its left bank, and startled the Union commander by opening with cannon upon the post at Gauley Bridge on the 1st of November. The demonstration was more noisy than dangerous. Floyd had no means of crossing the river. The ordnance stores at the post were moved into a gorge out of the range of fire, and a battery was established high up on Gauley Mount to reply to the enemy. Rosecrans had hopes of capturing Floyd, by turning his position from below by Benham's and Robert C. Schenck's (formerly Scammon's) brigades. Delays occured which Rosecrans attributed to failure to obey orders on the part of Benham. On the 10th detachments from my brigade at Gauley Bridge crossed the river and scaled the heights, attacking Floyd in front and securing a position on the top of the mountain. Floyd withdrew his artillery, and on the 12th, learning that Schenck and Benham were moving toward his rear, decamped, and did not cease his retreat till he reached the Holston Valley railroad.

Lee returned to Richmond, and portions of the troops on both sides were sent to other fields, where military operations in winter were thought to be more practicable. The remnant went into winter quarters, and though some combats occurred, the most noteworthy of which was Milroy's attack upon the Confederates in front of Cheat Mountain pass in December, these engagements did not change the situation. West Virginia had organized as a free State within the Union, and this substantial result of the campaign crowned it with success. The line of the Alleghanies became the northern frontier of the Confederacy in Virginia, and was never again seriously broken.

======================= ★★★ =======================

R. M. KELLY
Holding Kentucky for the Union

R. M. Kelly was a volunteer officer in the Union Army who served in Kentucky during 1861, in a period when the governor was trying to maintain the state's neutrality. Such a posture was impossible, for the state was of enormous strategic importance, as Lincoln—a

Kentuckian by birth—said, "I hope I have God on my side, but I must have Kentucky." Kelly's life is rather obscure, but his dry account of operations in Kentucky, which is taken from Battles and Leaders of the Civil War, *is highly accurate.*

The military situation in Kentucky in 1861 cannot be properly understood without a brief sketch of the initial political struggle which resulted in a decisive victory for the friends of the Union. The State Legislature had assembled on the 17th of January in called session. The governor's proclamation convening it was issued immediately after he had received commissioners from the States of Alabama and Mississippi, and was followed by the publication of a letter from Vice-President Breckinridge advising the calling of a State convention and urging that the only way to prevent war was for Kentucky to take her stand openly with the slave States. About this time the latter's uncle, the Rev. Dr. Robert J. Breckinridge, an eminent Presbyterian minister, addressed a large meeting at Lexington in favor of the Union. The division of sentiment is further illustrated by the fact that one of his sons, Colonel W. C. P. Breckinridge, followed his cousin into the Confederate army, while another son, Colonel Joseph C. Breckinridge, fought for the Union. The position of the Union men was very difficult. They knew that Governor Magoffin was in sympathy with the secession movement and that the status of the Legislature on the question was doubtful. The governor had under his orders a military force called the State Guard, well armed and disciplined, and under the immediate command of General Simon B. Buckner, a graduate of West Point. There was a small Union element in it, but a large majority of its membership was known to be in favor of secession. Suspicious activity in recruiting for this force began as soon as the governor issued his call for the Legislature, and it was charged that new companies of known secession proclivities could get arms promptly from the State arsenal, while those supposed to be inclined toward the Union were subjected to annoying delays. The State Guard at its strongest numbered only about four thousand men, but it was organized and ready while the Union men had neither arms nor organization to oppose it.

When the Legislature assembled it was soon ascertained that it was very evenly divided in sentiment. Old party lines promptly disappeared, and members were called as "Union" or "Southern Rights." In the Senate there was a safe majority against calling a convention. In the house on a test question the Union men prevailed by only one vote. There were some half-dozen waverers who always opposed any decisive step toward secession but were equally unwilling to give any active support to the Government. Outside pressure was brought to bear. Large delegations of secessionists assembled at Frankfort, to be speedily confronted by Union men, just as determined, summoned by telegraph from all parts of the State. Argument was met by argument, threat by threat, appeals to sentiment and prejudice on one side by similar appeals on the other. The leading public men of the State, however, had been trained in a school of compromises, and they long cherished themselves, and kept alive in the people, the hope that some settlement would be reached that would avert war and save Kentucky from becoming the battle-field of contending armies. This hope accounts in a large degree for the infrequency of personal affrays during those exciting days.

The struggle, kept up during three sessions of the Legislature, demonstrated that the State could not be carried out of the Union by storm, and terminated in adopting the policy of neutrality as a compromise. The Union men, however, had gained some decided advantages. They had consented to large appropriations for arming the State, but on condition that the control of military affairs should be taken from the governor and lodged in a military board of five members, the majority being Union men; they provided for organizing and arming Home Guards, outside of the militia force, and not subject, as such, to the governor's orders, and they passed an act requiring all the State Guard to take the oath required of officers, this measure being mainly for the purpose of allowing the Union members of that organization to get rid of the stringent obligations of their enlistment.

As in most compromises, the terms of the neutrality compromise were differently interpreted by the parties, but with both the object was to gain time. The secessionists believed that neutrality, as they interpreted it, would educate the people to the idea of a separation from the Union and result in alliance with the new Confederacy; the Union men expected to gain time to organize their forces, elect a new legislature in sympathy with their views, and put the State decisively on the side of the Government. Events soon showed that the Union men best understood the temper of the people. The Legislature adjourned May 24th, four days after the governor had issued his neutrality proclamation. At the special congressional election, June 20th, nine Union representatives were chosen to one secessionist by an aggregate majority of over 54,000 votes. The legislative election in August resulted in the choice of a new body three-fourths of whose members in each house were Union men.

Under the first call for troops, Kentucky was required to furnish four regiments for the United States service. These Governor Magoffin indignantly refused to furnish. Shortly afterward he was asked by the Secretary of War of the Confederacy for a regiment. He declined this request as beyond his power to grant. His course did not suit the more ardent of the young men on either side. Blanton Duncan had already procured authority to recruit for the Confederacy, and in various portions of the State men were publicly engaged in raising companies for him. Before the end of April he had started with a regiment for Harper's Ferry by way of Nashville. An incident connected with this movement shows how strong the belief still was that the war was to be short, and that Kentucky might keep out of it. As Desha's company of Duncan's regiment was leaving Cynthiana, Ky., by rail, one of the privates said to a friend who was bidding him farewell: "Be sure to vote for Crittenden [then the Union candidate for delegate to the Border State Conference] and keep Kentucky out of the fuss. We are just going to Virginia on a little frolic and will be back in three months." On the other side, immediately after Magoffin's refusal to furnish troops, J. V. Guthrie, of Covington, went to Washington and got authority for himself and W. E. Woodruff, of Louisville, to raise two regiments. They established a camp just above Cincinnati, on the Ohio side of the river, and began recruiting in Kentucky. They soon filled two regiments, afterward known as the 1st and 2d Kentucky, which were sent early in July to take part in the West Virginia campaign.

The Union Club in Louisville was an important factor in organizing Union sentiment. Originating in May, in six weeks it numbered six thousand members in that city, and spread rapidly through the State and into East Tennessee. It was a secret society, the members of which were bound by an oath to be true to the flag and Government of the United States.

One of the most striking figures of the period was Lieutenant William Nelson of the navy. He was a man of heroic build, six feet four inches high, and carrying lightly his weight of three hundred pounds; he had many accomplishments, spoke several languages, and was endowed with a strong intellect and a memory which enabled him to repeat, verbatim, page after page of his favorite authors. A fluent and captivating talker, when he wished to please, no man could be more genial and companionable, but he had a quick and impetuous temper and an overbearing disposition, and when irritated or opposed was offensively dictatorial and dogmatic. A native of Kentucky and an ardent friend of the Union, he visited the State several times in the course of the spring to watch the course of events. As a result of his observations he reported to Mr. Lincoln that the arms of the State were in the hands of the secessionists, and that the Union men could not maintain themselves unless they were also furnished with arms. Mr. Lincoln placed at his disposal ten thousand muskets with means for their transportation. Toward the end of April he met in consultation at Frankfort a number of the leading Union men of the State and arranged for the distribution of the arms. When, shortly afterward, the organization of the Union Home Guards began, it was from this source they were armed. In Louisville, on the initiative of J. M. Delph, the Union mayor, a brigade of two full regiments and a battery were organized, which were destined to play a very useful part.

When the Legislature of which he was a member had finally adjourned, Lovell H. Rousseau went to Washington and obtained authority to recruit a brigade, and, in order to avoid possibly injurious effects on the approaching election, established his camp on the Indiana shore, opposite Louisville.

Nelson, after making arrangements for the distribution of guns to the Union men of the State, was authorized by the President to do a similar service for the Union men of East Tennessee, and for an escort was empowered to recruit three regiments of infantry and one of cavalry in eastern Kentucky. He selected his colonels, commissioning them "for the Tennessee expedition" and appointing a rendezvous at Hoskin's Cross Roads, in Garrard county, on the farm of Richard M. Robinson, a stanch Union man, for the day after the legislative elections in August.

During this period of neutrality Kentucky history seemed to be repeating itself. As before its occupation by white men it was common hunting-ground for the Indian of the North and of the South on which by tacit agreement neither was to make a permanent home, so now it had become the common recruiting-ground of Northern and Southern armies on which neither was to establish a camp. The Kentucky secessionists had opened a recruiting rendezvous near Clarksville, Tennessee, a few miles from the Kentucky border, which they called Camp Boone, and recruits began to gather there early in July. Buckner resigned from the State Guard a few days after the battle of Bull Run and soon took his way southward. His example was followed by most of the higher officers, and the State Guard began rapidly to disintegrate. It was no uncommon sight in Louisville, shortly after this, to see a squad of recruits for the Union service marching up one side of a street while a squad destined for the Confederacy was moving down the other. In the interior, a train bearing a company destined for Nelson's camp took aboard at the next county town another company which was bound for Camp Boone. The officers in charge made a treaty by which their men were kept in separate cars.

On the day after the August election Nelson's recruits began to gather at his rendezvous. Camp Dick Robinson was situated in a beautiful blue-grass country, near where the pike for Lancaster and Crab Orchard leaves the Lexington and Danville Pike, between Dick's River and the Kentucky. By September 1st, there had gathered at this point four full Kentucky regiments and nearly two thousand East Tennesseeans, who had been enlisted by Lieutenant S. P. Carter. This officer, like Nelson, belonging to the navy, was a native of East Tennessee, and it was part of the original plan of the East Tennessee expedition that he should enter that section and organize men to receive the arms that Nelson was to bring. This was found to be impracticable, and he opened his camp at Barboursville and the men began to come to him.

In August, W. T. Ward, a prominent lawyer of Greensburg, commenced recruiting a brigade and soon had twenty-two companies pledged to rendezvous when he should obtain the necessary authority from Washington. In Christian county, Colonel J. F. Buckner, a wealthy lawyer and planter, recruited a regiment from companies which organized originally as Home Guards, but soon determined to enter the volunteer service. He established a camp five miles north of Hopkinsville, where a few companies remained at a time. Christian county was strongly Unionist, while all the counties west of it were overwhelmingly secessionist. Camp Boone was only a few miles from its southern border, and Fort Donelson about twenty miles south-west. Colonel Buckner had a 6-pounder cannon, which could be heard at Camp Boone and made his vicinity additionally disagreeable to those neighbors.

The neutrality proclaimed by Governor Magoffin on the 20th of May had been formally recognized by the Confederate authorities and treated with respect by those of the United States, but it was destined to speedy termination. It served a useful purpose in its time, and a policy that had the respectful consideration of the leading men of that day could not have been so absurd as it seems now.

On the 3d of September General Polk, who was in command in western Tennessee, caused Columbus, Kentucky, to be occupied, on account of the appearance of a body of Union troops on the opposite side of the Mississippi. Hearing of this, on the 5th General Grant moved from Cairo and occupied Paducah. A few days afterward General Zollicoffer advanced with four Confederate regiments through Cumberland Gap to Cumberland Ford. The Union Legislature had met on the 2d. Resolutions were passed on the 11th requiring the governor to issue a proclamation ordering the Confederate troops to leave the State. They were promptly vetoed and promptly passed over the veto, and the proclamation was issued. In spite of the governor's opposition, acts were passed putting the State in active support of the Government. The governor was reduced to a nullity. General Robert Anderson, who was assigned on May 28th to command the Department of Kentucky, was invited to remove his headquarters to Louisville, and the State's full quota of volunteers were called for. Recruiting was pushed with energy, and by the end of the year 28 regiments of infantry, 6 of cavalry, and 3 batteries had been organized.

On September 15th General Albert Sidney Johnston assumed command of the Confederate forces in the West, and at once ordered General Buckner with five thousand men from Camp Boone and another camp in the vicinity to proceed by rail and occupy Bowling Green. Buckner reached that point early on the 18th, having sent in advance one detachment by rail to seize the bridge over Green River at Munfordville, and another to go as far as Elizabethtown and bring back all the rolling-stock possible. This was successfully accomplished, a part of the advance detachment going as far as the bridge over the Rolling Fork of Salt River, within thirty-three miles of Louisville, and burning the bridge.

Buckner's movement was supposed in Louisville to have that city for its objective, and great excitement prevailed there. Rumor magnified his forces, but there was abundant ground for apprehension without that. General Anderson was in command, but he was without troops. The only forces in his department in Kentucky were the unorganized regiment of Colonel Buckner near Hopkinsville, the few hundred recruits gathered at Greensburg by General Ward, and Nelson's forces at Camp Dick Robinson,—none of which were ready for service,—the Home Guard Brigade of Louisville, and the scattered companies of Home Guards throughout the State. Opposite Louisville was Rousseau's camp, in which were some two thousand men not yet prepared for the field. Very few troops were in reach. Owing to the neutrality of Kentucky, the regiments recruited in Ohio, Indiana, and the North-west generally had been sent as fast as organized to the Potomac or Missouri armies. Fortunately, Governor Oliver P. Morton, of Indiana, had received information, about the 1st, which had led him to reserve a few regiments for Kentucky, and in response to General Anderson's appeal he hurried them forward. Anderson had learned of Buckner's intended advance the day it was made, and the non-arrival of the regular train from the south showed him that it had begun. The Home Guards of Louisville were at once ordered out for ten days, and, assembling at midnight, eighteen hundred of them under Colonel A. Y. Johnson, Chief of the Fire Department, started by rail for Muldraugh's Hill. Rousseau, with twelve hundred men, followed in a few hours. The whole force was under Brigadier-General W. T. Sherman, who had shortly before, at Anderson's request, been assigned to duty with him. On arriving at Lebanon Junction Sherman learned that Rolling Fork Bridge, a few miles farther on, had just been destroyed. The Home Guards debarked at the junction, and Rousseau moved forward to the bridge, finding it still smoking. A reconnoissance in force, carried for some distance beyond the river, found no enemy, and the burning of the bridge indicated that no farther advance was intended immediately.

General Sherman's army was rather a motley crew. The Home Guards did not wear regulation uniforms, and Rousseau's men were not well equipped. Muldraugh's Hill had been occupied for six weeks or more during the summer by a regiment of the State Guard, and the people in the vicinity were generally in sympathy with the rebellion. Sherman's attention was attracted to a young man, without any uniform, who was moving around with what he considered suspicious activity, and called him up for question. The young fellow gave a prompt account of himself. His name was Griffiths, he was a medical student from Louisville acting as hospital steward, and he had been called out in such a hurry that he had had no time to get his uniform. As he moved away he muttered something in a low tone to an officer standing by, and Sherman at once demanded to know what it was, "Well, General," was the reply, "he said that a general with such a hat as you have on had no right to talk to him about a uniform." Sherman was wearing a battered hat of the style known as "stovepipe." Pulling it off, he looked at it, and, bursting into a laugh, called out: "Young man, you are right about the hat, but you ought to have your uniform."

On the 20th, the 38th Indiana (Colonel B. F. Scribner) arrived, and soon after four other regiments. Sherman moved forward to Elizabethtown, not finding any available position at Muldraugh's

William Tecumseh Sherman was chided by a recruit about his battered "stovepipe" hat.

Hill. A few days afterward, having on October 8th succeeded Anderson, who had been relieved by General Scott in these terms, "To give you rest necessary to restoration of health, call Brigadier-General Sherman to command the Department of the Cumberland," Sherman ordered Rousseau to advance along the railroad to Nolin, fifty-three miles from Louisville, and select a position for a large force.

While Sherman was at Elizabethtown, Buckner, with several thousand men, moved rapidly to Rochester, on Green River, and destroyed the locks there, and then moved against Colonel Buckner's camp near Hopkinsville. Warned of his approach, Colonel Buckner directed his men, who had not yet been regularly enrolled, to disperse and make their way to the Union camp near Owensboro. They succeeded, but Colonel Buckner himself was taken pris-

oner. Occupying Hopkinsville after a slight skirmish with the Home Guards, Buckner left a garrison there under General Alcorn and returned to Bowling Green.

Rousseau's advance to Nolin and the arrival of large reënforcements there induced Johnston to move his headquarters from Columbus to Bowling Green, and on October 15th he sent Hardee with 1200 men from that place against Ward at Greensburg, who, hearing of Hardee's approach, fell back with his recruits 20 miles to Campbellsville.

No material change in this position of affairs in western Kentucky occurred while General Sherman remained in command, though there were several sharp skirmishes between bodies of Kentucky recruits and Confederate scouting parties in the Lower Green River country.

Feliz K. Zollicoffer.

In the mean time the East Tennessee expedition was not progressing. Nelson, whose arbitrary temper had made him enemies among influential politicians, was sent to eastern Kentucky to superintend recruiting camps, and Brigadier-General George H. Thomas took command at Camp Dick Robinson. Thomas was an ardent advocate of the movement on East Tennessee and bent all his energies to getting ready for it, but his command was not half equipped and was wholly without transportation; staff-officers were scarce, and funds were not furnished. More patient than Nelson, he was yet greatly tried by the importunities of the East Tennessee troops, and of the prominent politicians from that region, who made his camp their rendezvous, as well as by military suggestions from civilians more zealous than wise in such matters. The speech-making of distinguished visitors became a burden to him. On one occasion, when General Sherman visited his camp, Ex-Senator J. J. Crittenden, Senator Andrew Johnson, and Horace Maynard were there. A band came from the camp to serenade them, and the soldiers, not yet rid of their civilian characteristics, began calling for speeches from one after another. Thomas withdrew from the orators to the seclusion of a little room used as an office, on one side of the piazza from which they were speaking. One of his aides was writing in a corner, but Thomas did not see him, and began striding up and down the floor in growing irritation. At last Sherman, who was not then such an orator as he is now, finished speaking, and cries arose for "Thomas." He blurted out, "——— —this speech-making! I won't speak! What does a man want to make a speech for, anyhow?" Observing that he had an auditor, he strode from the room slamming the door behind him, and kept his own quarters for the rest of the evening.

Accustomed to the discipline of the regular army, and fresh from the well-organized army of General Patterson on the upper Potomac, Thomas had little confidence in the raw recruits whom, for lack of a mustering officer, he mustered in himself. He was willing to advance into East Tennessee with half a dozen well-drilled regiments, and asked for and obtained them, but came without transportation, and he had none for them. While he was struggling to get ready for an advance, Zollicoffer had made several demonstrations, and to oppose him Garrard's regiment had been thrown forward to a strong position on Wild Cat Mountain just beyond Rockcastle River, supported by a detachment of Wolford's cavalry. On the 17th of October, Garrard reported that Zollicoffer was advancing in force, and asked for reënforcements. Thomas hurried forward several regiments under General Schoepf, who had reported to him shortly before. Schoepf arrived with the 33rd Indiana, in time to help in giving Zollicoffer, who had attacked vigorously with two regiments, a decisive repulse. Zollicoffer retired, apparently satisfied with developing Garrard's force, and Thomas moved Schoepf with Carter's East Tennesseeans and several other regiments forward in pursuit, till stopped by order of General Sherman, at London.

On the 12th of November, Sherman, having received information from his advance that a large force was moving between him and Thomas, apparently toward Lexington, ordered the latter to withdraw all his forces north of the Kentucky River. Making arrangements to obey, Thomas at the same time sent an officer to Sherman, urging the impolicy of the move unless absolutely necessary, and controverting the information on which it was based. The order was revoked, but the revocation did not reach Schoepf until his troops had begun the movement.

The East Tennessee regiments had received it with an indignation that carried them to the verge of mutiny. They threw their guns to the ground and swore they would not obey. Many actually left the command, though they returned in a few days. It required all of Carter's influence to keep them to their standards, and hundreds of them wept as they turned their backs on their homes. Andrew Johnson was with them, and his indignation had added fuel to their discontent. He was so indiscreet that Thomas seriously contemplated his arrest. On the revocation of the order Carter returned to London, while Schoepf took position soon after at Somerset.

In September Colonel John S. Williams had begun to gather a Confederate force at Prestonburg, in eastern Kentucky, threatening incursions into the central part of the State. On the 8th of November General Nelson, who had advanced against him with two Ohio and detachments of several Kentucky regiments, with a part of his force encountered a large detachment thrown forward by Williams to cover his retreat, in a strong position by Ivy Creek. After a well-contested engagement Williams was forced from his position, and retired through Pound Gap into Virginia. Nelson with the Ohio regiments was then ordered to join the column in front of Louisville, where he was assigned to command the Fourth Division. On this expedition Nelson reported as part of his force, "thirty-six gentlemen volunteers," probably the latest appearance in history of that description of soldier. One of them, of strong bibulous propensities, acting as his private secretary, brought about an altercation between Nelson and a wagoner nearly as large, which narrowly missed fatal results. He was anxious to get the driver away from his wagon in which there was a jug of whisky, and directed him to Nelson's tent to find a big fellow who was employed to unhitch teams for tired drivers. He warned him that the big fellow was cross, but told him he must insist on his rights. The driver was just tipsy enough to be reckless, and he roused Nelson with little ceremony. There was a terrible outburst of fury on both sides, which brought interference just in time to prevent a conflict between the two giants, one armed with a sword, and the other with a loaded whip-handle. The aide, not reporting next morning was, after some search, found sound asleep in a wagon with the jug beside him. He was a noted wag, and Nelson, recognizing him at once as the author of the trick, dismissed him to his home.

A visit from Secretary Cameron and Adjutant-General Lorenzo Thomas, on their return from St. Louis in the latter part of October, resulted in the removal of General Sherman. In explaining the needs of his department to the Secretary, Sherman expressed the opinion that two hundred thousand men would be required for successful operations on his line. This estimate, which, as events showed, evinced remarkable foresight, then discredited his judgment. On their way to St. Louis, on the same tour, the Secretary had ordered General O. M.

Mitchel to take charge of the East Tennessee expedition, superseding General Thomas, but General Sherman succeeded in having the order recalled.

On November 15th, General Don Carlos Buell assumed command of the Department of the Ohio, enlarged so as to include the States of Ohio, Michigan, and Indiana. He was given the advantage, not enjoyed by his predecessors, of controlling the new troops organized in those States. By one of his first orders, General Thomas was directed to concentrate his command at Lebanon. The new commander began at once the task of creating an efficient army out of the raw material at hand. He organized the regiments into brigades and divisions, and subjected them to a system of drill and discipline the beneficial effects of which endured throughout the war.

The advance into East Tennessee remained a favorite project with the authorities at Washington. Buell's instructions presented Knoxville as the objective of his first campaign. McClellan wrote several times urging that the seizing of the East Tennessee and Virginia railroad was essential to the success of his plans, and that the political results likely to follow success in that direction made the movement of the first importance. Buell did not consider East Tennessee important enough to be his principal objective; he wanted it to be a subordinate feature in a great campaign. He submitted his plans to McClellan in a personal letter. They were comprehensive and required a large force, and it was already seen that Sherman's estimate was not so far out of the way. Buell proposed that a heavy column should be moved up the Tennessee and Cumberland rivers by steamer, to unite with another moving on Nashville, to the eastward of Bowling Green. Demonstrations were to be made in front of Columbus and Bowling Green, sufficient to keep the forces holding them fully occupied until their retreat was cut off by the marching columns. At the same time an expedition from Lebanon, moving by way of Somerset, was to be directed against East Tennessee. Until he was ready to move, he desired to do nothing to put the enemy on the alert. His brigades and regiments were allowed to remain in apparently objectless dispersion. He did not care if some isolated posts were occasionally raided by the enemy. But his regiments were frequently inspected and required to keep constantly ready for a movement the day and hour of which he proposed to keep to himself. The notion that Buckner or Zollicoffer contemplated an advance, which so frequently agitated the military mind before he came, was dismissed by him as idle. "I would as soon," he wrote to McClellan, "expect to meet the Army of the Potomac marching up the road, as Johnston."

His policy of quiet had to be laid aside when, early in December, Morgan and Helm burned the Bacon Creek bridge in his front. He advanced his lines to Munfordville and threw forward a small force beyond Green River. This resulted in a skirmish between a portion of the 32d Indiana, deployed as skirmishers, and Terry's Texas Cavalry—notable as one of the few fights of the war between infantry skirmishers in the open and cavalry.

Nothing else of moment occurred on Buell's main line until the capture of Forts Henry and Donelson compelled Johnston to retire from Bowling Green and leave the road to Nashville open. During November Buell reviewed Thomas's command at Lebanon, and advised with him about an attack on Zollicoffer, who to meet a rumored advance had left Cumberland Gap in charge of a strong garrison, had made his appearance on the Cumberland at Mill Springs, a few miles south-west of Somerset, had crossed the river, and after some picket-firing with Schoepf had intrenched himself on the north side.

General Thomas left Lebanon on the 1st of January. As far as Columbia there was a good turnpike; beyond, only mud roads. It rained incessantly, and artillery carriages and wagons sank to their axles in the soft soil. On one part of the route eight days were consumed in advancing forty miles.

On the 17th of January Thomas reached Logan's Cross Roads, ten miles north of Zollicoffer's intrenched camp (on the north side of the Cumberland, opposite Mill Springs) and about the same distance west of Somerset, with the 9th Ohio and 2d Minnesota of Robert L. McCook's brigade, the 10th Indiana of Manson's brigade, Kenny's battery, and a battalion of Wolford's cavalry. The 4th Kentucky, 10th Kentucky, the 14th Ohio, Wetmore's battery, and the 18th regulars were still detained in the rear by bad roads. Halting at the cross roads, Thomas communicated with Schoepf and ordered him to send across Fishing Creek to his camp the 12th Kentucky, the 1st and 2d East Tennessee regiments, and Standart's battery, to remain until the arrival of his delayed force. Hearing that a large wagon train, sent on a foraging expedition by Zollicoffer, was on a road about six miles from the camp of Steedman, of the 14th Ohio, he ordered that officer to take his own regiment and Harlan's 10th Kentucky and attempt its capture. On the evening of the 18th the 4th Kentucky, the battalion of Michigan Engineers, and the battery arrived and went into camp near the 10th Indiana.

THE BATTLE OF LOGAN'S CROSS ROADS (MILL SPRINGS)

A few days before this General George B. Crittenden had arrived at Zollicoffer's camp and assumed command. Hearing of the arrival of Thomas with part of his command, and believing that Fishing Creek, which was a troublesome stream at any stage of water, was unfordable from recent rains, he called a council of his brigade and regimental commanders to consider the propriety of making an attack on Thomas before he could be reached by Schoepf or his regiments in the year. There was little delay in coming to a decision. Their camp on the north side of the river was not tenable against a strong attack, and the means of crossing the river were so insufficient that a withdrawal without great loss could not have been effected, in the face of an enterprising enemy. The only chance for a satisfactory issue was to attack Thomas before he could concentrate. Crittenden ordered a movement to begin at midnight on the 18th in the following order: General Zollicoffer's brigade, consisting of two cavalry companies, a Mississippi regiment, three Tennessee regiments, and a battery in front; next, the brigade of General Carroll, composed of three Tennessee regiments and a section of artillery. An Alabama regiment and two cavalry regiments, intended as a reserve, closed the column. After a march of nine miles over muddy roads and through the rain, his cavalry about daylight encountered Wolford's pickets, who after firing fell back on the reserve, consisting of two companies of the 10th Indiana, and with them made a determined stand, in which they were promptly supported by Wolford with the rest of his battalion, and soon after by the rest of the 10th Indiana, ordered up by Manson, who had been advised by courier from Wolford of the attack. Colonel Manson proceeded in person to order forward the 4th Kentucky and the battery of his brigade and to report to General Thomas. On his way he notified Colonel Van Cleve, of the 2d Minnesota. As Manson dashed through the camp of the 4th Kentucky shouting for Colonel Speed S. Fry, and giving warning of the attack, the men, wearied with the muddy march of the day before, were just beginning to crawl out of their tents to roll-call. Forming rapidly, Fry led them at double-quick in the direction of the firing. Having no one to place him, on coming in sight of the enemy, he took position along a fence in the edge of the woods, with his right resting near the Mill Springs road. In front of him was an open field, across which the enemy were advancing from the shelter of woodland on the opposite side. A ravine ran through the open field parallel to Fry's front, heading near the road on his right, with steep sides in his front, but sloping gradually beyond his left. Before Fry's arrival Zollicoffer had deployed his brigade, and had forced Wolford and the 10th Indiana to fall back, almost capturing the horses of Wolford's men, who were fighting on foot. A portion of Wolford's command, under his immediate charge, and Vanarsdall's company of the 10th Indiana, rallied on the 4th Kentucky when it appeared, the remainder of the 10th falling back to its encampment, where it re-formed its lines. Fry was at once subjected to a severe attack. The enemy in his front crawled up under shelter of the ravine to within a short distance of his lines before delivering their fire, and Fry, mounting the fence, in stentorian tones denounced them as dastards, and defied them to stand up on their feet and come forward like men.

A little lull in the firing occurring at this juncture, Fry rode a short distance to the right to get a better view of the movement of the enemy in that direction. The morning was a lowering one, and the woods were full of smoke. As Fry turned to regain his position he encountered a mounted officer whose uniform was covered with a water-proof coat. After approaching till their knees touched, the stranger said to Fry: "We must not fire on our own men"; and nodding his head to his left, he said, "Those are our men." Fry said, "Of course not. I would not do so intentionally"; and he began to move toward his regiment, when turning he saw another mounted man riding from the trees who fired and wounded Fry's horse. Fry at once fired on the man who had accosted him, and several of his men, observing the incident, fired at the same time. The shots were fatal, and the horseman fell dead, pierced by a pistol-shot in his breast and by two musket-balls. It was soon ascertained that it was Zollicoffer himself who had fallen. In the mean time, the enemy were pressing Fry in front and overlapping his right. On his right front only the fence separated the combatants. The left of his regiment not being assailed, he moved two companies from that flank to his right. As he was making this change General Thomas appeared on the field, and at once placed the 10th Indiana in position to cover Fry's exposed flank.

The fall of Zollicoffer and the sharp firing that followed caused two of his regiments to retreat in confusion. Crittenden then brought up Carroll's brigade to the support of the other two, and ordered a general advance. Thomas met this by placing a section of Kenny's battery on the left of the 4th Kentucky, which was overlapped by Carroll's line, ordered the 12th Kentucky to the left of Kenny's two guns, and Carter with the two East Tennessee regiments, and Wetmore's battery still farther to the left, in front of the Somerset road. Standart's battery and Kenny's remaining guns were held in the rear of the center, and McCook's two regiments were ordered up, the 9th Ohio on the right of the 10th Indiana, and the 2d Minnesota in reserve behind the latter regiment and the 4th Kentucky. During these movements Kenny's section was so threatened that it was withdrawn some distance to the rear. There was little opportunity for the effective use of artillery on either side, and that arm played an insignificant part in the engagement, Thomas's superiority in that particular availing him little. Carroll's attack was pressed with great courage, and the ammunition of the 4th Kentucky and 10th Indiana beginning to fail, the 2d Minnesota was ordered to relieve them, which it did under severe fire. Both of McCook's regiments were admirably drilled and disciplined, and moved to the attack with the order and steadiness of veterans. Thomas's disposition of his troops had begun to tell. The advance of the 12th Kentucky on the left, the firing of Wetmore's battery, and the movement of Carter's East Tennesseeans checked the enemy's right, and it soon began to give back. The 2d Minnesota was slowly pushing forward over the ground that had been the scene of the most persistent fighting from the first, and the 9th Ohio, on the right, was forcing back the enemy through open ground, when, slightly changing direction, it made a bayonet charge against the enemy's left, which gave way in confusion. Their whole line then broke into a disorderly retreat. After replenishing

At Logan's Crossroads, General Thomas commanded the Federal troops.

The body of Zollicoffer is conveyed from the field at Mill Spring.

cartridge-boxes, Thomas pushed forward in pursuit. Within a few miles, a small body of the enemy's cavalry attempted to make a stand, but were scattered by a few shells from Standart. The road which the retreating force followed was strewn with evidences that the retreat had degenerated into a panic. A piece of artillery was found abandoned in a mud hole, hundreds of muskets were strewn along the road and in the fields, and, most convincing proof of all, the flying foe had thrown away their haversacks filled with rations of corn pone and bacon. Those were the days when stories of "rebel atrocities" in the way of poisoning wells and food were current, and the pursuers, who had gone into the fight breakfastless, were doubtful about tasting the contents of the first haversacks they observed. Their great number, however, soon became a guarantee of good faith, and the hungry soldiers seized on them with avidity. As Crittenden in his report mentioned the loss of all the cooked rations carried to the field as enhancing the distress of his subsequent retreat, the abundance of the supply obtained by the pursuing force may be inferred. On arriving near the enemy's intrenchments the division was deployed in line of battle, advancing to the summit of the hill at Moulden's, which commanded the enemy's intrenchments. From this point Standart and Wetmore's batteries kept up a cannonade till dark, while Kenny's on the left, at Russell's house, fired upon their ferry to keep them from crossing. The 14th Ohio and the 10th Kentucky had come up during the pursuit, and were placed in advance for the assault ordered for daybreak. General Schoepf arrived about dark with the 17th, 31st, and 38th Ohio.

At daybreak next morning Wetmore's Parrott guns, which had been moved to Russell's, began firing on the steamer which was evidently engaged in crossing troops, and it was soon abandoned and set on fire by the enemy. The assaulting columns moved forward, the 10th Kentucky and the 14th Ohio in advance, and reaching the intrenchments found them abandoned. In the bottom near the ferry-crossing were found 11 pieces of artillery, with their caissons, battery-wagons, and forges, hitched up and ready to move but abandoned by the artillerymen, more than 150 wagons, and over 1000 horses and mules. All the troops had escaped. The steep road on the other bank was strewn with abandoned baggage and other evidences of disorderly flight. The boats used for crossing having been destroyed by the retreating enemy, no immediate pursuit was possible; but during the day means were improvised for getting the 14th Ohio across for a reconnoissance and to secure abandoned property.

Thomas reported his loss in action as 39 killed and 207 wounded, the casualties being confined entirely to the 10th Indiana, 4th Kentucky, 2d Minnesota, 9th Ohio, and Wolford's cavalry. Colonels McCook and Fry were among the wounded. The enemy's loss he reported as 192 killed, 89 prisoners not wounded, and 68 prisoners wounded. Crittenden's report stated his own loss at 125 killed, 309 wounded, and 99 missing, much the heaviest loss being in the 15th Mississippi (Lieutenant-Colonel E. C. Walthall), of Zollicoffer's brigade, which had led the attack on Fry and fought through the whole engagement.

Besides the property mentioned above, a large amount of ammunition, commissary stores, intrenching tools, camp and garrison equipage and muskets, and five stands of colors were found in the camp. The demoralization was acknowledged by Crittenden in his report, in which he says: "From Mill Springs and on the first steps of my march officers and men, frightened by false rumors of the movements of the enemy, shamefully deserted, and, stealing horses and mules to ride, fled to Knoxville, Nashville, and other places in Tennessee." Of one cavalry battalion, he reported that all had deserted except twenty-five. On his retreat his sick-list increased greatly from lack of food and fatigue, and the effective force of his army was practically destroyed.

After entrance into his intrenchments had demonstrated the panic that existed in the enemy's forces, Fry said to Thomas: "General, why didn't you send in a demand for surrender last night?" Looking at him a moment as if reflecting, Thomas replied: "Hang it, Fry, I never once thought of it." At this time originated a saying often heard in the Western army afterward. A sprightly young prisoner slightly wounded was allowed the freedom of the camp. To some soldiers chaffing him about his army being in such a hurry as even to throw away their haversacks, he replied: "Well, we were doing pretty good fighting till old man Thomas rose up in his stirrups, and we heard him holler out: 'Attention, Creation! By kingdoms right wheel!' and then we knew you had us, and it was no time to carry weight."

Thomas's victory was complete, and the road was opened for advance into East Tennessee which he had so long endeavored to make and which was contemplated by his instructions, but the scarcity of provisions, the badness of the roads, and the difficulty of crossing the river made progress on that line impracticable, and shortly afterward Carter was ordered with his brigade against Cumberland Gap and Thomas to rejoin Buell's main column, and the East Tennessee expedition, which Nelson had devised and McClellan had strongly urged and Thomas had labored so to put in motion, was definitively abandoned.

While Thomas was marching against Zollicoffer, Colonel Garfield was driving Humphrey Marshall from the mountainous region along the Virginia border. With Marshall's retreat the last Confederate force was driven from the State, and Garfield with his brigade joined the army in Tennessee.

General George H. Thomas forced the Confederates out of Kentucky.

VI

THE FIRST WINTER

BULL RUN CONVINCED EVERYONE THAT THE WAR WAS NOT GOING TO BE OVER IN SIXTY days. Military preparations, already seemingly at fever pitch, were pressed with renewed vigor. It was a remarkable demonstration of will by both sides. Where at the beginning of 1861 the old Regular Army amounted to but 16,367 officers and men, by 1 July, on the eve of Bull Run, there were already nearly 300,000 under arms, both North (186,751) and South (112,040), a figure more than tripled by year's end, when not quite a million were enrolled, 575,917 in the Union ranks and 351,418 in those of the Confederacy. Bull Run had proven that the volunteers and militiamen who made up the new armies would fight, but it had also shown that they were not yet soldiers. Only time could make the farm boys and factory hands and office clerks into soldiers. So as the summer of 1861 turned into autumn and the autumn into winter, there was relatively little fighting but much marching and drilling as the troops acquired the skills of war.

★★★

GEORGE B. McCLELLAN

The Creation of the Army of the Potomac

George B. McClellan's success in West Virginia confirmed the high opinion in which he was held by General-in-Chief Winfield Scott, a brilliant but aged veteran of the War of 1812 and that with Mexico. At Scott's urging, Lincoln called McClellan to Washington and entrusted him with the organization of the defenses of the capital and of the principal army of the Republic. McClellan, a talented, indefatigable organizer, threw himself into the work with considerable skill and energy. He did his job well, but did not always agree with Scott, nor was he inclined to share the limelight with his aged superior. The following excerpts from Mc-

Clellan's Own Story (New York, 1887) give a good idea of the problems which had to be dealt with and the work that was necessary before the mass of raw manpower in the many camps around Washington could be turned into an army, as well as some idea of the unusual character of the armies being raised. McClellan's experience that autumn and winter were similar to those of General Joseph Johnston, his Confederate counterpart, who was also trying to whip an ill-disciplined, untrained mass of men into an army, not too many miles away in Northern Virginia.

At this juncture it would have been wise to adopt a definite policy with regard to the regular army— viz., either virtually break it up, as a temporary measure, and distribute its members among the staff and regiments of the volunteer organization, thus giving the volunteers all possible benefit from the discipline and instruction of the regulars, or to fill the regular regiments to their full capacity and employ them as a reserve at critical junctures. I could not secure the adoption of either plan, and a middle course was followed which resulted less favorably than either of the plans indicated; but it must be said that, even as things were, the regulars were in every way of immense benefit to the service. As a general rule the officers (and, of course, the non-commissioned officers) of the volunteer regiments were entirely ignorant of their duties, and many were unfitted, from their education, moral character, or mental deficiences, for ever acquiring the requisite efficiency.

These latter were weeded out by courts-martial and boards of examination, while the others were instructed *pari passu* as they instructed their men. The small number of regular officers available rendered it impossible to furnish all the staff officers from among them; so that a regiment was very fortunate if its colonel was a regular officer, and a brigade was lucky to have a regular as its commander. The generals were usually, and colonels always, obliged to appoint their staff officers from civil life, and instruct them as best they could. It speaks wonders for the intelligence and military aptitude of our people that so much was well done in this way on both sides. Many of these raw civilians, who were men of pride, intelligence, and education, soon became excellent officers; though these very men most keenly regretted their lack of a good military education in early life.

The frequent reviews I held at Washington were not at all for the benefit of the public, nor yet for the purpose of examining the individual condition of the men, although I did much of that even on these occasions—for a general with a quick eye can see things when riding at a gallop which would seem impossible to a civilian. But they were to accustom the regiments to move together and see each other, to give the troops an idea of their own strength, to infuse *esprit de corps* and mutual emulation, and to acquaint myself with the capacity of the general officers. These reviews also had a good effect in accustoming the troops to see me, although they saw so much of me in their camps and on the picket-lines that this was of minor importance. With new troops frequent reviews are of the greatest utility and produce the most excellent effect. Those I held did much towards making the Army of the Potomac what it became. Some persons, who ought to have known better, have supposed that in organizing the Army of the Potomac I set too high a model before me and consumed unnecessary time in striving to form any army of regulars. This was an unjustifiable error on their part. I should, of course, have been glad to bring that army to the condition of regulars, but no one knew better than myself that, with the means at my command, that would have been impossible within any reasonable or permissible time.

What I strove for and accomplished was to bring about such a condition of discipline and instruction that the army could be handled on the march and on the field of battle, and that orders could be reasonably well carried out. No one cognizant of the circumstances and possessed of any knowledge of military affairs can honestly believe that I bestowed unnecessary time and labor upon the organization and instruction of that army whose courage, discipline, and efficiency finally brought the war to a close.

In spite of all the clamor to the contrary, the time spent in the camps of instruction in front of Washington was well bestowed, and produced the most important and valuable results. Not a day of it was wasted. The fortifications then erected, both directly and indirectly, saved the capital more than once in the course of the war, and enabled the army to manœuvre freely and independently. The organization and discipline then acquired, and so much improved during the campaign of the Peninsula which converted the men into veterans, enabled the army to pass gloriously through the many sanguinary conflicts and harassing campaigns that proved necessary to terminate the war. They learned to gain victories and to withstand defeat. No other army we possessed could have met and defeated the Confederate Army of Northern Virginia. And, with all the courage, energy, and intelligence of the Army of the Potomac, it probably would not have been equal to that most difficult task without the advantage it enjoyed during its sojourn in the camps around Washington. . . .

A few days after reaching Washington Gen. Scott asked me what I intended to do in the way of organization. I replied that I wished the force under my command to be organized as and denominated an army instead of a geographical division; that I should first form brigades, then divisions, and, when in the field, army corps. My reason for postponing the formation of the latter was that with untried general officers it would be too dangerous an experiment to appoint any to such high and important commands without first proving them in actual campaign and in battle.

He objected to all I proposed, save the brigade formation, saying that under our system and regulations it would be impossible to administer the affairs of an "army," and that the retention of the system and nomenclature of geographical divisions and departments was an absolute necessity; he also objected to the formation of divisions as unnecessary, for the reason that in Mexico he had only brigades.

I called to his attention the fact that, all the world over, fighting forces were organized as armies; that I had done so in West Virginia; and that his force in Mexico was a very small affair in comparison with that soon to be collected in front of Washington. He did not change his views. So I quietly went to work in my own way. The result was that on the 20th of Aug. the order constituting the Army of the Potomac was issued; and in addition to the two departments originally under my command, the troops in the Shenandoah, Maryland, and Delaware were also included in the Army of the Potomac, the old departments being broken up and merged in the newly created army. Thus I had command of all the troops on the line of the Potomac and as far to the rear as Baltimore and Fort Delaware.

I intended to compose each division of three infantry brigades of four regiments each, four batteries, and one regiment of cavalry, which would have given a nominal strength of 12,000 infantry, 1,000 cavalry, and 24 guns, or an effective of about 10,000 infantry, 700 cavalry, and 24 guns. It was determined to collect whatever regular infantry could be obtained to form the nucleus of a reserve.

President Lincoln reviews the troops in Washington with members of his cabinet.

The measures taken from recruiting these regiments were so insuficient and the results so meagre that as late as the 30th of April, 1862, there were only 4,600 men in the 71 companies, regular infantry, on duty with the Army of the Potomac. These, together with the 5th and 10th N.Y. Volunteers, finally formed part of the 5th corps as a division under Brig.-Gen. Sykes, 3d U.S. Infantry.

The creation of an adequate artillery establishment for an army of so large proportions was a formidable undertaking; and had it not been that the country possessed in the regular service a body of accomplished and energetic artillery officers, the task would have been almost hopeless.

The charge of organizing this most important arm was confided to Maj. (afterwards Brig.-Gen.) William F. Barry, chief of artillery, whose industry and zeal achieved the best results. The following principles were adopted as the basis of organization:

During the autumn of 1861 . . . I spent my days chiefly in the saddle, rarely returning from my rides until late at night. Most of the night and the morning hours were given up to office-work.

Of course I rode everywhere and saw everything.

Not an entrenchment was commenced unless I had at least approved its site; many I located myself. Not a camp that I did not examine, not a picket-line that I did not visit and cross, so that almost every man in the army saw me at one time or another, and most of them became familiar with my face. And there was no part of the ground near Washington that I did not know thoroughly.

The most entertaining of my duties were those which sometimes led me to Blenker's camp, whither Franklin was always glad to accompany me to see the "circus," or "opera," as he usually called the performance. As soon as we were sighted Blenker would have the "officer's call" blown to assemble his polyglot collection, with their uniforms as varied and brilliant as the colors of the rainbow. Wrapped in his scarlet-lined cloak, his group of officers ranged around him, he would receive us with the most formal and polished courtesy. Being a very handsome and soldierly-looking man himself, and there being many equally so among his surroundings, the tableau was always very effective, and presented a striking contrast to the matter-of-fact way in which things were managed in the other divisions.

In a few minutes he would shout, *"Ordinans numero cins!"* whereupon champagne would be brought in great profusion, the bands would play, sometimes songs be sung. It was said, I know not how truly, that Blenker had been a non-commissioned officer in the German contingent serving under King Otho of Greece.

His division was very peculiar. So far as "the pride, pomp, and circumstance of glorious war" were concerned, it certainly outshone all the others. Their drill and bearing were also excellent; for all the officers, and probably all the men, had served in Europe. I have always regretted that the division was finally taken from me and sent to Fremont. The officers and men were all strongly attached to me; I could control them as no one else could, and they

would have done good service had they remained in Sumner's corps. The regiments were all foreign and mostly of Germans; but the most remarkable of all was the Garibaldi regiment. Its colonel, D'Utassy, was a Hungarian, and was said to have been a rider in Franconi's Circus, and terminated his public American career in the Albany Penitentiary. His men were from all known and unknown lands, from all possible and impossible armies: Zouaves from Algiers, men of the "Foreign Legion," Zephyrs, Cossacks, Garibaldians of the deepest dye, English deserters, Sepoys, Turcos, Croats, Swiss, beer drinkers from Bavaria, stout men from North Germany, and no doubt Chinese, Esquimaux, and detachments from the army of the Grand Duchess of Gerolstein.

★★★

JOHN N. OPIE
Relieving the Monotony of Camp Life

John N. Opie, the youthful Virginia volunteer who wrote "Joining the Army," found soldiering an agreeable career, and certainly better than analytical geometry. But it was boring, despite, or perhaps because of, training, drill, and fatigue duty, particularly during the winter. Like

many a soldier before and since, Opie and his comrades found ways to pass the time, as can be seen in this excerpt from his A Rebel Cavalryman with Lee, Stuart, and Jackson *(Chicago, 1899).*

Nothing of a military nature worth relating happened this fall, the time spent in camp being dull and monotonous. At night I generally obtained the countersign by establishing a post of my own, or by wedging in between two sentinels when their backs were turned. A piece of chalk made good imitation shoulder straps, which could not be easily distinguished at night; then all that remained was to obtain the sword of some officer, and there was a full-fledged lieutenant—sword, shoulder-straps, and countersign. The objective point, Winchester; the attraction, the beautiful girls of the town. There was much dancing and love-making; but when it came to asking pa or ma we sought other worlds to conquer, as we were too young to seriously contemplate matrimony. On one occasion, three of us agreed to address simultaneously three ladies of our acquaintance, two of whom were old maids and the other a young girl about sixteen. We drew lots for choice, and called on the ladies, and each one of us proceeded to make love to the lady who had fallen to this lot. The old maids were highly incensed, and left the room, but the young girl, being unsuspect-

ing, replied that she would "ask ma." We three young rascals soon left in disorder, never to return.

Almost all soldiers are great scamps, and most of them are fond of whiskey; and the following was the manner in which they obtained it in Winchester: General Jackson was a most devout Christian, a Presbyterian of the strictest sect, and detested liquor. The old fellow thought that he had made it impossible to procure it. It was only sold at the drugstores, upon the order or prescription of a surgeon, countersigned by the colonel of a regiment, and general of brigade. A soldier wrote an order or prescription for a pint, quart, or gallon, as the thirst required, to which he signed the surgeon's name, another signed the colonel's, and still another that of General Garnett, the brigade commander; then one of the boys, representing a hospital clerk, went to a drugstore in the town, and soon produced the pain-killer.

On one occasion, we were not compelled to go through this red-tape performance. Our company officers received from home three kegs of fine old rye, and invited the other officers of the regiment to their tent to partake with them. We were not ex-

Troops find diversions in Sutler's Store in Harpers Ferry.

pected, and, consequently, were offended. Securing two tin buckets, we went to the rear of the tent, which was crowded with officers, who were compelled to stand up for the want of space. We pulled up two or three tent pins, rolled out a keg, filled our two buckets with the old rye, and then rolled back

the keg, and replaced the tent pins. We then made a campfire that resembled Vesuvius, and raised Cain; but, as the officers of the regiment were engaged in the same meritorious business, we escaped punishment. The next morning, the regimental colors were found lashed to the tallest tree in the camp.

While we were in this camp, I witnessed a very amusing incident. Not far from our camp was a flour-mill, about which was a large dam. On this occasion, I saw an Irishman seated on the ground, smoking his pipe and arranging the cartridges in his box. Presently, having fixed the cartridges to his satisfaction, he arose, and, pushing his cartridge box back into place, started to walk away. When he had gotten about fifty yards from the dam, there was an explosion in his rear. The astounded man looked around in all directions, to ascertain from whence it came, when another explosion occurred, whereupon he realized that his cartridge box was on fire; and, instead of unbuckling his belt and dropping it, he made for the mill dam, leaping high in the air at every explosion, until, finally, reaching the bank, he made one terrific plunge and disappeared beneath the surface of the water. Finally he reappeared upon the surface and I assisted him to the shore. I had hysterics for a week.

⭐⭐⭐

BÉLA ESTVÁN
A Christmas Story

Béla Estván (see "A Troublesome Regiment") spent the winter of 1861–1862 in West Virginia. Here, an excerpt from his War Pictures *from the South (New York, 1863) tells something about the tragedy of war and the common humanity of man.*

On the 23d December, 1861, I rode back, after inspecting the outposts of our division of the Confederate army. It was a cold, dreary day; the snow fell in heavy flakes, so that my cloak soon had the appearance of ermine. Silently I rode along the banks of the New River, and the stillness around only seemed to make more audible the roar of the waters as they splashed over the rocks in the stream.

No joyous shout greeted me from the camp; none of the gay excitement of a soldier's life was visible. A few groups might be seen sitting silently and musingly round their watch fires, worn out and careless at what was going on or of what might happen next: most of the men were in their huts, and everything appeared cold and cheerless. Why so? Our proud hopes of victory were for the moment at an end; we were compelled to give way before the all-powerful enemy; we were beating a retreat—and the retreat of

an army, even if performed in the best order, has, as every soldier who has been at the wars well knows, something discouraging in it. Winter added to the dreariness. Here, in cold and snow, were encamped the sons of those Southern districts, where the sun is always bright and warm; where the green meadows are never covered with snow or ice. Some cast dreary looks at the summit of Hawk's Nest, where the once beloved, now hostile banner of the Republic of the United States unfolded its stars to the wind. Many joyful reminiscences of home and former times were awakened in the breasts of the soldiers on beholding the flag, under whose powerful protection their own section of the community had also grown great and prosperous and they themselves had lived in comfort. Tattered and hungry lay encamped the sons of the South, here, in Western Virginia, deprived of their former prosperity and

West Virginia Cavalry takes a break.

content, lying on the hard ground with their rifles by their side, eager to aid in lowering that flag for which their forefathers had shed streams of blood, perhaps to become, instead of free citizens, the subjects of some foreign adventurer or native despot.

My mind also was disturbed by these sad reflections; but a soldier's heart must not brood over sorrow, and I urged my horse to a quicker pace along the river side to rejoin my regiment. The dark night and the roaring stream were not congenial to lively thoughts; in vain did I endeavor to recall the happy dreams of my youth: they were dispelled by darker thoughts more in keeping with the shades of the night. How could it be otherwise? It was now thirteen years that I had been away from my native home, and now, drawn into the whirlpool of events, I found myself, almost against my will, serving in the ranks of a foreign army, and fighting for a cause with which neither my head nor heart could thoroughly sympathize.

Occupied with these rather depressing reflections, I reached my tent. I threw off my cloak and sat down by the fire; nature claimed her rights, and, with a physical enjoyment which for a moment set aside mental annoyance, I warmed myself at the glowing embers.

Suddenly I heard the voice of a friend calling out my name. It was General Henningsen, who soon joined me. "Here," he said, "are despatches for the Secretary of War, and which must be taken by a trustworthy hand immediately to Richmond. Will

you take them?" I jumped up at once, ordered a fresh horse to be saddled, shook the General warmly by the hand, and, accompanied by an orderly, set out on my mission. "Keep a sharp lookout," shouted Henningsen after me, for he knew I had resolved to take the shortest road, through a defile which might probably be occupied by the enemy. A few shots, indeed, were fired at me from the heights; but, happily, owing to the darkness of the night, they missed their mark, and once through the pass we were safe.

It was only on the evening of the following day that I reached the little town of Petersburg. What a contrast it offered to the monotonous life in camp! Cheerful-looking houses, with well-lit shops, and busy people going to and fro, making purchases or looking in at the shop windows. Merry children, with their parents, buying Christmas gifts.

My path now took me through a dark street, where I was suddenly brought to a standstill. It was blocked up by a detachment of soldiers.

"What's the matter here?" I shouted; "why do you stop up the road?" "We are waiting for a sure conveyance," was the reply, "to send these d——— Yankees on to Salisbury, as they cannot march any farther."

I hastily got off my horse, ordered my orderly lancer to see the horses properly attended to, and accosted the prisoners. Here I found men of every nation, as is common in some regiments of the United States army. Germans, Poles, Hungarians, Frenchmen, Italians, and Irishmen were all mixed up together, each, in his own tongue, trying to describe his misfortunes, and beseeching my assistance. Many of the poor fellows lay wounded and footsore on the ground. It made my heart bleed to see them. What a contrast was this scene of misery to the gay shops of the town! What a Christmas Eve!

With a round English oath, I asked the officer in command of the detachment why he did not get shelter for his prisoners for this one night, at least. He answered insolently, "That the vile dogs were not worth the trouble."

Convinced that if I was to give a distinct order it would wholly fail of effect upon so coarse a nature, and that the brutal officer would have found a hundred pretexts not to provide a shelter, I went myself in search of one, and succeeded in getting the large outhouses at the railway station arranged as best I could; and I then ordered the lieutenant to follow me with his men.

The prisoners, who numbered about 120 men, now lay down on benches and dry sacks, sheltered, at least, by walls, from the inclemency of the night. Good fires were lit, and the railway authorities sent in food for the hungry men. I gave twenty-five dollars to two subalterns, and sent them into the town for rum, sugar, and lemons, and the courage of the poor fellows gradually revived as the hope of better days dawned within them. On my taking leave they gave me hearty cheer.

I remounted my horse, and was off for Richmond. I had spent my Christmas Eve!

Here I must be allowed to anticipate events, by introducing an incident that some time after pleasantly recalled this Christmas Eve to my mind.

Months had passed. Heaven had protected me. I had escaped without harm from the many sanguinary engagements which, as we shall see by and by, took place in the first half of 1862, when I was suddenly attacked by the yellow fever in the swampy ricefields of Savannah. With death in my heart, I had myself conveyed to Richmond for medical advice. The doctors were not wanting in good counsel; but the apothecaries' stores were exhausted. By the advice of my physician, I asked for leave and a free pass to the North, where the change of climate might restore me to health. This being granted, I reached the outposts of the Union without difficulty, and received a hearty welcome from the general in command, who allowed me to continue my journey to New York unmolested. In fact, what was there to fear from a man who was more dead than alive?

I regained my health, nevertheless, in a wonderfully short time; and going down the railway one day, in 6th Avenue, New York, with a friend, I was suddenly addressed by a soldier with only one arm, with the question: "Are you not a colonel in the Confederate army?" "Yes, yes," I replied, hastily, fancying he wished to pick a quarrel with me, and seek revenge for his lost limb. "Well, then, Colonel," he said, "I am happy that I still have one hand left thankfully to shake yours, for I am one of the prisoners for whom you provided a never-to-be-forgotten Christmas Eve at Petersburg."

★★★

ETHEL LYNN BEERS
All Quiet Along the Potomac

Ethel Lynn Beers, a sensitive young woman from New York, was moved to poetry by the newspaper headline, "All Quiet Along the Potomac," which appeared frequently in the autumn of 1861, usually followed by a subhead dealing with some minor incident or other. One day the subhead read "A Picket Shot." The incongruity of the headline, which suggested nothing of importance, and the subhead, which reported a personal tragedy of overwhelming consequence, *prompted Beers to write a sad poem, "The Picket Guard." This appeared in* Harper's Weekly *in November of 1861. The poem soon came to the attention of James Hewitt, a noted journalist, poet, and musician who was serving as an officer in the Confederate Army. Hewitt set "The Picket Guard" to music. The song, popularized as "All Quiet Along the Potomac," soon became popular on both sides, dealing, as it did, with the pain and suffering of the war.*

All quiet along the Potomac," they say,
"Except now and then a stray picket
Is shot, as he walks on his beat to and fro,
By a rifleman hid in the thicket.

'Tis nothing—a private or two now and then
Will not count in the news of the battle;
Not an officer lost—only one of the men,
Moaning out, all alone, the death-rattle."

All quiet along the Potomac to-night,
Where the soldiers lie peacefully dreaming;
Their tents in the rays of the clear autumn moon,
Or the light of the watch-fire, are gleaming.
A tremulous sigh of the gentle night-wind
Through the forest leaves softly is creeping;
While stars up above, with their glittering eyes,
Keep guard, for the army is sleeping.

There's only the sound of the lone sentry's tread,
As he tramps from the rock to the fountain,
And thinks of the two in the low-trundle-bed
Far away in the cot on the mountain.
His musket falls slack; his face, dark and grim,
Grows gentle with memories tender,
As he mutters a prayer for the children asleep,
For their mother; may Heaven defend her!

The moon seems to shine just as brightly as then,
That night, when the love yet unspoken
Leaped up to his lips—when low-murmured vows
Were pledged to be ever unbroken.
Then drawing his sleeve roughly over his eyes,
He dashes off tears that are welling,
And gathers his gun closer up to its place,
As if to keep down the heart-swelling.

He passes the fountain, the blasted pine-tree,
The footstep is lagging and weary;
Yet onward he goes, through the broad belt of light,
Toward the shade of the forest so dreary.
Hark! was it the night-wind that rustled the leaves?
Was it moonlight so wondrously flashing?
It looked like a rifle . . . "Ha! Mary, good-bye!"
The red life-blood is ebbing and plashing.

All quiet along the Potomac to-night;
No sound save the rush of the river;
While soft falls the dew on the face of the dead—
The picket's off duty forever!

Union family from Western Missouri seeks refuge in St. Louis.

SOURCES

Beauregard, Pierre G. T. "The First Battle of Bull Run." In *Battles and Leaders of the Civil War*, edited by Robert U. Johnson and Clarence C. Buel, vol. 1, pp. 196-219. New York, 1887.

Chester, James. "Inside Sumter in '61." In *Battles and Leaders of the Civil War*, edited by Robert U. Johnson and Clarence C. Buel, vol. 1, pp. 51–73. New York, 1887.

Cox, Jacob D. "McClellan in West Virginia." In *Battles and Leaders of the Civil War*, edited by Robert U. Johnson and Clarence C. Buel, vol. 1, pp. 126–148. New York, 1887.

——————. "Ohio Goes to War." *op. cit.*, vol. 1, pp. 89–98.

"Declaration of Causes Which Induced the Secession of South Carolina." In *The Rebellion Record: A Diary of American Events, with Documents, Narratives, Illustrative Incidents, Poetry, etc.*, edited by Frank Moore, vol. 1, pp. 3ff.

Dicey, Edward. "The Union Creates an Army." In *Six Months in the Federal States*, vol. 2, pp. 5–12. London, 1863.

Doubleday, Abner. "From Moultrie to Sumter." In *Battles and Leaders of the Civil War*, edited by Robert U. Johnson and Clarence C. Buel, vol. 1, pp. 40–46. New York, 1887.

Estván, Béla. "A Christmas Story." In *War Pictures from the South*, pp. 171–175. New York, 1863.

——————. "A Troublesome Regiment." *op. cit.*, pp. 163–164.

Fry, James B. "McDowell's Advance to Bull Run." In *Battles and Leaders of the Civil War*, edited by Robert U. Johnson and Clarence C. Buel, vol. 1, pp. 171–193. New York, 1887.

Gibbon, John. "The Rumblings of Civil War Reach a Frontier Garrison." In *Personal Recollections of the Civil War*, pp. 36ff. New York, 1928.

Goss, Warren Lee. "Going to the Front." In *Battles and Leaders of the Civil War*, edited by Robert U. Johnson and Clarence C. Buel, vol. 1, pp. 149–159. New York, 1887.

Kelly, R. M. "Holding Kentucky for the Union." In *Battles and Leaders of the Civil War*, edited by Robert U. Johnson and Clarence C. Buel, vol. 1, pp. 373–392. New York, 1887.

Lee, Stephen D. "The First Step in the War." In *Battles and Leaders of the Civil War*, edited by Robert U. Johnson and Clarence C. Buel, vol. 1, pp. 74–81. New York, 1887.

Lewis, John H. "Virginia Goes to War." In *Recollections from 1860–1865*, pp. 20–23. Washington, 1895.

Lincoln, Abraham. "A House Divided." In *The World's Greatest Speeches* edited by Lewis Copeland, pp. 309–315. New York, 1942.

McClellan, George B. "The Causes of the Civil War." In *McClellan's Own Story: The War for the Union*, pp. 29ff. New York, 1887.

——————. "The Creation of the Army of the Potomac." *op. cit.*, pp. 97ff.

Nicolay, John G. "Lincoln Calls for Volunteers." In *The Oubreak of the Rebellion*, pp. 73–75. New York, 1882.

Opie, John N. "Joining the Army." *A Rebel Cavalryman with Lee, Stuart, and Jackson*, pp. 14–24. Chicago, 1899.

——————. "Relieving the Monotony of Camp Life." *op. cit.*

Redpath, James. "John Brown's Speech on Being Sentenced to Death." *The Public Life of Captain John Brown*, pp. 261–263. Boston, 1860.

Snead, Thomas L. "The First Year of the War in Missouri." In *Battles and Leaders of the Civil War*, edited by Robert U. Johnson and Clarence C. Buel, vol. 1, pp. 262–277. New York, 1887.

Wherry, William M. "Wilson's Creek and the Death of Lyon." In *Battles and Leaders of the Civil War*, edited by Robert U. Johnson and Clarence C. Buel, vol. 1, pp. 289–297. New York, 1887.